Sexuality and the Reading Encounter

Identity and Desire in Proust, Duras, Tournier, and Cixous

EMMA WILSON

CLARENDON PRESS · OXFORD
1996

Oxford University Press, Walton Street, Oxford OX2 6DP
Oxford New York
Athens Auckland Bangkok Bombay
Calcutta Cape Town Dar es Salaam Delhi
Florence Hong Kong Istanbul Karachi
Kuala Lumpur Madras Madrid Melbourne
Mexico City Nairobi Paris Singapore
Taipei Tokyo Toronto
and associated companies in
Berlin Ibadan

Oxford is a trade mark of Oxford University Press

Published in the United States
by Oxford University Press Inc., New York

British Library Cataloguing in Publication Data
Data available

Library of Congress Cataloging in Publication Data
Wilson, Emma.
Sexuality and the reading encounter/Emma Wilson.
Includes bibliographical references and index.
1. French fiction—20th century—History and criticism. 2. Sex in
literature. 3. Books and reading—Psychological aspects.
4. Identity (Psychology) I. Title.
PQ673.W55   1996   843´.91093538—dc20   95-44944
ISBN 0-19-815885-8

1 3 5 7 9 10 8 6 4 2

Typeset by Best-set Typesetter Ltd., Hong Kong
Printed in Great Britain
on acid-free paper by
Bookcraft Ltd.
Midsomer Norton, Avon

For MY PARENTS
and for J.

Reading is eating the forbidden fruit,
making forbidden love, changing eras,
changing families, changing destinies,
and changing day for night.

Hélène Cixous

Preface

In his recent study of French autobiography, Michael Sheringham remarks: 'The reader's place in the text, realized in different ways (through an implied reader, a narratee, the orientation towards "reception", or the prominence of epistemic desire) marks the point of "application" through which the fictional world engages with and encompasses the real.'[1] I allude to Sheringham's comments here since they have served aptly to concentrate my mind on the ways in which my own study has arisen out of a prolonged fascination with precisely this 'point of "application"', this intersection between the actual and the imaginary, which I will come to term here the reading encounter. The reading encounter is evidently an expression which affords various interpretations, a number of which will be my concern in the pages that follow. Before embarking on a more detailed analysis of the participants in this encounter and the spaces, real and imaginary, in which it might take place, I want to pause a moment to reveal a few motivations for the writing of this study as a whole. Indeed by way of introduction to the analyses which are the products of my own encounters with both fictional and theoretical texts, I will mention several points of 'application' which I hope will serve to show the ways in which I have seen my own work attempt at least to some degree to engage with the real.

This study was largely reworked and completed in Cambridge in the summer of 1994, at a time when Michael Howard's amendment to the Criminal Justice Bill was going through Parliament in Britain, arousing public comment and some dissension. This amendment specifies that when deciding whether to give a certificate to a video (or deciding what kind of certificate to give) the British Board of Film Classification must 'have special regard (among the other relevant factors) to any harm

---

[1] Michael Sheringham, *French Autobiography: Devices and Desires* (Oxford, 1993), 25.

that may be caused to potential viewers or, through their behaviour, to society by the manner in which the work deals with—(a) criminal behaviour; (b) illegal drugs; (c) violent behaviour or incidents; (d) horrific behaviour or incidents; or (e) human sexual activity'.[2] The amendment came as a response to David Alton's campaign on video violence, and of course in the horrified aftermath of the murder of James Bulger.

In the context of this apparent and distressingly necessary admission of the possible deleterious effects of the viewing of violence, it is surprising and potentially disturbing that 'human sexual activity' should be included in the cautionary list. As Philip Dodd puts it: 'All the anxiety was about violence, but, with sad predictability, "human sexual activity" has climbed aboard.'[3] My interest here does not lie in debating whether the representation of 'human sexual activity' may so readily be equated with the representation of violent and horrific behaviour. I am concerned rather with the implicit assumption that the representation of 'human sexual activity' may cause 'harm' to viewers. The amendment appears, despite the caution of its wording, a fairly open avowal that viewers may be vulnerable to the videos they watch. We may note that a further clarification is made in the following terms: 'any behaviour or activity referred to in subsection (1)(a) to (e) above shall be taken to include behaviour or activity likely to encourage it'.[4]

Following this argument, we may be led to consider also, it seems, that readers may be the victims of the texts they so readily consume. Some may disagree with this notion of the equivalence of media, suggesting indeed that scopic pleasures demand identification more readily, that the visual media more coercively prescribe a complicit viewing position. Yet it will be important to my argument in this study to maintain that the pleasures of viewing and of reading are at least coextensive. Indeed the reading of texts of desire will be seen to depend on an economy of vision which necessarily engages the reader in a complicit and potentially voyeuristic encounter. In this sense I will suggest that the analyses of viewing and spectatorship

[2] *Criminal Justice and Public Order Act 1994* (London, 1994), 74.
[3] Philip Dodd, 'Editorial: Dog Days', *Sight and Sound*, 4/8 (Aug. 1994), 3.
[4] *Criminal Justice and Public Order Act*, 74.

which have preoccupied recent film theory have specific relevance to theorists of the reading process. Thus a reckoning with the dangers of viewing has, in my view, its own importance to any critic intent on assessing the risks (and pleasures) of the reading encounter. I would argue, then, that the implications of the Howard amendment are of great relevance to theorists of textual consumption, as well as to viewers of videos. I would suggest, however, that a complacent censoring of fictions has its own dangers, and that the 'harm' done by representations needs urgently to be reassessed. Can we really accept the far-reaching implications of a positive verdict on the contagion of fiction, the responsibility of the author and the ethics of reading?

This leads me to the questions which underlie this study and which will be rethought throughout. In the first place, I will ask whether the text can really be shown to form the reader. And, on the other hand, whether the reader can really form the text. How far does the reader's control extend?

Since this is largely a study of fictions of desire, I will question in what ways the reader is implicated in representations of desiring relations. Do gender and sexuality determine the reader's patterns of identification in fictions of desire? Is s/he free to cross-dress at will as s/he reads? Is identification formative? Does reading depend on the reader's own identity category? And is the reader's sexuality as much the product as the pre-condition of the reading encounter?

I first came to think about many of these questions in the context of my doctoral thesis on reading and sexuality in the work of the (living) writer Michel Tournier. Troubled by the complexities of a reading encounter overshadowed by the presence of a writer who, despite some evident debts to post-structuralist theory, never seems quite to have succumbed to the death of the author, I was reluctant to contact Tournier. Persuaded eventually that this would be in the interest of my project, I wrote to him and a correspondence ensued, followed by an interview at Gallimard. Of some relevance to this study are the apparently generous words of Tournier in a letter to me where he expressed himself thus: 'Vous êtes une lectrice comme je les aime: possessive et créatrice. Je ne conçois mes histoires que comme des points de départ pour la rêverie du lecteur. Rien ne doit limiter sa liberté.'[5] I was less sceptical then, and am more so now, over precisely this issue of the reader's freedom (and over the implications of Tournier's comment). And thus I was led to the following questions: Can fiction be seen in this way to feed its reader's fantasies? Is the reader free to possess the text as s/he desires? Is the pleasure of the text dependent on a more subtle and transferential play of power and constraint? What indeed is the relation between writer and reader as they meet in the illusory space of the reading encounter?

In some senses I would have wished this study to be more phenomenological in nature and to chart the experiences of a series of 'real' readers with individual texts. The scope of my project is, unfortunately, not broad enough to encompass this and I can offer here in effect only my own affective journey through these fictions of desire. However, my work has inevitably been rarefied by and will reflect my experiences of teaching some of the texts to which I have devoted specific attention here. Undergraduate reactions to the texts of Proust, Duras, Tournier, and Cixous have been a source of continual fascination to me, and the diversity of my students' readings, and their subversion of many fixed assumptions of gendered reading patterns, have frequently served as lessons to me. I offer this study up, then, as, in some senses, the fruit of these shared interpretations.

Shoshana Felman, in a study of reading and sexual difference, comments that 'reading is a rather risky business whose outcome and full consequences can never be known in advance'.[6] It is with these words of caution that I shall embark on this account of imagined and real reading encounters.

[5] Michel Tournier, in a letter to me (6 Apr. 1990). Translations are my own unless otherwise stated. ('You are the sort of reader I like: possessive and creative. I think of my stories only as starting-points for the reader's day-dreams. Nothing must limit his/her freedom.')

[6] Shoshana Felman, *What does a Woman Want? Reading and Sexual Difference* (Baltimore, 1993), 5.

Acknowledgements

I would like to thank the editors of *French Studies* and *Dalhousie French Studies* for permission to draw on material used in articles for those journals. Part of Chapter 5, which has appeared in article form, is reprinted by permission from the *Romanic Review*, 87, 1 (January 1996). Copyright by the Trustees of Columbia University in the City of New York. I am especially grateful to Andrew Lockett and Jason Freeman of Oxford University Press for their encouragement and invaluable advice at various stages in the writing of this book. I am greatly indebted also to Leslie Hill, whose astute and clear-sighted comments helped me re-form and clarify my ideas. Thanks are due as well to Laurien Berkeley, Helen Gray, Vicki Reeve, and Sophie Goldsworthy for their help in the production of this book. Michel Tournier was kind enough to answer my questions in an informal interview in Paris in 1990: I am very grateful to him.

I have been thinking about some of these ideas for almost ten years now, since I was first inspired as an undergraduate by the teaching of J. Ann Duncan. I have since benefited from the judicious and generous guidance of my research supervisors Rosemary Lloyd and Alison Finch. Discussions with Colin Davis have rarefied and changed my thoughts on Tournier. I owe a great deal to them all. I am very grateful also to the Master and Fellows of Corpus Christi College and to colleagues in the French Department in Cambridge for their support and example. Amongst the many people to whom I am indebted, I would like to thank in particular Ann Caesar, Peter Collier, Nick Corbyn, David Cresswell, Jenny Davey, Patrick Higgins, Anna Lawrence, Tim Seaton, and Meryl Tyers. Josephine Lloyd has been a tender and thoughtful friend in the years I have been working on this book: I am very grateful to her. Finally, I'd like to thank my parents, Millar and Jacqueline Wilson, for the love and freedom they've given me.

Sexuality and the
Reading Encounter

PQ673 WIL

DATE DUE FOR RETURN

Contents

I

The Reading Encounter

In this thin transparent air I feel able to perceive in her
unmoving form the signs of that invisible movement that
reading is, the flow of gaze and breath, but, even more, the
journey of words through the person . . .

(Italo Calvino, *If on a Winter's Night a Traveller*)

Chercher à envoûter l'autre,
à l'embarquer dans son rêve.
L'effleurer de quelques gestes et le noyer dans les mots.
Jouer la passion pour
éveiller la compassion.
Comme dans les films qui apprennent la vie . . .
Comme dans les livres qui sont plus beaux que la vie.[1]

(Colette Dubois, *'La Maman et la putain' de Jean Eustache*)

• *Day for Night*

'Avant de faire l'amour vraiment, on le fait d'abord au cinéma.'[2]
These lines, spoken in Marguerite Duras's novel *Un Barrage
contre le Pacifique*, focus the reader's mind on the possibilities
of previewing existence in fictions. For Duras, film prefigures
reality; it performs the desire which will be replayed and com-
memorated by her characters. Hers are texts obsessed with
relations between viewing and desire, between fictions and their
lived re-enactment. The cinema becomes a privileged space and

---

[1] 'To seek to bewitch the other, | to set him sail on his dreams. | Touch him lightly
and drown him in words. | Play at passion to | arouse compassion. | As in films which
teach how to live . . . | As in books which are lovelier than life . . .'

[2] Marguerite Duras, *Un Barrage contre le Pacifique* (Paris, 1950), 199 ('Before
really making love, you make love first in the cinema'). See Joël Magny, 'Le Cri de
l'écran', in *Marguerite Duras* (Paris, 1992), 15–34, for a reading of this text with
relation to Duras's cinema.

films are shown by Duras to play a prominent role in the formation of identity.[3] Her works entirely invert the hierarchical relation between reality and fiction, revealing, with unusual candour, the seductive power of fictional identifications and celluloid images. Suzanne, one of Duras's adolescent heroines and fictive *alter egos*, finds herself drawn into the artificial night of the movie-house and revelling in 'les rêves de l'écran plus vrais que la vie'.[4] Duras explores the libidinal investment in viewing a film, showing how her young spectator engages in a scenario of fascinated wish-fulfilment, identifying with the characters on screen: 'On voudrait bien être à leur place. Ah! comme on le voudrait.'[5] More radical still is Duras's analysis of memory and displacement: Suzanne and her brother spend 'des journées entières au cinéma'; their fascination is such that 'ils parlaient encore des films qu'ils avaient vus avec autant de précision que s'il se fût agi de souvenirs de choses réelles qu'ils auraient vécues ensemble'.[6]

In no uncertain terms, Duras shows an infrastructure of fictions upholding the tenuous existences of her characters. She explores a dependency on fiction, an inability to divorce fiction from reality, a desire to perform and perfect a fictional identity. Repeatedly in her texts, fiction appears to supersede reality and to take on the power to form identity. What we might question is whether, implicitly, Duras is seeking this power herself in her fictions? Do her representations of reading and viewing encounters self-consciously betray their own desire to form the reader?

---

[3] The term 'identity' will recur with great frequency in this study and thus it may be useful at the outset to designate the ways in which it will be used here. Identity will be linked broadly to the notion of selfhood and will be seen to be dependent on the adoption of specific subject positions. Inevitably in a study of this nature my concern is primarily with the issue of gender identities and sexual identities, although the ways in which these intersect with and construct a more general sense of the 'self' will be drawn into question. Identity will be understood to be potentially multiple, dissociated, and non-self-identical. This notion depends on both a Lacanian reading of identity as integrally fictitious, and on a post-structuralist view of identity as constructed and diverse. Following Judith Butler, I see identity as the effect of a performance and of a set of identifications rather than an attribute or series of attributes inhering in the individual subject.

[4] Duras, *Un Barrage contre le Pacifique*, 122–3 ('the dreams on the screen which are more real than real life').

[5] Ibid. 189 ('we would so like to be in their place. Oh how we long to be!').

[6] Ibid. 123 ('they still talked about the films they had seen with as much precision as if they were memories of real things they had experienced together').

How, indeed, does the reader react to a text which draws attention to its power to displace and even dispossess the reader's reality?

These are questions which might relate also to the work of Proust, who, most notoriously in *A la recherche du temps perdu*, has created a tortured phenomenology of reading which traces the intertwining of text and experience, imagination and sensation; as the narrator says of the novelist: 'voici qu'il déchaîne en nous pendant une heure tous les bonheurs et tous les malheurs possibles dont nous mettrions dans la vie des années à connaître quelques-uns'.[7] Proust's narrator claims that a book touches and troubles its reader, 'à la façon d'un rêve mais d'un rêve plus clair que ceux que nous avons en dormant et dont le souvenir durera davantage'.[8] A fiction is seen to displace a dream, where, in Duras's text, film screens memory. Fictions are shown not merely to mimic or conceal reality, but to heighten and re-present it in accelerated and previously inaccessible forms. The reading of a text, the viewing of a film, is revealed by both Proust and Duras to be not recreational but experiential. And this itself may explain in part why so much emphasis is laid in both their texts on the viewing arena, on the scene of reading. In these spaces of solitude and desire, the reading encounter takes on a formative power and becomes a privileged subject in their fictions.

In *A la recherche du temps perdu*, the narrator describes the ephemeral light and fragmented images of the enclosed room where he lies, 'un livre à la main, dans ma chambre qui protégeait en tremblant sa fraîcheur transparente et fragile contre le soleil de l'après-midi derrière ses volets presque clos où un reflet de jour avait pourtant trouvé moyen de faire passer ses ailes jaunes, et restait immobile entre le bois et le vitrage, dans un coin, comme un papillon posé'.[9] In Duras, cinema offers the

[7] Marcel Proust, *A la recherche du temps perdu* (Paris, 1989), i. 84: *In Search of Lost Time*, trans. C. K. Scott Moncrieff and Terence Kilmartin, rev. D. J. Enright (London, 1992), i. 100 ('for the space of an hour he sets free within us all the joys and sorrows in the world, a few of which only we should have to spend years of our actual life in getting to know').

[8] *A la recherche*, i. 84: *In Search of Lost Time*, i. 100 ('as might a dream, but a dream more lucid and more abiding than those which come to us in sleep').

[9] *A la recherche*, i. 82: *In Search of Lost Time*, i. 97 ('with a book in my hand. My room quivered with the effort to defend its frail, transparent coolness against the afternoon sun behind its almost closed shutters through which, however, a gleam of

extinguishing of light and immersion in 'la salle noire de l'après-midi, la nuit des solitaires';[10] yet we are told too that 'la nuit était venue pendant la séance et c'était comme si ç'avait été la nuit de la salle qui continuait, la nuit amoureuse du film'.[11] In these two accounts of the experience of reading or viewing, Proust and Duras dwell on the indistinct borders between exterior and interior, between the inner stage of fictional re-enactments and the outside world it apparently displaces. The description of literal location is used in each case paradoxically to dissolve stability and to play out a series of shifts between the imaginary and the real. Indeed these shifts hold an intricate metaphorical relation to the thematics of reading and viewing both Proust and Duras explore, since each is concerned with that intimate and ambiguous encounter which takes place between text and reader, film and viewer, where the imaginary entirely permeates the real.

The untroubled comparison between reading and viewing implicit in my comments above may be contentious: critical studies of reading and spectatorship have, of course, largely diverged. My purpose in aligning the activities of reading and viewing, and eliding difference between them, is variously motivated. The model of reception (both visual and verbal) that I am adopting depends crucially on the notion of 'identification'. This is a usefully fluid and polyvalent term, and in this study I intend to call a number of its meanings into play. As Malcolm Bowie reminds us, identification is one of those terms that Freudian diction shares with both philosophical discourse and colloquial speech.[12] In this study as a whole I will be laying

daylight had contrived to insinuate its golden wings, remaining motionless in a corner between glass and woodwork, like a butterfly poised upon a flower'). For a fine reading of Paul de Man's analysis of the use of metaphor in this passage, see Jonathan Culler, 'The Problem of Metaphor', in T. E. Hope (ed.), *Language, Meaning and Style* (Leeds, 1981), 5–20: 11–12.

[10] Duras, *Un Barrage contre le Pacifique*, 188 ('the dark picture-house in the afternoon, the night of solitary people').

[11] Ibid. 190 ('night had fallen during the screening and it was as if the dark of the picture-house spread outside, the amorous night of the film').

[12] Bowie explains the psychoanalytic role of the term identification very clearly, saying: 'If the ego can be thought of as having components, as capable of 'coming apart' into building materials that are smaller and simpler than itself, then the infant's earliest identifications are those components. The identification of oneself with another being is the very process by which a continuing sense of selfhood

emphasis on a Lacanian interpretation which privileges identification as scopic activity dependent on the recognition and assimilation of an (alien) image or series of images which will become constitutive of the self.

My aim is to test, and indeed contest, the differences between the notion of identification used in its fullest psychoanalytic sense, and the notion of identification used more commonly with relation to reading a text or viewing a film where we speak of the possibility of 'identifying' with a specific character, emotion, or spectatorial position. Identification in this latter sense is, of course, used fairly loosely to refer to both media, but my desire to relate reading and viewing is inspired by more than this. I think it is telling that analysis of the reading of fictions of desire is perhaps necessarily dependent on questions of viewpoint and voyeurism which are by virtue of the very specificity of their terminology, visual in nature. Further, desiring reading may be seen to demand a process of visualization which is not exclusively in response to the visual stimuli and verbal images offered in the text. The text may engage its reader in a process of fantasy construction and voyeuristic participation as it literally arouses his/her imagination. The text may thus offer the reader new images of him/herself as desiring subject with which to identify, and new scenarios for the performance of an identity category.

In this sense I would argue that for the reader, as well as the spectator, the self may be *re-viewed* and identification may thus precede, endorse, or disrupt a fiction of stable identity. In the studies which follow, texts will themselves be seen to provide an imaginary stage upon which identity may be enacted and an imagined screen for the projection of vicarious desires. And this imagined screen viewed and revisited in the reading process is possibly all the more productive of fictive *imagos*, and adopted identifications, since unlike the real screens of movie-houses, its images are unfixed, subjective, and ephemeral, as liable to metamorphosis and re-formation as identity itself.

This imaginary encounter will be my subject here. I will make a series of readings of texts which privilege reading encounters,

becomes possible, and it is from successive assimilations of other people's attributes that what is famously called the ego or the personality is constructed Malcolm Bowie, *Lacan* (London, 1991), 30–1.

decoding protagonists and hermeneutic desires. My interest is not solely, however, in the disclosing of allegories of reading. My aim is not to show that reading is itself the all-absorbing subject of these fictions. The reader will not be seen directly, in Baudelairean terms, as a complicit or resistant double of the reading hero/ine. Rather, I will look at how these apparently specular relations may go awry, at how the reader may exceed the parameters of his/her pre-inscribed role. In the very fabric of their representations, the texts I will study all reveal the reading encounter to be volatile, affective, unknowable, distorting, and transformative. And in this sense they may be seen to prefigure the external reader's experience, yet necessarily to preclude the possibility of delimiting or controlling this. Thus I will argue that these texts testify at once to the freedom of the reader *and* to the formative power of the reading encounter. And in analysis of the reading of these texts, we may be led to reflect further on how far the act of reading might itself redirect reality.

• *Reading as Encounter*

The expression 'the reading encounter' necessitates further analysis. What is this encounter and who are its protagonists? Where does it exist between the imaginary and the real, the writer and the reader?

Implicit in the expression is the notion that reading is an interpersonal, transactional activity, dependent on the participation of (unequal?) partners. Ostensibly this encounter may be said to be purely solipsistic: the reader in solitude and control constructs his/her own interpretation of a text radically divorced from its author's orbit. Readers have indeed assumed the power to act thus. Yet it is noticeable that the orphan reader is frequently disinclined entirely to adopt his/her enfranchised status.

In a much fetishized fragment from *Le Plaisir du texte*, Barthes reminds us: 'Comme institution, l'auteur est mort: sa personne civile, passionnelle, biographique, a disparu; dépossédée, elle n'exerce plus sur son œuvre la formidable paternité dont l'histoire littéraire, l'enseignement, l'opinion avaient à charge d'établir et de renouveler le récit.'[13] And Foucault comments famously: 'la marque de l'écrivain n'est plus que la singularité de son absence; il lui faut tenir le rôle du mort dans le jeu de l'écriture'.[14] The death of the author effectively overshadows the texts I will be discussing here. Indeed the denial of the author's paternity is a necessary prerequisite for this rereading of reception. No longer does the author address his (feminine?) reader as 'vous qui tenez ce livre d'une main blanche, vous qui vous enfoncez dans un moelleux fauteuil'.[15] Balzac may, through his use of an omniscient narrator, assume paternal control over his text, yet noticeably even here in *Le Père Goriot* he appears both to desire and demand the reader's response, declaring: '*All is true*, il est si véritable, que chacun peut en reconnaître les éléments chez soi, dans son cœur peut-être.'[16] The reader subtly becomes the guarantor of the text's veracity. The reader's acceptance, as much as reception, is seen as necessary to the text's success. This implicit privileging of the role of the reader is pursued further by Proust, who, in his denigration of biographical criticism and defence of the occlusion of the public self of the author, states, 'un livre est le produit d'un autre *moi* que celui que nous manifestons dans nos habitudes, dans la société, dans nos vices';[17] and he continues: 'Ce moi-là, si nous voulons essayer de le comprendre, c'est au fond de nous-mêmes, en essayant de le recréer en nous, que nous

---

[13] Roland Barthes, *Le Plaisir du texte* (Paris, 1973), 45: *The Pleasure of the Text*, trans. Richard Miller (Oxford, 1990), 27 ('As institution, the author is dead: his civil status, his biographical person have disappeared; dispossessed, they no longer exercise over his work the formidable paternity whose account literary history, teaching, and public opinion had the responsibility of establishing and renewing').

[14] Michel Foucault, 'Qu'est-ce qu'un auteur?', *Bulletin de la Société française de philosophie*, 63/1 (1969), 73–104: 78 ('the mark of the writer is no longer anything other than the singularity of his absence; he must play the role of the dead man in the game of writing').

[15] Honoré de Balzac, *Le Père Goriot* (Paris, 1966), 26: *Père Goriot*, trans. A. J. Krailsheimer (Oxford, 1991), 2 ('you . . . holding this book in soft white hands, sinking into a comfortable armchair').

[16] *Le Père Goriot*, 26: *Père Goriot*, 2 ('*All is true*. So true that everyone can recognize its elements in his own circle, perhaps in his own heart').

[17] Marcel Proust, *Contre Sainte-Beuve* (Paris, 1954), 127: *Against Sainte-Beuve*, trans. John Sturrock (London, 1994), 12 ('a book is the product of a self other than that which we display in our habits, in company, in our vices').

pouvons y parvenir'.[18] Proust calls for a specular relation between author and reader, an intimate identification between the
two, an incorporation, indeed, of the author by the reader. And
these are points to which I shall return. Suffice it to say, here,
that where *A la recherche du temps perdu* may pre-date the
other texts which will be examined in this study, and which have
all been produced more or less consciously in the context of
post-structuralist criticism, this should be understood as testimony to the role Proust's theoretical and fictional accounts of
the reading encounter have played in paving the way for the
liberation of the reader. Proust's text might be said indeed
perpetually to undermine its own authority as it lays itself so
openly in the hands of its interpreter.

Where the death of the author transforms the way we may
conceive of the reading encounter, where the denial of paternity
is necessary to the reader's filial liberty, it seems important to
stress as well that this fictional demise by no means ensures the
total absence of the author. And here we might return once
more to the passage from *Le Plaisir du texte* quoted above. We
may note that in this text, the avowal of loss is radically modi-
fied as Barthes continues: 'mais dans le texte, d'une certaine
façon, *je désire* l'auteur: j'ai besoin de sa figure (qui n'est ni
sa représentation, ni sa projection), comme il a besoin de la
mienne'.[19] It seems that this further implication of the apparent
death of the author has not been fully realized. Barthes leaves
reading relations resting upon two potentially incompatible
phantom desires. For Barthes, an imaginary encounter between
writer and reader is a requisite of reading, as it is also of writing.
What has changed radically from previous configurations,
however, is the power structure implied within the reading
encounter. Stripped of control of his text, the paternal author
may very well be prey to his reader. The hierarchical relation of
author to reader is permanently troubled, and this will be seen
to have important implications for questions of reading and
sexuality.

[18] *Contre Sainte-Beuve*, 127: *Against Sainte-Beuve*, 12 ('if we want to try and
understand this self, it is deep inside us, by trying to re-create it within us, that we
may succeed').

[19] Barthes, *Le Plaisir du texte*, 45–6: *The Pleasure of the Text*, 27 ('but in the text,
in a way, *I desire* the author: I need his figure (which is neither his representation nor
his projection), as he needs mine').

Barthes himself elaborates on the tenuous, desiring position of the writer as he himself assumes the position of author in *Le Plaisir du texte*, writing: 'Écrire dans le plaisir m'assure-t-il— moi, écrivain—du plaisir de mon lecteur? Nullement. Ce lecteur, il faut que je le cherche, (que je le "drague"), *sans savoir où il est*.'[20] In this configuration, we are led to realize how far the writer needs and desires the reader, as the sexual implications of Barthes's use of the term 'draguer' amply indicate. In *Le Plaisir du texte* Barthes sensitizes the reading process, tantalizes his desired reader, and theorizes textual seduction.

Following Barthes, my argument here will depend in part on a primary recognition that reading entails the mobilization of desire, that, for the reader, meaning is an object of desire, and that libidinal energy is redirected in the desire to know, and enjoy, a text. As Malcolm Bowie specifies in his essay 'Proust, Jealousy, Knowledge': 'Baudelaire has spoken of "une extase *faite de volupté et de connaissance*". Roland Barthes, reminding us that the very notion of pleasure has come to seem politically and intellectually suspect, wondered in *Le Plaisir du texte*: "et pourtant: si la connaissance elle-même était *délicieuse*?".'[21] Reading will be construed and constructed as a desiring activity. This is itself reflected further in the texts discussed where, in Proust and Cixous, for example, reading is itself revealed to be both sensual and erotic. Conversely, desiring relations within these texts will be seen to be peculiarly dependent on the decoding of signs and on dramas of (re)cognition.

In this sense I have selected texts which reflect (upon) what I see as the desiring process of reception. This choice of fictions of desire is entirely deliberate. As Raymond Jean suggests in *Lectures du désir*: 'la vie érotique elle-même peut très bien marquer assez fortement une œuvre pour donner, par son propre système de signes, une assez belle illustration de ce qu'est le travail du désir dans un texte'.[22] Developing this point, I will argue that the

---

[20] *Le Plaisir du texte*, 11: *The Pleasure of the Text*, 4 ('Does writing in pleasure guarantee—guarantee me, the writer—my reader's pleasure? Not at all. I must seek out this reader (must "cruise" him) *without knowing where he is*').

[21] Malcolm Bowie, *Freud, Proust and Lacan: Theory as Fiction* (Cambridge, 1987), 63.

[22] Raymond Jean, *Lectures du désir* (Paris, 1977), 12 ('the erotic life can very well mark a book fairly strongly, giving, by means of its own sign system, a fairly fine illustration of how desire works in a text').

representation of erotic relations serves also to illustrate the possible desires activated in the reading encounter.

It should be said at the outset, however, that the argument I am developing with relation to the reading encounter and the formative power of fictions could have, in effect, far broader implications and application and is not particular to or solely proved by fictions of desire.[23] While I will be limiting my readings to representations of desire, and to theorizations of the construction of sexuality, the theoretical framework of this work relates more generally to notions of fiction, interpretation, and identity. As I will go on to show, this work is intended ultimately to re-view the role of the reading encounter in identity formation. That I have concentrated so specifically on the formation of sexual identity reflects, however, a debt to Freudian psychoanalysis and a conviction that the construction of sexuality is the most powerful and diverse, fictive and controlling, constitutive part of an individual's relation to others and to him/herself.

Here I want to return for a moment to Barthes's phrase about the desiring reader where he states: 'Ce lecteur, il faut que je le cherche, (que je le "drague").'[24] Barthes's words, despite their sexual innuendo, are in fact potentially free from gender assumption. It could be argued, certainly, that Barthes introduces here a scenario of a gay pick-up into his imagining of reading relations. The reader who has witnessed the hopeless and poetic encounters of *Incidents* will be only too ready to flesh out the

[23] In a rather different context, Shoshana Felman looks to map out relations between the textual and the real, between identity, writing, and reading, in *Testimony: Crises of Witnessing in Literature, Psychoanalysis, and History* (New York, 1992). Here she claims that her book will form 'the first stage of a theory of a yet uncharted, nonrepresentational but performative, relationship between art and culture, on the one hand, and the conscious or unconscious witnessing of historical events, on the other' (p. xx). Felman's argument relates to the necessity of testimony to survival. She attempts to demonstrate how far the production of a text (or testimony), and the engagement with a fiction, has the power to affect and protect the survivor. In her study, she writes as reader, not survivor, and shows how for herself, as reader and teacher, working on Holocaust texts has brought her up against 'the shock of the unintelligible in the face of the attempt at its interpretation' (p. xx). This experience is shown to be transformative for Felman, and her students, and her book becomes, in effect, a testimony to the power of this encounter. The theories behind Felman's study come close to my own in terms of the recognition that art can be a means of reassessing reality, and in terms of the notion that a textual encounter may be transformative.

[24] See n. 20.

bare bones of the scenario presented in *Le Plaisir du texte*.[25] Yet it should be recognized that despite the latent homosexuality and luxuriating homoeroticism of many of Barthes's texts, his theorization of the tangential relations between the desire involved in textual production and the thematics of sexuality, pursued through *S/Z*, *Le Plaisir du texte*, and *Fragments d'un discours amoureux*, gains importance through its implicit denial of distinctions between homosexual and heterosexual desire. Barthes employs sexual metaphors in his theorization of reading relations, but he undoes any certainty on the part of the reader as to the gender of the subject or object of desire. Where the reading encounter is, for Barthes, of shattering eroticism, he works to deny any fixed configurations of relations between gender, power, and pleasure.

This is not so readily the case with some other theorists of desiring reading, and it is with reference to their work that I wish to analyse, and undo, some explicit and implicit assumptions about masculinity and femininity, activity and passivity, and the compulsory heterosexuality of the reading encounter. By way of an introduction to these I intend to discuss Michel Tournier's essay on reading, 'Le Vol du vampire', which serves particularly well to illustrate the complex relations between writer, text, and reader involved in the reading encounter.

• *Vampire Texts*

'Le Vol du vampire' is, one might argue, a tale of seduction. Tournier, like Barthes, endeavours to present to the reader a myth of textual consumption as erotic encounter. Despite its recourse to anecdote and its leisurely pace, the essay is of specific importance in terms of its redefinitions of the role of the decoder, and its privileging of bodily emotion and sensation as part of the reading process. Paul Ricœur writes in his essay 'The Metaphorical Process as Cognition, Imagination and Feeling': 'feelings—I mean poetic feelings—imply a kind of *époché* of our bodily emotions. Feelings are negative, suspensive experiences in relation to the literal emotions of everyday life. When we read,

---

[25] See Roland Barthes, *Incidents* (Paris, 1987).

we do not literally feel fear or anger.'[26] This is an argument which evidently runs counter to that which I am developing here. And Tournier's theories of the reception of his texts, read in this context, tend effectively to disturb Ricœur's concept of the non-literal nature of poetic feelings. Tournier might be said to take a view such as Ricœur's as a constraint within and against which he writes. He suggests indeed that his texts desire a suspension of disbelief on the part of the reader, a participation in a sexual act which is imaginary yet whose affective associations are very real. Tournier's fiction offers a painful pleasure, an illusion of reality, as it plays with its power to make the reader respond.

'Le Vol du vampire' images the reading encounter as one between lovers engaged in a symbiotic, yet sado-masochistic embrace. Tournier's essay on reading readily grafts itself on to the corpus of texts which explore the seduction, sexuality, and sensitizing of reading relations. The essay opens with a discussion of why writers produce fiction. Tournier stresses here that he writes to be read and to disperse his texts; as he admits: 'Oui, la vocation naturelle, irrépressible, du livre est centrifuge. Il est fait pour être publié, diffusé, lancé, acheté, lu.'[27] Here the 'livre'

---

[26] Paul Ricœur, 'The Metaphorical Process as Cognition, Imagination and Feeling', in Sheldon Sacks (ed.), *On Metaphor* (Chicago, 1978), 141–57: 155. Ricœur is quoted in English here since this essay is based on a paper read in English at the symposium 'Metaphor: The Conceptual Leap', sponsored by the University of Chicago Extension, Feb. 1978.

[27] Michel Tournier, 'Le Vol du vampire', in *Le Vol du vampire* (Paris, 1983), 11–27: 12: 'The Flight of the Vampire', trans. Ninette Bailey and Michael Worton, *Paragraph*, 10 (Oct. 1987), 4–12: 5 ('Yes, the natural, irrepressible vocation of the book is centrifugal. It is made to be published, distributed, launched, bought, read'). 'Le Vol du vampire' has inspired various readings. Colin Davis, for example, concentrates on the problematics of mastery and control. His text reacts coolly against what he diagnoses as 'an impossible double bind' where the reader is exhorted 'to create freely on the one hand, but to obey and lionize the author on the other' (*Michel Tournier: Philosophy and Fiction* (Oxford, 1988), 123). Davis is troubled by the very duplicity of 'Le Vol du vampire'. He sees the latent violence and authorial aggression as symptomatic of the failure of the writer's adherence to negative hermeneutics and of an implicit denial of Tournier's stated belief in the primacy of the reader. Michael Worton, in his exciting essay 'Use and Abuse of Metaphor in Tournier's "Le Vol du vampire"' (*Paragraph*, 10 (Oct. 1987), 13–28), perpetuates play between pain and pleasure, seeing vampirism as a dialectic of desire and aggression. Worton appears to enjoy the attack on decoding he detects in Tournier's texts, and so postulates a hypothetical model of textual seduction involving disorientation and disease. He reveals how the vampire metaphor itself is open to mutiple interpretations, and should not necessarily be equated with violation.

maintains its status as paper product, published, bought, and read. There follows, however, a subtle drift in Tournier's conceptualizations. He claims that: 'Un livre écrit, mais non lu, n'existe pas pleinement. Il ne possède qu'une demi-existence.'[28] This recognition of the half-life of the book opens out a series of metaphors showing the book to be part animate and to have acquired a potential carnality in Tournier's image patterns. Borrowing the language of phenomenology, Tournier now describes the book as 'une virtualité, un être exsangue, vide, malheureux'.[29] The images are then given more substance and Tournier unfurls his vampire metaphor as the bloodless beings become 'une nuée d'oiseaux de papier, des vampires secs, assoiffés de sang'.[30] The paper text is transformed into a sentient body in an act of conceptual metamorphosis.

The text, incarnate, is animated by desire. The virtuality thirsts for substance 'dans un appel à l'aide pour exister'.[31] The vampires lust for blood and 'se répandent au hasard en quête de

Mireille Rosello, in a reading of 'Le Vol du vampire' in her book L'In-différence chez Michel Tournier (Paris, 1990), explores alternative significations of the text's sexual metaphors. She rereads Tournier's images as marking the supremacy of the patriarchal signifier and the stamp of the author. Sexuality is textualized in a vigorous deconstruction of the text. My reading may be seen to differ from each of these in its raising of the question of the insecurity and potential victimization of the writer.

[28] Tournier, 'Le Vol du vampire', 12: 'The Flight of the Vampire', 5 ('A book which is written but not read does not fully exist').

[29] 'Le Vol du vampire', 12: 'The Flight of the Vampire', 5 ('a potentiality, a bloodless, empty, miserable being'). For expositions of a phenomenological approach to reading, see particularly Wolfgang Iser, 'The Reading Process: A Phenomenological Approach', in The Implied Reader (Baltimore, 1974), 274–94, and 'Interaction between Text and Reader', in Susan Suleiman and Inge Crosman (eds.), The Reader in the Text (Princeton, 1980), 106–19. In these essays Iser stresses both the virtuality of the work of art and the great importance of the actions involved in responding to a text.

[30] Tournier, 'Le Vol du vampire', 12: 'The Flight of the Vampire', 5 ('a flock of paper birds, parched, bloodthirsty vampires'). The choice of vampire as metaphor for the text neatly fits Tournier's series of winged creatures: the holy dove in Le Vent Paraclet, the butterfly signifier in Gaspard, Melchior et Balthazar, the goatskin kite in Vendredi ou les limbes du Pacifique. It may also be relevant that, in popular culture, the vampire is often seen as an image of the rapist. Christopher Frayling, studying stereotypes of the rapist, notes: 'the visual metaphor was usually the knife, although in the most famous rape fantasy it was the canine teeth' ('The House that Jack Built: Some Stereotypes of the Rapist in the History of Popular Culture', in Sylvana Tomaselli and Roy Porter (eds.), Rape (Oxford, 1986), 174–215: 174).

[31] Tournier, 'Le Vol du vampire', 12: 'The Flight of the Vampire', 5 ('in a call for aid—to exist').

lecteurs'.[32] In Tournier's configuration, then, the text claims the reader as partner in a sexual act which depends on the imperative need for the exchange of fluid. The vampire settles on the reader to suck his/her blood in an act of oral seduction close to rape. Tournier images this seduction in terms of violence and appropriation, saying: 'A peine un livre s'est-il abattu sur un lecteur qu'il se gonfle de sa chaleur et de ses rêves.'[33] This language of violence is not uncommon in theorizations of textual reception, as we shall see below.

In 'Le Vol du vampire', Tournier pursues his (sexual) fantasies of his text's reception, but the linearity of his argument is disrupted. It might be suggested that here he refuses to choose between conflicting compulsions. In one way Tournier entertains a paternal tenderness for his text and observes its flourishing and growth. He reveals that in the text 'les intentions de l'écrivain et les fantasmes du lecteur' mingle 'comme sur le visage d'un enfant les traits de son père et de sa mère'.[34] In an essay which apparently upholds the polarity and hierarchy of sexual difference and authorial authority, the writer is shown as father of the text and the reader as mother. The child they produce might be seen as a metatextual incarnation of the adored children of Tournier's fictions. He is at once the result of the sexual act and the forbidden object of desire.

Tournier's novels move between paedophilia and promiscuity. In a similar pattern, his fantasy of his text's activity gravitates towards an image of aggressive, repeated penetration. The image of predatory extraction becomes one of violent and promiscuous insemination. In the fantasy Tournier has produced, his reader receives the thrust of his texts, taking on the (gendered?) role of victim and passive recipient. Yet, noticeably, this role is by no means fixed. The metaphor of sucking and satiation mutates and the power relation between text and reader is inverted: 'la lecture terminée, le livre épuisé, abandonné par le lecteur, attendra un autre vivant afin de

[32] 'Le Vol du vampire', 13: 'The Flight of the Vampire', 5 ('fly in all directions in search of readers').

[33] 'Le Vol du vampire', 13: 'The Flight of the Vampire', 5 ('As soon as a book has swooped down on a reader, it gorges itself on his warmth and on his dreams').

[34] 'Le Vol du vampire', 13: 'The Flight of the Vampire', 5 ('the intentions of the author and the fantasies of the reader' mingle 'just as the features of both the father and the mother merge into each other in their child's face').

féconder à son tour son imagination'.[35] The vision of the text swelling with the reader's blood is suspended and copied. The two parts of the metaphor exist like mirroring twins, equal but opposite one to another. The text cannot be resolved into an image of symbiosis, of mutual transfusion, since this is absent from both configurations, and works to deny the conflicting relations of dominance and dependence that Tournier describes.

In a Derridian deconstruction this conflict of the equal but opposite is written out in a play of elision, fusion, and dissemination; to pursue the sexual metaphor, in Sarah Kofman's words: 'chaque sexe, comme chaque texte l'un à l'autre agglutiné, devient indécidable, parle la langue et dans la langue de l'autre: ni féminin ni masculin, ni castré ni non castré, non parce que bisexué mais parce que battant entre les sexes, parce que sexe toujours déjà double, qui gaine et bande doublement obéissant à un *double Bind*'.[36] The nature of the double bind in Tournier's texts is rather different. He depends on the simultaneous retention of conflicting images and tenets. Readings of his texts exist in the clash between mutually exclusive statements: deconstruction happens in the apposition rather than in the contamination and interpenetration of separate concepts. Tournier's play of contradictions offers a painful pleasure, in the way that Barbara Johnson shows (more generally): 'Division, contradiction, incompatibility, and ellipsis . . . thus stand as the challenge, the enigma, the despair, and the delight of both the lover and the reader of literature.'[37]

Following Johnson, I would claim that these painful pleasures are necessary to the affective enjoyment of texts. I would add further that one particular and elusive pleasure derives from what I have called previously the encounter between two potentially incompatible phantom desires: that of the writer

---

[35] 'Le Vol du vampire', 13: 'The Flight of the Vampire', 5 ('once the reading is over, the book exhausted, abandoned by its reader, will wait for another living being in order to fertilize in turn his imagination').

[36] Sarah Kofman, *Lectures de Derrida* (Paris, 1984), 144 ('Each sex, like each text stuck one to another, becomes undecidable, speaks the language and in the language of the other: neither male nor female, neither castrated nor uncastrated, not because it is bisexual, but because it goes between the sexes, because sex is always already double, doubly masking and blindfolding, obeying a double Bind').

[37] Barbara Johnson, *The Critical Difference* (Baltimore, 1980), 20.

for the phantom reader and that of the reader for the absent writer.

The writer's desire is amply illustrated in Tournier's text and it is seen to be peculiarly troubling. In 'Le Vol du vampire', the writer is seen as the master of his text, which he conceives and confects 'pour un certain public'.[38] The writer recognizes the text's need of a reader to exist, and the (sexual) exchange between text and reader is mediated by the writer's act of publishing the text. The writer endows the text with its centrifugal force, consciously releasing a horde of paper vampires. On the one hand we might suggest here that the writer is constructed as pander, or Pandarus, permitting and creating the proliferation of passionate acts. Yet the power and prowess this suggests is undermined by other images of the writer as victim of his own predatory texts.

In *Le Vent Paraclet*, whose essays pre-date 'Le Vol du vampire', we find the same language of blood-letting and release when Tournier writes of his work: 'Et quand elle me lâche, quand gorgée de ma substance elle commence à rouler de par le monde, je gis exsangue, vidé, écœuré, épuisé, hanté par des idées de mort.'[39] Here the writer is left by his texts. His blood is sucked as his reader's blood will be sucked; he is emptied by the force of his fiction. The passive writer, victim of fiction, comes to mirror the passive reader, possessed by the vampire text. Both reader and writer play 'female' roles as they are enjoyed by the phallic text. If the text's recipient is gendered female, the doubling author may appear to hold an illusory femininity himself. From this perspective we may reread the image of the writer releasing his texts. Pandarus may be replaced by Pandora, who unknowingly lets out a swarm of evils into the world.[40]

Tournier's essay works ostensibly, at first, to uphold a gendered pattern of reading relations. The author as master desires a female reader who will receive the phallic text. This

[38] Tournier, 'Le Vol du vampire', 12: 'The Flight of the Vampire', 4 ('for a specific public').

[39] Michel Tournier, *Le Vent Paraclet* (Paris, 1977), 179: *The Wind Spirit*, trans. Arthur Goldhammer (London, 1991), 153 ('And when it has fed on me and sucked my blood, when it begins to make its own way in the world, I lie wan, drained, disgusted, exhausted, and obsessed with thoughts of death').

[40] For references to Pandora, see Hesiod, *Theogony*, lines 570–612, and *Works and Days*, lines 47–105, in *The Homeric Hymns and Homerica* (London, 1967).

configuration evidently runs counter to Tournier's many statements about the freedom of the reader.[41] Indeed in his gestures
towards interpretative liberty he appears to undermine the possibility of upholding this fixed gender configuration. Further,
taking apart the image patterns of Tournier's writings on reception, we have seen that the author is far from confident of his
paternity. The author is seen to become, indeed, a mirror image
of his desired reader. Yet this specular relation offers no security
of identity. For Tournier, the reading encounter emerges as a
charged and shattering contest of power, a fearful play with
reality and illusion.

• Reading and Psychoanalysis

I want to pause here to consider one further implication of the
possible feminization of the role of the writer. One problem
which arises in attempts to analyse the reading encounter is to
define the part played by the text as it mediates relations between producer and consumer. In suggesting the instability and
insecurity of the author's paternity, I want to consider further
the question of whether the text may be read as fetish, as
substitute phallus for the castrated mother-author.

The fetish can be seen both to affirm and to deny the fact of
castration. As Freud claims in his essay 'Fetishism': 'both the
disavowal and the affirmation of the castration have found their
way into the construction of the fetish itself.'[42] Deleuze, rereading Freud, writes that 'le fétiche est l'image ou le substitut d'un
phallus féminin, c'est-à-dire un moyen par lequel nous dénions
que la femme manque de pénis'.[43] Looking at Freud's theory of
the motivation for the choice of specific fetish, he continues: 'Le
fétichiste élirait comme fétiche le dernier objet qu'il a vu, enfant,

---

[41] For a reading of Tournier which forms a critique of the notion that Tournier
offers his reader interpretative freedom, see Colin Davis, 'Les Interprétations', in
Arlette Bouloumié and Maurice de Gandillac (eds.), *Images et signes de Michel
Tournier* (Paris, 1991), 191–206.

[42] Sigmund Freud, 'Fetishism', in *The Standard Edition of the Complete Psychological Works of Sigmund Freud* (London, 1981), xxi. 147–57: 156.

[43] Gilles Deleuze, *Présentation de Sacher-Masoch* (Paris, 1967), 28 ('the fetish is
the image of or a substitute for the female phallus, in other words the means by
which we deny that women do not have a phallus').

avant de s'apercevoir de l'absence.'[44] The relevance here of these theories of fetishism derives from the play they suggest between presence and absence, fiction and suspension of disbelief. By replacing the phallus, the fetish is a substitute which demands an engagement with both illusion and reality. This type of double-think, I suggest, is necessary to and a component of the reading encounter as the reader is troubled at once by desire, doubt, and identification. In *Le Plaisir du texte* Barthes, indeed, uses a metaphor of the castrated mother to express the willing duplicity of certain readers: 'Beaucoup de lectures sont perverses, impliquant un clivage. De même que l'enfant sait que sa mère n'a pas de pénis et tout en même temps croit qu'elle en a un (économie dont Freud a montré la rentabilité), de même le lecteur peut dire sans cesse: *je sais bien que ce ne sont que des mots, mais tout de même* . . .'.[45]

I would argue that it is in this suspension of disbelief, the acceptance of the text as phallus, not fetish, this susceptibility to a phantom desire, that the reading encounter acquires its power.

Textual seduction may be seen to involve a form of double-think which may heighten our awareness of the parallels between reading relations and the transference-love of psychoanalysis. Elizabeth Wright suggests indeed: 'Transference and countertransference might be regarded as the "reader theory" of psychoanalysis.'[46] She concludes her analysis in the following terms: 'Readers do not only work on texts, but texts work on readers, and this involves a complex double dialectic of two bodies inscribed in language.'[47] This recognition that texts work on readers is of course readily aligned with the analysis of reading relations I am developing here.

I would argue that the question of transference raises precisely the issues of illusion and reality which are manipulated in the reading encounter. In an analysis of Freud's essay 'Observations

[44] Gilles Deleuze, *Présentation de Sacher-Masoch* (Paris, 1967), 28–9 ('The fetishist would choose as a fetish the last object he has seen as a child before becoming aware of this absence').

[45] Roland Barthes, *Le Plaisir du texte*, 76: *The Pleasure of the Text*, 47 ('Many readings are perverse, implying a split, a cleavage. Just as the child knows its mother has no penis and simultaneously believes she has one (an economy whose validity Freud has demonstrated), so the reader can keep saying: *I know these are only words, but all the same* . . .').

[46] Elizabeth Wright, *Psychoanalytic Criticism: Theory in Practice* (London, 1984), 15.   [47] Ibid. 17.

on Transference-Love', John Forrester writes that transference 'could only be "discovered" by the physician accepting the relationship as exactly that—a relationship, whose components are real—and not dismissing it as an "illusion", or "fantasy" or a "lie"'.[48] While the emotions are real, the engagement is not: the analyst controls the charged relationship which depends strongly on the belief in what should also be known to be an illusion. As Forrester says: 'the aim of the analyst is always double: to entice or attract, and then to decline and evade, to defer and delay'.[49] To effect a cure, psychoanalysis depends in this sense on the formative power of a fictional encounter. The analysand must engage with that fiction, identify him/herself as an active participant in that fiction. The fiction itself must be controlled by the analyst, and finally relinquished by the analysand. But it is important to note that the formative effects of the engagement with that fiction should be felt, even after the illusion has been revealed.

It is with reference then to the acknowledgement of the formative effects of a fictional encounter that I am making this comparison between reading relations and transference-love. And this leads me to look at how the position I am adopting here will in fact diverge from conventional models of psychoanalytic criticism. Broadly speaking, a model from psychoanalytic theory and practice has been used to reread reading relations. By way of example we might cite Wright's summing up of Shoshana Felman's argument in 'Turning the Screw of Interpretation'. As Wright puts it: 'The reader begins as analyst and ends up as analysand, reactivating his past traumas.'[50] In this framework, the reader's traumas necessarily pre-exist the reading encounter, which becomes itself potentially (though not necessarily effectively) therapeutic. In terms of the argument I am developing here, my concern is to question how far the comparison between identification in reading and the transference-love of psychoanalysis may reveal in each case how far the construction of a fiction of desire which masquerades, in the

[48] John Forrester, 'Rape, Seduction and Psychoanalysis' in Tomaselli and Porter (eds.), *Rape*, 57–83: 78. Forrester makes a reading of Freud's essay 'Observations on Transference-Love' (in *Standard Edition*, xxi. 157–73).

[49] Forrester, 'Rape, Seduction and Psychoanalysis', 79.

[50] Wright, *Psychoanalytic Criticism*, 131.

confined spaces of the clinical session and the reading encounter, as 'real' experience, may in fact reveal the fragile and mutable bases of identity formation and psychoanalytic cure. My aim in pursuing this analogy is to stress how the encounter and identification with a fiction may potentially also propagate and reform delusion as much as effect cure.

But, of course, it would be perverse not to acknowledge that there are dangerous and telling differences between reading relations and the transference-love of psychoanalysis. Freud counsels that 'psychoanalytic treatment is founded on truthfulness'[51] and he prescribes methods for the analyst to adopt, saying for example that 'he must keep firm hold of the transference-love, but treat it as something unreal'.[52] We may be sceptical as to whether this is always achieved in the psychoanalytic session, but this debt to truthfulness remains at least a theoretical aim. The author of fictions, contrarily, has no debt to an ideal of truthfulness and apparently no duty to a suffering patient. The concept of truth, in Tournier's fiction, for example, is taken apart by the very strategy of upholding opposing truths. For Proust, as I will discuss later, truth is entirely eradicated for narrator and reader alike in the desiring quest for knowledge of Albertine. For Duras, the perpetual renarration of events, both fictional and biographical, corrodes any possibility of stability and certain meaning.

Writers such as Tournier appear to enjoy the elaborate possibilities of lies, and their perpetual unsettling of the reader's security. He quotes, with relish, Cocteau's statement: 'je suis un mensonge qui dit toujours la vérité'[53] and admits: 'il y a des phrases de Cocteau que je n'aurai jamais fini de caresser et de redire parce qu'elles sont inépuisables'.[54] Tournier displays evident pleasure in dissimulation and it may be seen as pervasive in the mutant metaphors of 'Le Vol du vampire'.

The injection of lies into persuasive discourse is doubly dis-

---

[51] Freud, 'Observations on Transference-Love', 166.

[52] Ibid.

[53] Tournier, 'Le Vol du vampire', 14: 'The Flight of the Vampire', 6 ('I am a lie which always tells the truth').

[54] Michel Tournier, 'Qu'est-ce que la littérature?', interview with Jean-Jacques Brochier, *Magazine littéraire*, 179 (Dec. 1981). 80–6: 83 ('there are some of Cocteau's sayings which I will never get tired of cherishing and repeating since they are inexhaustible').

turbing. On the one hand, lies trouble the enjoyment of a text, as Leo Bersani claims: 'By initiating a designifying mobility within a text, the author's silent, insistent voice undoes that security of statement by which we can so easily be seduced, and possessed.'[55] Yet the very seduction of fiction may be seen as consisting of a play of lies and elusive enticement. Baudrillard describes the 'puissance immanente de la séduction de tout ôter à sa vérité et de le faire rentrer dans le jeu, dans le jeu pur des apparences, et là de déjouer en un tournemain tous les systèmes de sens et de pouvoir'.[56] Bersani stresses the pain of a destabilized text; Baudrillard takes pleasure in the evacuation of truth and the play of artifice. Lies lead the reader into a volatile realm of dis-ease whether it be painful or pleasurable, deluded or illusory.

So what can we conclude then about the issue of the impact of fiction, and of the author's responsibility? Does the reading encounter do potential harm to the reader? Can the reader accommodate the violence and subversion frequently implicit in contests of authorial control and interpretative mastery?

In the case of Tournier, it might be said that it is the author's (avowed) desire that the reader succumb to the disease of his texts. Tournier writes at least that he seeks to touch and con-taminate his readers; as Colin Davis suggests: 'Whereas Sartre's reader is *fascinated* by the text, Tournier's is *infected* as if by a contagious disease'.[57] Tournier's ideal is one of infiltration and injection, entering the reader in order to rouse in him/her a mirroring desire. Reading is created as compulsion in a coercive experience of coupling. Tournier is apparently obsessed with 'le rêve de toute création qui est de devenir contagieuse'[58] and he states that 'toute création se veut-elle fondamentalement

---

[55] Leo Bersani, *The Freudian Body: Psychoanalysis and Art* (New York, 1986), 67.

[56] Jean Baudrillard, *De la séduction* (Paris, 1979), 20: *Seduction*, trans. Brian Singer (London, 1990), 8 ('The capacity immanent to seduction to deny things their truth and turn it into a game, the pure play of appearances, and thereby foil all systems of power and meaning with a mere turn of the hand'). See also Ross Chambers, who writes: 'Seduction as a narrative tactic takes the form of recruiting the desires of the other in the interests of maintaining narrative authority' (*Story and Situation: Narrative Seduction and the Power of Fiction* (Minneapolis, 1984), 215).

[57] Davis, *Michel Tournier*, 122.

[58] Tournier, *Le Vent Paraclet*, 199: *The Wind Spirit*, 171 ('the dream of all creation, which is to become contagious').

contagieuse et en appelle-t-elle à la créativité des lecteurs'.[59] The reading of the text is imaged as disease, but this disease is seen to inspire the desire and the creativity of the reader. The uneasy reader, in search of textual freedom, unleashing his/her creativity, leaves him/herself uncomfortably open to the possibility of pain and mutation.

• *Body and Text*

The dissemination of dis(-)ease throughout Tournier's texts leads to an insidious interest in deformations of reality. Tournier's explorations of eroticism are provocatively twisted; his *corps de jouissance* bears signs of mutilation. This fascination with the rarefying of pleasure through pain will be seen to recur in all the texts I will examine in this study. What I am interested to question is whether pain is a necessary correlative of the pleasure of the reading encounter. An analysis of various theorists of reading may lead us to suggest that this is indeed the case.

Barthes offers an ambiguous engagement with the possibilities of pain in pleasure in the fragmented pieces which form *Le Plaisir du texte*. He attacks his own discourse with the 'maximum of disintegrative violence'[60] Barbara Johnson describes in her reading of *S/Z*. *Le Plaisir du texte* sets afloat conflicting expressions of sexuality dependent on the proximity of rapture and rupture. One way in which Barthes images the text is as a body, and this is particularly significant in the context of this analysis of reading as encounter. Where, for Tournier, the reading encounter is dominated by the text as phallus, denying, yet commemorating castration, for Barthes, the text is fragilized body, at once adored and mutilated by the desiring reader. Barthes's conceptualization opens out further possibilities of violence and desire in the relation between sentient reader and sensitized fiction. His intimations of this intimacy in reading render relations between reader and text all the more intense.

[59] Tournier. 'Le Vol du vampire', 13: 'The Flight of the Vampire', 5 ('in its desire to have a contagious effect, every literary work of art appeals to the creativity of its readers').
[60] Johnson, *The Critical Difference*, 7.

Barthes exploits this intensity, perpetually flexing and redressing the complex power play inherent in this interdependence and desire.

The figuring of the text in the form of a body has itself been fetishized as a device. Ricœur writes: 'The very expression "figure of speech" implies that in metaphor, as in other tropes or turns, discourse assumes the nature of a body by displaying forms and traits which usually characterize the human face, man's "figure"; it is as though the tropes gave to discourse a quasi-bodily externalization.'[61] Barthes appropriates the bodily metaphor readily applied to and associated with the tropes which generate the text. His figurative language fleshes out the text, lets it appear in bodily form, yet it is necessarily a body that may be stripped, flayed, and dissected: 'le texte lui-même, structure diagrammatique, et non pas imitative, peut se dévoiler sous forme de corps, clivé en objets fétiches, en lieux érotiques'.[62]

In the discourse of deconstruction, if the text appears as a body, it is in effect to be disclosed and dissected. Derrida writes of 'cette violence nécessaire', saying: 'Si nous distinguons le texte du livre, nous dirons que la destruction du livre, telle qu'elle s'annonce aujourd'hui dans tous les domaines, dénude la surface du texte'.[63] Denuding the text, denying its integrity and authority, becomes an obsessive pleasure of writing and reading practice. Sarah Kofman goes so far as to see the Derridian text as fractured flesh: 'corps morcelé, atopique, décentré, bousculant sens dessus dessous le logos traditionnel, tel serait le texte derridien'.[64] Her Lacanian metaphor for the text is supplemented by an analysis of the affective effects of Derrida's écriture: 'Comme les organes génitaux féminins, elle inquiète,

---

[61] Ricœur, 'The Metaphorical Process as Cognition, Imagination and Feeling', 142.

[62] Barthes, Le Plaisir du texte, 89: The Pleasure of the Text, 56 ('the text itself, a diagrammatic and not an imitative structure, can reveal itself in the form of a body, split into fetish objects, into erotic sites').

[63] Jacques Derrida, De la Grammatologie (Paris, 1967), 31: Of Grammatology, trans. Gayatri Chakravorty Spivak (Baltimore, 1976), 18 ('If I distinguish the text from the book, I shall say that the destruction of the book, as it is now underway in all domains, denudes the surface of the text').

[64] Kofman, Lectures de Derrida, 25 ('the body in pieces, atopic, decentred, turning the traditional logos upside down, this is what the Derridian text would be like').

méduse, pétrifie.'[65] It is noticeable here that the text grows affinities with the castrated body of the mother, as it does also with the disintegrated mirror image of the self. The fear and recognition of castration and violence against the self are revealed as determining features of the generation and creative deconstruction of the body of the text.

Where Barthes's reading of the textual body depends on unveiling, cleaving, and division, the language he selects to express the tensions of the reading process is itself shadowed with the implication of sado-masochistic pleasure. Barthes refers to Sade, writing: 'Sade: le plaisir de la lecture vient évidemment de certaines ruptures (ou de certaines collisions).'[66] In the collisions which occur in Le Plaisir du texte, Barthes engages with 'la dialectique de l'attendrissement et de la haine'.[67] He shows how reading can be inscribed as corporeal, and how the experiences of the body re-created in the reading process are both painful and pleasurable: 'Chaque fois que j'essaye d'"analyser" un texte qui m'a donné du plaisir, ce n'est pas ma "subjectivité" que je retrouve, c'est mon "individu", la donnée qui fait mon corps séparé des autres corps et lui approprie sa souffrance ou son plaisir: c'est mon corps de jouissance que je retrouve.'[68]

Jouissance is found in the fusion of suffering and pleasure. The body's rapture collides pain and sensual stimulation. Yet, whilst Barthes's pleasure in the text seems dependent on these ambivalent divisions—as he writes indeed: 'Je m'intéresse au langage parce qu'il me blesse ou me séduit'[69]—the relation he describes between text and reader is not inherently conflictual.

[65] Ibid. 26 ('Like the female genital organs, it troubles, dumbfounds, petrifies').

[66] Barthes, Le Plaisir du texte, 14: The Pleasure of the Text, 6 ('Sade: the pleasure of reading him clearly proceeds from certain breaks (or certain collisions)'). Revealing Barthes's interest in the broken and fragmented, Stephen Ungar writes: 'Edges, seams, joints and flaws promote a metaphoric equivalence of text and body which removes reading from science and resituates it in pleasure, a transition discernible in the fragmentary nature of Barthes's own text' (Roland Barthes: The Professor of Desire (London, 1983), 59).

[67] Barthes, Le Plaisir du texte, 75–6: The Pleasure of the Text, 47 ('the dialectic of tenderness and hatred').

[68] Le Plaisir du texte 98–9: The Pleasure of the Text, 62 ('Whenever I attempt to "analyse" a text which has given me pleasure, it is not my "subjectivity" I encounter but my "individuality", the given which makes my body separate from other bodies and appropriates its suffering or its pleasure: it is my body of bliss I encounter').

[69] Le Plaisir du texte, 62: The Pleasure of the Text, 38 ('I am interested in language because it wounds or seduces me').

In this account of the reading encounter, Barthes may be seen to differ radically from Tournier, and from some other theorists of reception.

- ## *Interpretative Mastery*

The reading encounter is all too frequently imaged in terms of aggression. Susan Sontag writes (in 1964); 'the contemporary zeal for the project of interpretation is often prompted not by piety toward the troublesome text (which may conceal an aggression) but by an open aggressiveness, an overt contempt for appearances'.[70] This aggressive encounter is itself not free from implications with relation to gender. Naomi Schor finds it significant that Sontag's essay reveals 'an assimilation of interpretation to (masculine) forms of aggression and mastery: rape and imperialism'.[71]

This machismo of interpretation flourishes in the critical discourse of Harold Bloom, who contends that 'Whether sublimation of sexual instincts plays a central part in the genesis of poetry is hardly relevant to the reading of poetry . . . But sublimation of aggressive instincts is central to reading and writing poetry.'[72] As the (male) poet metaphorically aggresses his literary forbears, so the (male) critic seeks to dominate the text he reads. Elizabeth Freund quotes an apt example from R. P. Warren, who, in developing a theory of reading, likens a poem to the monstrous Orillo in Boiardo's *Orlando Inamorato*: 'There is only one way to conquer the monster: you must eat it, bones, blood, skin, pelt and gristle. And even then the monster is not dead, for it lives in you, is assimilated into you, and you are different, and somewhat monstrous in yourself for having

[70] Susan Sontag, 'Against Interpretation', in *A Susan Sontag Reader* (Harmondsworth, 1983), 95–101: 98.

[71] Naomi Schor, 'Fiction as Interpretation/Interpretation as Fiction', in Suleiman and Crosman (eds.), *The Reader in the Text*, 165–82: 182.

[72] Harold Bloom, *The Anxiety of Influence* (New York, 1973), 115. Bloom pursues his theories of competitiveness, usurpation, and 'misprision' in *Agon: Towards a Theory of Revisionism* (New York, 1982). See also, for example, Stanley Fish, who claims that 'the text and the reader are independent and competing entities whose spheres of influence and responsibility must be defined and controlled' (*Is there a Text in this Class? The Authority of Interpretive Communities* (Cambridge, Mass., 1980), 12).

eaten it.'[73] For Warren the text is monster, as for Tournier the text is vampire: the text is created in metaphor as potential, fantastical aggressor who finds his(?) mirror image in the combative heroic reader who attempts to 'appropriate it by a violent act of mastery and incorporation'.[74] This image of reading as appropriation is familiar in reception theory; Starobinski writes of Jauss, for example: 'Jauss affirme ainsi que la réception des œuvres est une appropriation active.'[75] Yet whilst attempting to appropriate and conquer the text, it seems that the reader must remain aware that in the act which reading becomes, s/he is also possessed by the text.

If the engagement of reading is constructed as aggressive encounter, then it may need to be recognized that the reader is potentially at risk from the text. The reader, violently feminized, becomes the vessel or victim of the text in multiple configurations of reading relations. Sartre says of reading: 'c'est une possession: on prête son corps aux morts pour qu'ils puissent revivre'.[76] Iser claims that 'the reader will be "occupied" by the thoughts of the author'.[77] Georges Poulet, in his essay 'Phénoménologie de la conscience critique', describes in a series of emotive metaphors a tense and violent scene of reading. For Poulet, the reader becomes 'la proie du langage'[78] experiencing a take-over of 'le fond subjectif de [s]on être'.[79] The work defines the content of his consciousness, takes hold of it, appropriates it. He concludes that 'une œuvre littéraire, tant qu'opère en elle cette insufflation de vie provoquée par la lecture, devient elle-même, aux dépens du lecteur dont elle annule la vie propre, une manière d'être humain'.[80] The imagery constructs a reader who

---

[73] R. P. Warren, quoted in Elizabeth Freund, *The Return of the Reader: Reader Response Criticism* (London, 1987), 55.

[74] Ibid.

[75] Jean Starobinski, in a preface to Hans Robert Jauss, *Pour une esthétique de la réception* (Paris, 1978), 15 ('Jauss affirms thus that the reception of texts is an active appropriation').

[76] Jean-Paul Sartre, *Qu'est-ce que la littérature?* (Paris, 1972), 36 ('it's a form of possession: we lend our bodies to the dead so they can live again').

[77] Iser, *The Implied Reader*, 293.

[78] Georges Poulet, 'Phénoménologie de la conscience critique', in *La Conscience critique* (Paris, 1971), 275–99: 279 ('the prey of language').

[79] Ibid. 282 ('the subjective basis of [his] being').

[80] Ibid. 285 ('a literary work, as long as this breath of life reading creates flows through it, becomes in itself a form of human being, at the expense of the reader, whose own life it suspends').

collaborates in his/her suffering. Where Poulet writes 'je me livre, pieds et poings liés, à la toute-puissance du mensonge'[81] he appears to enter eagerly into the sado-masochistic exchange of reading. The prey desires the aggression of the predator. The reader is, in Tournier's terms, 'l'indispensable collaborateur de l'écrivain'.[82] Yet, as Poulet admits, the work exists at the expense of the reader: despite collusion, reading is seen as invasion. The existence of the text within the reader is a charged transgression, an erotic, desired violation. The (male) reader enjoys the forbidden, alluring pleasure of passivity and penetration.

Barthes attempts to explode this preoccupation with the model of combat, power relations, activity, and passivity, which haunts the image of coupling ubiquitous as metaphor for reading relations. He stresses: 'Je ne suis pas nécessairement *captivé* par le texte de plaisir; ce peut être un acte léger, complexe, ténu, presque étourdi,'[83] and he continues to specify: 'Le plaisir du texte (la jouissance du texte) est au contraire un effacement brusque de la *valeur* guerrière.'[84] Barthes's work seeks not to reverse or reorientate power relations, but to shatter the prescribed active–passive dyad of sexual metaphors. Pain and suffering are seen to be always already present within the sensation of pleasure: their existence is not dependent on the aggression of sexual power play and the feminization of the reader.

And it is Barthes's model that I want, in part, to adopt in the readings that follow. My aim will be to show that the configuration of reading as (sexual) encounter should not depend on a

[81] Ibid. 279 ('my wrists and ankles tied, I deliver myself up to the supreme power of falsehood'). Here Poulet uses overt imagery of bondage; another type of bonding also proliferates in reader response criticism, as Wayne C. Booth suggests: 'the receiver's process of interpretation is itself part of what is communicated; the activity of interpretation, performed at the speaker's command, produces a "bonding" which is part of the "meaning"' ('Ten Literal "Theses"', in Sacks (ed.), *On Metaphor*, 173–4: 173). The supposedly benign bond of reading becomes bound up with connotations of constraint.

[82] Tournier, 'Le Vol du vampire', 12: 'The Flight of the Vampire', 5 ('the writer's indispensable collaborator').

[83] Barthes, *Le Plaisir du texte*, 41–2: *The Pleasure of the Text*, 24 ('I am not necessarily *captivated* by the text of pleasure; it can be an act that is slight, complex, tenuous, almost scatterbrained').

[84] *Le Plaisir du texte*, 50: *The Pleasure of the Text*, 30 ('The pleasure of the text (the bliss of the text) is on the contrary like a sudden obliteration of the warrior *Value*').

fixed hierarchy of power or fixed gender roles. It depends neither entirely on the intention of the writer, nor exclusively on the desire of the reader. It depends instead on a frequently incompatible specular relation between two unequal couples: the author and his/her imagined reader, and the reader and his/her imagined author. It is indeed in this play of incompatibilities that the multiple potential of the reading encounter may be realized. Yet it is also in this incompatibility that we find pain as the necessary correlative of the pleasure of the reading encounter. Both writer and reader may be tantalized or traumatized by the illusory nature of their desires, by the tenuous pleasures of engagement in an imaginary encounter. Both writer and reader may be haunted by their absent, yet menacing and seductive, counterpart. And while this nexus of power and pleasure may be cross-cut with relations of gender, of similarity and difference, these are effectively destabilized in the necessary challenge posed both to the writer's authority and to the reader's freedom.

In the discussion of texts which follows I have attempted to illustrate how far assumptions about gendered reading, about relations of activity and passivity, about homosexuality and heterosexuality, can be subverted and even exploded in the reading encounter both represented and performed. In some senses it may seem that I am launching a familiar attack on authorial control, and linking this all too readily with patriarchy, paternity, and phallocentrism. However, my aim is not to theorize or argue for an alternative, non-conflictual *lecture féminine*, dependent on reciprocity or, indeed, on celebration. My aim is to suggest that the reading encounter is at once interrelational and conflictual, and that it depends not on pre-constructed identities, but on the very performance of identity in the process of reading. And in this sense, my work is specifically informed by contemporary queer theory, as I shall go on to show in the next chapter.

2

Identity and Identification

Le problème n'est pas de découvrir en soi la vérité de son sexe mais c'est plutôt d'user désormais de sa sexualité pour arriver à des multiplicités de relations.[1]

(Michel Foucault, 'De l'amitié comme mode de vie')

Je te cherche par-delà l'attente
Par-delà moi-même
Et je ne sais plus tant je t'aime
Lequel de nous deux est absent.[2]

(Paul Éluard, Capitale de la douleur)

• The Queer Reader

In Le Temps retrouvé Proust, meditating on identification and desire, makes reference to the potential of a queer reader. He begins in definite terms: 'l'écrivain ne doit pas s'offenser que l'inverti donne à ses héroïnes un visage masculin'.[3] Indeed Proust specifies that it is only by configuring the desire represented in the text in the terms of his own libidinal investment that the 'inverti' may come to realize fully the pleasure of the text. This is made clear with reference to the text's most notorious 'inverti', Charlus. As the narrator notes: 'si M. de Charlus n'avait pas donné à l' "infidèle" sur qui Musset pleure dans la Nuit d'Octobre ou dans le Souvenir le visage de Morel, il n'aurait ni pleuré, ni compris, puisque c'était par cette seule

---

[1] 'The difficulty doesn't lie in discovering the truth of one's sex in itself, but rather in using one's sexuality thenceforth to achieve a multiplicity of relations.'

[2] 'I search for you beyond waiting | Beyond myself | And I love you so much I no longer know | Which one of us is absent.'

[3] Marcel Proust, A la recherche du temps perdu (Paris, 1989), iv. 489: In Search of Lost Time, vi. 273 ('the writer must not be indignant if the invert who reads his book gives to his heroines a masculine countenance').

voie, étroite et détournée, qu'il avait accès aux vérités de l'amour'.[4] It is noticeable here that Proust makes use of an example of homosexual desire in order to introduce one of the prime theories of reading put forward within *A la recherche du temps perdu*. The recognition of the ability of the 'inverti' to construe the text in terms of his own patterns of desire, and indeed the avowal of the seeming necessity for this interpretative agility, frame the famous phrase where Proust states: 'En réalité, chaque lecteur est quand il lit, le propre lecteur de soi-même.'[5]

This statement itself, and the way in which it is framed in the text, are of specific relevance to my argument here. In the chapter that follows I will stress that it is of some considerable significance that Proust should make use of the dislocating experience of the queer reader, who reads against the constraints of a socially and textually coercive heterosexual matrix, in order to develop a theory of reception which undermines authorial intention and authority, and privileges instead the act of the interpreter.

Proust allows the act of reading to become a means of measuring and rereading the self. As the text states: 'L'ouvrage de l'écrivain n'est qu'une espèce d'instrument optique qu'il offre au lecteur afin de lui permettre de discerner ce que, sans ce livre, il n'eût peut-être pas vu en soi-même.'[6] The encounter with the text is seen to allow and even necessitate an occasion for self-analysis. I want to suggest here that, following the implications of the text still further, we may see the act of reading as not only a means to self-scrutiny, but also a means of self-creation. In this sense the reading encounter may then be said to be formative: the reader not only recognizes in the text what s/he knows to be true of him/herself, in him/herself, s/he also may be able to perceive aspects of the self which were previously occluded and

---

[4] *A la recherche*, iv. 489: *In Search of Lost Time*, vi. 273 ('if M. de Charlus had not bestowed upon the "traitress" for whom Musset weeps in *La Nuit d'Octobre* or *Souvenir* the features of Morel, he would neither have wept nor have understood, since it was only along this path, narrow and indirect, that he had access to the verities of love').

[5] *A la recherche*, iv. 489: *In Search of Lost Time*, vi. 273 ('In reality every reader is, while he is reading, the reader of his own self').

[6] *A la recherche*, iv. 489–90: *In Search of Lost Time*, vi. 273 ('The writer's work is merely a kind of optical instrument which he offers to the reader to enable him to discern what, without this book, he would perhaps never have perceived in himself').

unknown. It is the encounter with and the liberation of these aspects of the self, which, we may conclude, work to transform the reader, allowing him/her to be effectively changed by the work of the text.

Proust stresses that the reading encounter may not always have this self-enhancing, revelatory effect: 'le livre peut être trop savant, trop obscur pour le lecteur naïf, et ne lui présenter ainsi qu'un verre trouble avec lequel il ne pourra pas lire'.[7] And this may be read as an important cautionary remark with relation to the argument I am developing here. Where I am attempting to argue that fiction may be formative, that the reading encounter may change the self, this depends precisely on the engagement of the reader and his/her response and the responsibility s/he takes as s/he reads. In this sense my argument relates not so much to the essential nature of the reading encounter, if such it has, but to its potential, and to the ways in which it may be understood to be both reactive and performative.

Proust's account of queer reading appears on the whole entirely affirmative. He follows up his caution about the 'naïve' reader with the riposte: 'Mais d'autres particularités (comme l'inversion) peuvent faire que le lecteur a besoin de lire d'une certaine façon pour bien lire';[8] he continues: 'l'auteur n'a pas à s'en offenser, mais au contraire à laisser la plus grande liberté au lecteur en lui disant: "Regardez vous-même si vous voyez mieux avec ce verre-ci, avec celui-là, avec cet autre"'.[9] Like Tournier, Proust makes a claim for the reader's freedom and his/her ability to read the text as s/he desires. While Proust may seek to open out the possibilities of reading, where his text may work indeed to construct the self-critical, cautious, and perceptive reader it describes (and this we shall go on to see in Chapter 3), the process of appropriating the text, and viewing it from the reader's singular, subjective, and desiring angle of vision,

[7] *A la recherche*, iv. 490: *In Search of Lost Time*, vi. 273–4 ('The book may be too learned, too obscure for a simple reader, and may therefore present to him a clouded glass through which he cannot read').

[8] *A la recherche*, iv. 490: *In Search of Lost Time*, vi. 274 ('And other peculiarities can have the same effect as inversion. In order to read with understanding many readers require to read in their own particular fashion').

[9] *A la recherche*, iv. 490: *In Search of Lost Time*, vi. 274 ('the author must not be indignant at this; on the contrary, he must leave the reader all possible liberty, saying to him: "Look for yourself, and try whether you see best with this lens or that one or this other one"').

may be more troubled than Proust's texts tend to suggest. And this relates not so much to issues of intention and authority as to those of the social construction of sexuality.

Proust's account of reading in *Le Temps retrouvé* recalls an earlier passage from *La Prisonnière* where he has previously made reference to the reading habits of the Baron de Charlus. Here again it is revealed that the reader's sexuality guides the reading encounter, and that the queer reader, paradoxically secure in his divergent sexual identity, fits the fiction to his inclination and deftly swaps the gender of his object of desire. Proust describes this reader as 'l'inverti qui n'a pas pu nourrir sa passion qu'avec une littérature écrite pour les hommes à femmes, qui pensait aux hommes en lisant les *Nuits* de Musset'.[10] We may note here that Proust has no thought of the female reader, and her position in reading, and this is an issue we shall return to in a reading of Albertine. Further, even in his seeming championing of the possibilities of queer reading we may note an added insinuation of constraint. The text might be read to imply that the passion of the 'inverti' might be all the more satisfyingly nourished in the consumption of a fiction which mirrored his desire. The effects of imposing a non-heterosexual frame on a text need to be considered further. Does the non-heterosexual frame imposed by the 'invert' subvert the text he reads? Does Proust encourage his own reader to impose his/her frames on the text of indeterminate desires he presents to us? Is the reader free to do this?

It is important to my argument here to stress that the implications of Proust's account of subversive reading are more insidious than the text ostensibly suggests. While Proust concentrates on the imaginary reader's ability to twist and turn the text to his own taste, and this is the fragment of the discussion which resurfaces in *Le Temps retrouvé*, in *La Prisonnière* he may also be seen to reveal the power of the fiction to form the reader. On rereading we may become aware that the text stresses, more poignantly, the difficulties of maintaining and pursuing heterosexual identifications within homosexual practice. To quote the passage from *La Prisonnière* in full: 'l'inverti qui n'a pas pu

---

[10] *A la recherche*, iii. 747: *In Search of Lost Time*, v. 274 ('The invert who has been able to feed his passion only on a literature written for women-loving men, who used to think of men when he read Musset's *Nuits* . . .').

nourrir sa passion qu'avec une littérature écrite pour les hommes à femmes, qui pensait aux hommes en lisant les *Nuits* de Musset, éprouve le besoin d'entrer de même dans toutes les fonctions sociales de l'homme qui n'est pas inverti, d'entretenir un amant, comme le vieil habitué de l'Opéra des danseuses, d'être rangé, d'épouser ou de se coller, d'être père'.[11] I would argue that, however wryly, Proust posits a relation between the normative function of social conditioning and the formative power of fictions. While heterosexual identifications and aims may not be entirely the product of the fictions the reader has consumed, the insidious effect of these fictions in their work in upholding and mirroring social practice should not be overlooked.

• *New Subjectivities*

One of the central issues in this study is, precisely, that of the relation between the formative power and the normative potential of fictions. Can reading be formative and not normative? Is the reader free to identify with the position of the desiring subject as s/he will?

Making a critique of reader response theory, Tania Modleski argues that the view that meaning resides in readers as they interact with the text, and the view that this meaning may be determined within the larger context of the interpretative community to which readers belong, has limitations for feminist criticism. She specifies here one problem with such a formulation which lies in the assumption that 'an *already-existent* meaning exists *somewhere*, and that the critic's only job is to locate it'.[12] She argues that a fully politicized feminist criticism aims rather at 'bringing into being *new* meanings and *new* sub-

---

[11] *A la recherche*, iii. 747: *In Search of Lost Time*, v. 274 ('. . . feels the need to enter in the same way into all the social activities of the man who is not an invert, to keep a lover, as the old frequenter of the Opéra keeps ballet-girls, to settle down, to marry or form a permanent tie, to become a father').

[12] Tania Modleski, quoted in D. N. Rodowick, *The Difficulty of Difference: Psychoanalysis, Sexual Difference and Film Theory* (New York, 1991), 137. The quotation from Modleski comes from her article 'Some Functions of Feminist Criticism; or, The Scandal of the Mute Body', *October*, 49 (Summer 1989), 3–24.

jectivities'.[13] She goes on to suggest that feminist criticism 'may be said to have a performative dimension—i.e., to be *doing* something beyond restating already existent ideas and views'.[14] In this second chapter, my aim is to move on from analysis of the author, of his/her loss of authority, and his/her imaginary relation to the reading encounter. My interest here is in the reader, in the reanalysis of gendered positions in the response to texts, and in the rereading of notions of sexual identity. I tend to subscribe to Modleski's view that feminist criticism should aim at bringing into being new subjectivities, and I intend to look at how the production of new subjectivities and identities, through the assumption of transgressive reading positions, may itself be a formative experience. And it is in this sense that the reading encounter itself may be said to be doing something, to be performative.

Drawing on Modleski, as he sums up *The Difficulty of Difference*, D. N. Rodowick states: 'Subjectivity is defined by social and historical processes that are irreducible to singular categories, and its forms and potentialities are always in flux. Only on this basis can we recognize and defend the multiple possibilities of identity and desire, in film as well as other discourses and practices, that challenge patriarchal and capitalist ideologies.'[15] It is the question of the multiple possibilities of identity and desire, and the challenge they pose to the regulatory matrix of heterosexuality, that strikes me as important. It is by means of a rethinking of subjectivity that we may come to a further understanding of sexuality and the reading encounter.

Subjectivity, and its relation to identity and identification, have largely been brought into question in contemporary feminist criticism and queer theory. I want to dwell further here on the implications this has for the study of the reading encounter. In her introduction to *Inside/Out: Lesbian Theories, Gay Theories*, Diana Fuss makes use of the image of the invertible knot, seeing it as a kind of shorthand notation 'for the nodular problems [her] book seeks to disentangle and reweave: the entwining of identification and desire, of sexual difference and sexual differences, of heterosexuality and homosexuality, and,

---

[13] Tania Modleski, quoted in Rodowick, *The Difficulty of Difference*, 138.
[14] Tania Modleski, quoted ibid.
[15] Ibid. 140.

finally, of inside and out'.[16] In my own terms, I also want to examine relations between identification and desire, and the relations between the construction of identity through identification, and the act of identifying with a fictional text. This itself will be related to a mapping of desire dependent on the notion of a continuum between homosexual and heterosexual, and a study of sexual identity constructed in transaction and interrelation. This will be seen to relate to issues of knowledge and disclosure, to what Eve Kosofsky Sedgwick has come to call the epistemology of the closet.[17]

The notions of inside and out, adopted by Fuss, raise the issue of space and sexuality, and the interrelation between the two. The concept of a space, metaphorical or textual, where reading takes place is central to the conceptualization of reading as encounter. I would argue also that the notion of a stage where a sexual identity is enacted (or concealed) is central to the theorizing of sexual identities as performative, and as constructed in performance. In each case the privileged space depends on a play of inside and out. On the one hand, the reader (in Proust's terms) internalizes the text, interacts with it and relates it to him/herself. On the other hand, the identity of the desiring subject (in Butler's terms, as we shall go on to see) is constructed as the product of the performance s/he enacts. In this study, I am arguing for the possible conflation of these two spaces, for the recognition that they may, at times, be one and the same. This entails necessarily the recognition that identity is dependent on identification with a fiction, and that reading may be understood as performative, and as performance.

• Queer Theory

As we shall see, many of the questions raised in this study interrelate with those posed by current queer theory. I am referring here to the body of work which has largely been produced over the last decade. Paul Julian Smith suggests that Eve

---

[16] Diana Fuss (ed.), 'Inside/Out', in *Inside/Out: Lesbian Theories, Gay Theories* (New York, 1991), 1–10: 8.
[17] Eve Kosofsky Sedgwick, *Epistemology of the Closet* (Hemel Hempstead, 1991).

Kosofsky Sedgwick's *Between Men: English Literature and Male Homosocial Desire* 'is generally thought to have inaugurated a theoretically informed body of lesbian and gay studies'.[18] Paul Julian Smith's own book *Laws of Desire: Questions of Homosexuality in Spanish Writing and Film 1960–1990*, one of the recent works published in this field in Britain, offers in its introduction an excellent and compact account of current critical issues. I myself don't intend to try to present an overview of the work produced in the last ten years but, rather, to signal the specific debates in which it will be necessary to engage, and to stress the place of queer theory within the field of French Studies. As Smith reveals in his introduction to *Laws of Desire*, despite the wealth of writing and films on the topic of homosexuality in contemporary Spain there has as yet been little Hispanic response to the burgeoning of lesbian and gay studies in the USA. Smith's own work breaks new ground for Hispanic Studies, offering new and enabling frameworks for textual and cultural analysis.

In French Studies the case is rather different since texts by French theorists and cultural critics have in part formed and informed current debate. The most important work has, however, so far been carried out in the field of theory, and less close attention has been paid to the interface between queer theory and French representations of eroticism and performances of sexual identity. A notable and fine exception here is Jonathan Dollimore's work on Gide in *Sexual Dissidence: Augustine to Wilde, Freud to Foucault*,[19] yet there are inevitably still many lacunae. Of the texts I will study here, it is of course *A la recherche du temps perdu* which has thus far figured most frequently in the work of queer theorists. Analysis of this work has in some cases proved pivotal in the work of Bersani, Sedgwick, Silverman, and others, as I shall go on to show in Chapter 3. The centrality of Proust to the analyses of these critics has allowed me to engage with their arguments when discussing specific issues related to knowledge, identity and

[18] Paul Julian Smith, *Laws of Desire: Questions of Homosexuality in Spanish Writing and Film 1960–1990* (Oxford, 1992), 9 n.

[19] (Oxford, 1991.) For considerations of sexuality and French textuality, see George Stambolian and Elaine Marks (eds.), *Homosexualities and French Literature: Cultural Contexts/Critical Texts* (Ithaca, NY, 1979) and Michael Worton and Judith Still (eds.), *Textuality and Sexuality* (Manchester, 1993).

sexuality in *Sodome et Gomorrhe* and *La Prisonnière*. However, while texts by the other authors I am examining in some detail, by Duras, Cixous, and Tournier, have been discussed very frequently by both critical theorists and critics of French literature, they have thus far largely escaped analysis in the context of queer theory. This is a situation which I am, evidently, attempting to remedy and I will argue that the work of these authors re-presents and refocuses some of the issues which are crucial to the analysis of performative identities and liminal sexualities.

• *Rereading Identity*

It is necessary to raise here a pressing question with relation to sexuality and the reading encounter, which is that of the interdependence of fiction and identity. One of the most radical insights of contemporary queer theory, informed by Lacanian psychoanalysis, relates precisely to the rereading of identity. In her chapter 'The Question of Identity Politics' in *Essentially Speaking: Feminism, Nature and Difference*, Diana Fuss comments that recent gay theory has rejected any adherence to a natural, essential or universal gay identity and emphasized instead 'the way in which the homosexual subject is produced not naturally but discursively, across a multiplicity of discourses'.[20] Her aim in this chapter is to relate this problematizing of assertions of identity to the important question of 'identity politics'. She stresses that 'identity is rarely identical to itself but instead has multiple and sometimes contradictory meanings';[21] and she continues that '[her] own position will endorse the Lacanian understanding of identity as alienated and fictitious'.[22]

Fuss seeks to chart the differences within identity, but is keen to stress that the deconstruction of identity does not necessarily imply the disavowal of identity, and this indeed is an issue we need to pursue. Fuss makes the important point that 'fictions of identity . . . are no less powerful for being fictions'.[23] We might add to this, following Judith Butler, that fictions of identity may

---

[20] Diana Fuss, *Essentially Speaking: Feminism, Nature and Difference* (New York, 1990), 97.
[21] Ibid. 98.   [22] Ibid. 102.   [23] Ibid. 104.

well be powerful since they are, furthermore, all to which we will ever have access. As Butler writes in 'The Lesbian Phallus', with reference to Lacan's theory of the mirror stage: 'The body in the mirror does not represent a body that is, as it were, before the mirror: the mirror, even as it is instigated by that unrepresentable body "before" the mirror, produces that body as its delirious effect—a delirium, by the way, which we are compelled to live.'[24]

It is important to Fuss to maintain that the deconstruction of identity is seen in no way to disable identity politics. She argues, indeed, that 'such a view of identity as unstable and potentially disruptive, as alien and incoherent, could in the end produce a more mature identity politics'.[25] Her argument is close to that of Butler, who suggests at the end of *Gender Trouble*: 'The deconstruction of identity is not the deconstruction of politics; rather, it establishes as political the very terms through which identity is articulated.'[26] While, in political terms it seems highly important to endorse this point of view, it might be added that the recognition of identity as fictive, dissociated, and non-self-identical may hold its own traumas. And here we might come back to our previous quotation from 'The Lesbian Phallus' and to the notion of delirium. In this essay Butler seeks, as she says, 'the critical release of alternative imaginary schemas for constituting sites of erotogenic pleasure'.[27] In so doing, she depends on the crucial, and ultimately persuasive, argument that the 'bodily ego produced through identification is not *mimetically* related to a preexisting biological or anatomical body'.[28] Whilst looking towards remapping and release, Butler does not perhaps pay enough attention to the necessary telling and troubling disorientation this recognition inevitably produces. And here we might dwell further on the negative affective connotations of her so very apt choice of the word 'delirium' and all it might imply. The realization of the ways in which self, identity, and bodily ego are only ever the product of identification with a fiction or

---

[24] Judith Butler, *Bodies that Matter: On the Discursive Limits of 'Sex'* (New York, 1993), 91.

[25] Fuss, *Essentially Speaking*, 104.

[26] Judith Butler, *Gender Trouble: Feminism and the Subversion of Identity* (New York, 1990), 148.

[27] Butler, *Bodies that Matter*, 91.

[28] Ibid.

fantasm is, quite possibly, inescapably alienating. In this alienation, identity dwells. But what about its effects on the reading
encounter?

In a lucid and challenging critique of questions of reading and
gender, Diana Fuss puts forward in fairly brief terms 'a theory of
reading based on the shifting grounds of subjectivity'.[29] It is in
many senses an attractive theory, opening up the bounds of
textual interpretation and strategically undermining any notion
of 'essential readers'. She concludes, in terms I would in part
choose to endorse, that 'if we read from multiple subject-
positions, the very act of reading becomes a force for dislocating
our belief in stable subjects and essential meanings'.[30] While this
notion, like that of Modleski quoted earlier, is itself integral to
my argument, I think Fuss, like Butler, tends rather to underes-
timate the ways in which instability and dissension can also
work to disable and disenfranchise. In this sense, in theorizing
the reading encounter, it seems that its full conflictual potential
should not be overlooked.

In questioning Fuss's proposition, we may be lead to ask
whether her theory of reading can be readily related to texts
which deal within a pre-established economy of desire. Where
the act of reading may indeed dislocate our belief in stable
subject positions, is there a difference in the reading of texts
which manifestly desire and necessitate a displaced reader and
of those which uphold unified identity and a hierarchy of
(gendered) subject positions? Further, how are the differing
hierarchies of homosexuality and heterosexuality to be mapped
on to the seeming polarities of gendered reading Fuss herself
attempts to deconstruct? Take the case, for example, of a text
which dramatizes a scenario of heterosexual desire, focused
through the gaze of a male desiring subject. Is it possible to
equate the experience of a male reader who identifies himself as
homosexual, and who may readily adopt the position of subject
of desire, but seek to change the gender of his object of desire
(much the scenario outlined by Proust indeed), with that of a
female reader who identifies herself as heterosexual, and who
thus may identify with the pattern of desiring relations represented, but not with the position of male desiring subject? And

[29] Fuss, *Essentially Speaking*, 35.
[30] Ibid.

this is to say nothing of the reader who may identify herself as lesbian, respond to the female object of desire, yet find herself disempowered by the difference between her relation to the heterosexual matrix and that of the male desiring subject represented in the text.[31] And this is only one such possible scenario where sexuality, as well as gender, may be seen to trouble and re-present the reading encounter.[32]

For Fuss, reading from multiple subject positions may work to dislocate our belief in stable and 'essential' identity. Her reader is seen to undo effectively any notion of an implied reading position or a hierarchy of responses. I would argue, however, that even in the assumption of multiple subject positions there still may be an implicit hierarchization of these subject positions, relating precisely to their similarity and assimilability to the patterns of desire represented in and upheld by the text. Of course it should not necessarily be assumed that a reader who finds his/her desires reflected in the text is in a privileged position. Indeed one issue I will examine, with rela-

---

[31] In *Homos* (Cambridge, Mass., 1995), discussing the (not untroubled) coming together of lesbians and gay men, Leo Bersani writes: 'With heterosexual women we at least share their desires, just as straight men, while ignorant of *how* a lesbian desires, turn in their desires toward many of the same images to which a woman loving women would be drawn' (p. 65). Here I think it's telling to note the seeming ease with which the first statement is made, and that further qualification is added when speaking of and for lesbians and straight men. In a sense both statements seem problematic. Can a female viewer of, say, Gus Van Sant's film *My Own Private Idaho* be said to respond in the same way to images of River Phoenix and Keanu Reeves as a male viewer who identifies as gay? Surely she is necessarily positioned differently even if in some senses she does 'share' the male viewer's desire? And I choose this film since it works significantly to cut across divisions between straight and gay. The case for difference would surely be stronger still in the case of films which more readily deal within an overtly homosexual or heterosexual economy.

[32] In rereading the final draft of this book I became aware how far the schema I am adopting and the models I am borrowing take little account of the possibility of a reader (male or female) who identifies as bisexual. It might be suggested that this is the blind spot within these analyses. The bisexual reader offers a troubling conundrum indeed. Is s/he positioned both necessarily within and without the regulatory matrix of heterosexuality? The reader who identifies as bisexual may know, recognize, and mirror multiple desiring reading positions. But perhaps by virtue of the very refusal of unity in his/her sexual identity category, s/he will always be troubled (or exhilarated) by the possibility of an imperfect identification? It should perhaps be questioned further, and evidently beyond the confines of this study, whether the troubling of identity categories, the refusal of intelligibility and coherence in these categories, *necessarily* requires the admission of a bisexual libidinal investment (above and beyond the primary bisexuality posited by Freudian theory) and indeed the performance of such desiring acts.

tion specifically to the work of Cixous, is the very problem of mirroring complicity between the author's projected protagonist and the text's desired reader. It might be argued indeed that distance and difference from the text's inscribed patterns of desire may create a self-conscious and objective reader who will not fall victim to the text's seduction. But this latter point depends on an assertion that the reader's sexuality, and his/her desire and patterns of identification, pre-exist and prescribe his/her reading of the text. And this is an assertion which, as will be seen below, I am disinclined to make.

If we are to accept Fuss's persuasive point that identity is unstable, disruptive, alien, and incoherent, it seems, as we have seen, that we are by implication subscribing to the Lacanian view that the ego is constructed in relation to an *imago*, and a mirror image, which may in its seductive unity be the guarantor of cohesion, but which may also, by virtue of its very alterity, entirely undo any secure sense of self.[33] And we return here again to Butler's notion of the delirium by and with which we are compelled to live. Now, this drama of identity formation may be seen to rest upon an uneasy act of identification with an alien (but not necessarily alienating) image of the self. This act of identification depends of course on the internalization of the alien image, and the transformation, or if we follow Butler the very construction, of the self with relation to that alien image.

I wish to argue that this process is itself dangerously assimilable with the reading encounter. In this sense the notion of identification applied to reading needs to be understood in its full psychoanalytic sense. Laplanche and Pontalis define identification as follows: 'processus psychologique par lequel un sujet assimile un aspect, une propriété, un attribut de l'autre et se transforme, totalement ou partiellement, sur le modèle de celui-ci'.[34] In this sense, identification is seen to change, or in Butler's

---

[33] See Jacques Lacan, 'Le Stade du miroir comme formateur de la fonction du Je', in *Écrits* (Paris, 1966), 93–100: 'The Mirror Stage as Formative of the Function of the I', in *Écrits: A Selection*, trans. Alan Sheridan (London, 1977), 1–7. See also Malcolm Bowie's reading of this essay in his *Lacan* (London, 1991), 17–43.

[34] Jean Laplanche and J.-B. Pontalis, *Vocabulaire de la psychanalyse* (Paris, 1973), 187: *The Language of Psychoanalysis*, trans. Donald Nicholson-Smith (London, Karnac, 1988), 205 ('Psychological process whereby the subject assimilates an aspect, property or attribute of the other and is transformed, wholly or partially, after the model the other provides').

terms to create, the subject. Is it not possible that identification with a text may have the same effect?

This certainly appears to be the case in the drama of reading Proust embeds in *A la recherche du temps perdu*, as discussed above. The dislocated identification with the text of desire allows Charlus to appropriate it to his own taste, but leaves him also the victim of the reading encounter. But in Proust's configuration, the queer reader's desire is seen to exist prior to his reading of the text. His patterns of identification are seen to be marked out and in some senses predestined. The social construction of Charlus's desire is, however, seen to be the product of the texts he reads and of the desiring positions they prescribe. The experience of queer reading is seen not only to re-create the text, but also to re-create the reader. Proust shows the construction of Charlus's identity to be transformed by the reading encounter; he shows how identification with the position of desiring subject in a fiction allows that subject position to be internalized, to become a construct of the reader.

We need to question whether this is necessarily the case for all experiences of dislocated identification in reading. How, for example, does the male reader who identifies himself as heterosexual respond to reading the narrative of Alexandre's queer and incestuous passions within Tournier's *Les Météores*? Tournier claims that 'l'audace des *Météores*, c'est de nommer l'hétérosexualité'[35] and he specifies that 'Alexandre en devenant mon seul point de vue m'a dévoilé la société hétérosexuelle'.[36] One of the purposes of the text's thematics of origins and artifice, models and copies, is certainly, it seems, to prefigure Butler's revelatory statement that 'gay is to straight *not* as copy is to original, but, rather, as copy is to copy'.[37] But does Tournier's novel achieve this deconstruction of hierarchical relations of straight and gay in part through the dislocated experience of the straight reader?

Here I would argue that it is important not to ignore the effects of social conditioning and of the regulatory matrix of

[35] Michel Tournier, *Le Vent Paraclet* (Paris, 1977), 257: *The Wind Spirit*, 219 ('The bold stroke in *Gemini* was to call heterosexuality by its name').

[36] *Le Vent Paraclet*, 256: *The Wind Spirit*, 218 ('Alexander served as my vantage-point on heterosexual society').

[37] Judith Butler, *Gender Trouble*, p. 31.

heterosexuality. The reader who identifies himself as hetero-sexual finds his identity perpetually reconstructed and reaf-firmed through a seductive encounter with fictions which deal within a heterosexual libidinal economy. In this sense I believe we still cannot afford to overlook the implications for the read-ing of fiction of what Laura Mulvey describes in film as the 'masculinization' of the spectatorial position imposed by 'in-built patterns of pleasure and identification'.[38] Identification with the position of a queer desiring subject may provide its own valuable dislocation, its own potential reorientation of desire. The effect of this dislocated identification may be different in the case of each individual reader. And here we might consider D. N. Rodowick's useful rereading of theories of spectatorship where he notes that 'textual analysis has accomplished much in suggesting how positions of identification and meaning are coded by film texts',[39] yet adds, 'but in my view, one must accept fundamentally that these positions exist only as potentialities that are ultimately undecidable with respect to any given specta-tor'.[40] While potentially readily accepting Rodowick's point of view, I think it must be said that if the possibility that identifi-cation with a fiction constructs identity is accepted, then the viewing position of any given spectator is necessarily at least in part not only afforded, but created, by the film s/he views or the book s/he reads.

Thus, given the widespread 'masculinization' of the spec-tatorial position in narrative cinema, and the equivalent, and some might say inevitable, privileging of heterosexuality within fictions of desire (although not necessarily those treated in this study), I would argue that the status of the straight reader who identifies with the subject position of a gay protagonist is by no means equivalent to that of the queer reader who consumes straight fiction.

To return then to Fuss's argument: although it may be more than desirable that the act of reading becomes a force for dis-locating our belief in stable subjects, I am far less confident than Fuss that the reader is (or even perhaps should be) unconstrained in his/her choice of subject position and identifi-

---

[38] Laura Mulvey, *Visual and Other Pleasures* (London: Macmillan, 1989), 29.
[39] Rodowick, *The Difficulty of Difference*, viii.
[40] Ibid. viii.

cation. Fuss, like Butler, appears to look towards the recognition of identity categories as fictional and shifting in order to undo hegemonic relations between male and female, homosexual and heterosexual. As Butler says in a statement about historical identities of sexual style, which might well be related here to the issue of sexuality and the reading encounter: 'The repetition of heterosexual constructs within sexual cultures both gay and straight may well be the inevitable site of the denaturalization and mobilization of gender categories.'[41] What I would argue with is the assumed correlation here between 'denaturalization' and 'mobilization'.[42] It must surely remain questionable whether the recognition that identity is dependent on the internalization of a fiction, that identity is essentially performative, will necessarily have any significant effect on the performance of those gender roles and sexual identities which have become compulsory within the regulatory matrix of heterosexuality, desirable though this might be. And for this reason I am less confident than Fuss that the experience of multiple identification necessarily enjoyed in reading will have any impact on the social construction of identity. It could even be argued that the constraint of reading against the heterosexual matrix holds its own seductive power.

• *Performative Reading*

Despite the reservations expressed above, I in no sense wish to deny the importance and impact of the work of Judith Butler in radicalizing notions of gender identity and sexuality. This has in

[41] Butler, *Gender Trouble*, 31.

[42] Reading Bersani's *Homos* whilst correcting the final draft of this book, I was interested to note that Bersani voices similar qualms to my own on this point, as he questions the power of 'denaturalizing the epistemic and political regimes that have constructed us'. Bersani continues: 'The power of those systems is only minimally contested by demonstrations of their "merely" historical character. They don't need to be natural in order to rule; to demystify them doesn't render them inoperative' (p. 4). But Bersani makes use of his qualms, and other significant quibbles it seems, to attack the deconstruction of identity enacted so forcefully by Butler and other queer theorists. My own position is, in fact, far closer to that of Butler than Bersani. As should be clear in this study, I entirely subscribe to Butler's project to trouble identity categories.

many ways invaluably enabled and influenced my own study of sexuality and the reading encounter. Above all Butler's work is influential here in terms of the emphasis she places on notions of performance and performativity.

Crucial to Butler's work, and my own following her, is the recognition that there is 'no gender identity behind the expressions of gender; that identity is performatively constituted by the very "expressions" that are said to be its results'.[43] Here Butler, like Fuss, works to attack the foundational illusions of identity. She argues that the inner truth of gender is a fabrication, that genders can be neither true nor false, but are only produced as the truth effects of a discourse of primary and stable identity. For Butler, gender is an act; she argues that 'as in other ritual social dramas, the action of gender requires a performance that is *repeated*'.[44] Hence she concludes: 'Gender ought not to be construed as a stable identity or locus of agency from which various acts follow; rather, gender is an identity tenuously constituted in time, instituted in an exterior space through a *stylized repetition of acts*.'[45]

Butler suggests that the gendered body has no ontological status 'apart from the various acts which constitute its reality'.[46] This leads to the proposition that 'if that reality is fabricated as an interior essence, that very interiority is an effect and a function of a decidedly public and social discourse, the public regulation of fantasy through the surface politics of the body, the gender border control that differentiates inner from outer, and so institutes the "integrity" of the subject'.[47] In these terms, identity is the product of a series of acts, of engagement in a perpetual performance which is regulated in a public and social arena. It is crucial to my argument here that the act of reading is itself seen to require the performance of an identity constituted by the discourse with which the reader engages. The reader may thus assume an identity which is constructed as s/he reads. If it is acknowledged that, in Butler's terms, all identities are thus assumed or fabricated, the proximity between reading

---

[43] Butler, *Gender Trouble*, 25.   [44] Ibid. 140.
[45] Ibid.   [46] Ibid. 136.   [47] Ibid.

as performance and the performance of identity is particularly striking.

The notion of reading as the performance of an identity has already been raised implicitly by Fuss in *Essentially Speaking* where she introduces the possibility of readers adopting multiple subject positions. What I want to argue here is that reading should be understood not only as performance but also as performative. Butler herself is particularly cautious about the relations between performance and performativity. In 'Critically Queer' she argues that, despite her suggestion that gender is performed, 'in no sense can it be concluded that the part of gender that is performed is therefore the "truth" of gender'.[48] She warns that 'the reduction of performativity to performance would be a mistake'[49] and she clarifies this by explaining that 'performance as bounded "act" is distinguished from performativity insofar as the latter consists in a reiteration of norms which precede, constrain, and exceed the performer and in that sense cannot be taken as the fabrication of the performer's "will" or "choice"'.[50] The act of reading may constitute a performance where the reader assumes the subject position with which s/he chooses to identify: this appears to be Fuss's model of the reading encounter. Yet it should be recognized too that reading can also be a performative act: and this has rather different implications. I would argue that as the reader identifies with a text s/he encounters a set of constraints which (pre)determine his/her reading position. Thus reading is performative in so far as the text provides a script which may determine and regulate the performance of identity in the reading encounter. The text may itself encourage or deny the norms of the regulatory matrix of heterosexuality. The reader him/herself may choose a dissident or resistant position with relation to the text s/he encounters. But the differences between these differing positions cannot be ignored. If it is acknowledged that a reader may destabilize the regulatory matrix of the text s/he reads, it should also be recognized that the reader's own identity may be malleable and fragile. In the performance of desire which reading may be seen to require, an identity may be constructed performatively through identification with a certain subject

---

[48] Butler, *Bodies that Matter*, 234.   [49] Ibid.   [50] Ibid.

position and internalization of a coded pattern of behaviour. In this sense the text may change the reader as much as the reader may change the text.

In 'Critically Queer' Butler speaks of the impossibility of 'ever fully inhabiting the name by which one's social identity is inaugurated and mobilized'[51] and she concludes that this implies 'the instability and incompleteness of subject formation'.[52] Recognizing this, we might wonder about the seductive potential of fictions which offer the illusion of a complete and stable subject. How readily may the reader be drawn to identify with a figure in fiction in whom, precisely, s/he does not recognize the shifting and perpetually unsettling instabilities of subjectivity? In fact, all the fictions I will study here refuse this delusory fantasy of stable subject formation and fixed identities. The texts of Proust, Cixous, Duras, and Tournier, in their very disparity, may perhaps most closely resemble each other in the desire to show identity in process, as perpetually unknowable, and as suicidally dependent on the unreliable reciprocation of an often elusive Other. In these texts the reader contends with identities represented which are as unstable as his/her own. If the text acts as mirror, it certainly offers no cohesive image of the self. What needs to be questioned is how disabling this experience may be for the reader.

For Butler, the instability of identity is seen ultimately to be enabling. In uncovering the imitative structure of gender, she may work to destabilize the regulatory matrix of heterosexuality. It should not be overlooked, however, that instability is also seen as a source of pleasure by Butler. In her essay 'Imitation and Gender Insubordination' she goes some way towards offering her readers a performance of her own identity when, speaking about identity categories as sites of necessary trouble, she admits: 'if the category were to offer no trouble, it would cease to be interesting to me: it is precisely the *pleasure* produced by the instability of those categories which sustains the various erotic practices that make me a candidate for the category to begin with'.[53] A similar libidinal investment in instability is found, of course, in the drama of Proust's narrator's desire

---

[51] Ibid. 226.   [52] Ibid.

[53] Judith Butler, 'Imitation and Gender Insubordination', in Fuss (ed.), *Inside/Out*, 13–31: 14.

for Albertine, as we shall see in the next chapter. Butler's theory depends, in a manner surprisingly reminiscent of Proust, on an economy which equates trouble with interest, and pleasure with instability. The dissociated subject whose identifications and concomitant desires challenge the heterosexual matrix is endowed by Butler not only with dissident potential, but also with erotic power. S/he is, simply, more sexy.

What Butler has at times overlooked, although this is in part redressed in the later *Bodies that Matter*, is the (unsettling) possibility that the regulatory matrix of heterosexuality may itself be idealized and eroticized. A heterosexual identity may be replicated imperfectly by the desiring subject, and s/he may find him/herself the victim of those very imperfections. The instability of identification may be a source not (only) of pleasure, but (also) of disorientation and distress.

• *Trans-sex Identification*

Feminist theorists of spectatorship have spoken of the necessity for a 'trans-sex identification' on the part of the female viewer who chooses to be the subject rather than the object of the gaze. Laura Mulvey concludes that: 'the spectator's fantasy of masculinization [is] at cross-purposes with itself, restless in its transvestite clothes'.[54] Mary Ann Doane takes up the image of the transvestite, commenting: 'the transvestite wears clothes which signify a different sexuality, a sexuality which, for the woman, allows a mastery over the image and the very possibility of attaching the gaze to desire'.[55] Where Doane may be seen to stress empowerment by means of 'trans-sex identification', Griselda Pollock tends rather to emphasize the pain and constraint of this imperfect identification. She sums up the situation, stating: 'to look at and enjoy the sites of patriarchal culture we women must become nominal transvestites. We must assume a masculine position or masochistically enjoy the sight of women's humiliation.'[56] Mulvey, Doane, and Pollock all, in

[54] Laura Mulvey, *Visual and Other Pleasures* (London, 1989), 37.
[55] Mary Ann Doane, 'Film and the Masquerade: Theorising the Female Spectator', *Screen*, 23/3–4 (Sept.–Oct. 1982), 74–87: 81.
[56] Griselda Pollock, *Vision and Difference: Femininity, Feminism and the Histories of Art* (London, 1988), 85.

their different ways, suggest that this identification is compulsory, whether the adoption of a displaced viewing position is seen to empower or disable the female spectator.

Following Butler, we might argue that playing the role of the 'nominal transvestite' is paradoxically liberating. The female spectator as transvestite, taking on the appearance and attributes of the hallowed possessor of the male gaze, comes effectively to destabilize and denaturalize his position of authority. The possibility for a female spectator to view a female object of desire serves further to parody and disturb gender polarities in much the same way as the assumption of 'butch' and 'femme' identities (as discussed by Butler). Further, the recognition that a viewing position is constructed rather than given allows for the potential recognition that the decoder may play multiple roles (and here we draw close to Fuss once more).

But where I have expressed some anxieties about whether multiple roles can so easily be adopted, I think more caution is also needed in alluding to the possibility of trans-sex identifications. D. N. Rodowick has voiced some qualms over the theorizing of female spectatorship in these terms. Rodowick seeks to reveal that in all sexed subjects, the processes of identification comprise 'constantly permutable ratios'[57] between masculine and feminine, active and passive, sadistic and masochistic. Although Rodowick endorses both Laura Mulvey and Teresa de Lauretis's accounts of identification as oscillation, for him, 'the characterization of this form of identification as "transvestite" or "transsexual" is unfortunate with its suggestion of opposed, self-identical forms that can be reversed or transgressed'.[58] Rodowick appears to see the imagery of transvestism and transsexualism upholding rather than undoing sexual difference.

I would argue, however, that Rodowick's own account, in its attempt effectively to undo sexual difference, pays too little attention to established and often still inescapable social hierarchies of gender and sexuality. Readers are necessarily constructed in relation to these matrices: their freedom of choice is necessarily constrained. The necessity of reading from a displaced, 'denaturalized' position may itself be peculiarly unset-

---

[57] Rodowick, *The Difficulty of Difference*, 136.
[58] Ibid., p. x.

tling, and not in any way afford the destablization of the regulatory matrix.

The position of the transvestite and transsexual as one of
troubling imperfection is revealed in documentary evidence. We
might consider, for example, Jennie Livingston's film *Paris is
Burning*. Livingston offers a view of Harlem's gay ball scene,
and its extravagant multitude of costumes and personae. Here
what is at stake, it seems, is a matter of convincing dissimulation. Livingston analyses the adoption of the clothes, manner,
and attributes of a particular role, be it cross-gendered or across
class and colour barriers. What is essential is the desire to 'pass',
to reach the elusive and illusory state of 'realness'. Where in
Gender Trouble Butler stresses: 'in imitating gender, drag implicitly reveals the imitative structure of gender itself—as well as
its contingency',[59] in *Bodies that Matter*, when she provides a
specific analysis of *Paris is Burning*, she is rather more ambivalent about the revelatory power of drag, saying: '*Paris is Burning* documents neither an efficacious insurrection nor a painful
resubordination, but an unstable coexistence of both.'[60] Butler
now emphasizes pain as well as pleasure, specifying: 'The film
attests to the painful pleasures of eroticizing and miming the
very norms that wield their power by foreclosing the very re-
verse-occupations that the children nevertheless perform.'[61] I
would argue, further, that the film testifies to the constraints and
not the destabilization of the regulatory matrix of heterosexual
and, in this case, white capitalist society. It might be argued that
in the Harlem ball scene as Jennie Livingston shows it, performance and cross-dressing are only in quite a small part parodic:
the dance-floor is more readily recognized as a stage for the
enactment of fantasies (to be a businessman, a preppy, a
supermodel) which *cannot* be put into 'real' practice. In the ball
scene there is little implicit critique of the normalized categories
adopted. Masquerade is seen tellingly as a product of poverty
and racial injustice; cross-dressing is seen often as the prelude to
taking the perilous (and expensive) path to becoming a 'real'
woman. An imperfect identification and enactment of a role has
dangerously material consequences. In this sense, the murder of

---

[59] Butler, *Gender Trouble*, 137.
[60] Butler, *Bodies that Matter*, 137.
[61] Ibid.

the young prostitute Venus is framed in such a way in *Paris is Burning* as to seem the suicidal result of living on gender borders and playing with 'reality'.[62]

Paris is Burning might be understood not only to stage the pleasures of instability, but also to emphasize the imbalance, the injustices, and the seduction of the hierarchical system mimed and fetishized on the dance-floor. A comparable idealization of binary gender divisions and of heterosexuality is revealed in the testimonies of transsexuals analysed by Sandy Stone in her 'The *Empire* Strikes Back: A Posttranssexual Manifesto'. Stone notes that these testimonies all 'reinforce a binary, oppositional mode of gender identification'[63] and that each author constructs 'a specific narrative moment when their personal sexual identification changes from male to female'.[64] What is noteworthy here also is the seeming evidence Stone gives of how identity can be in part constructed with relation to a text. She talks about the influence exerted by Harry Benjamin's work *The Transsexual Phenomenon*, published in 1966, telling how Benjamin's book was the researchers' standard reference. She reveals: 'when the first transsexuals were evaluated for their suitability for surgery, their behaviour matched up gratifyingly with Benjamin's criteria'.[65] She goes on to comment, candidly: 'it took a surprisingly long time—several years—for the researchers to realize that the reason the candidates' behavioural profiles matched Benjamin's so well was that the candidates, too, had read Benjamin's book'.[66]

In many ways Stone's manifesto makes comparable points to Livingston's film on the issue of 'passing' and attaining 'realness'. For the transsexual, 'passing' implies living successfully in the gender of choice, and even being perceived as a 'natural' member of that gender. Here again a perfect identification and an illusory stable subject position is sought; Stone comments: 'The highest purpose of the transsexual is to erase him/herself, to fade into the normal population as soon as possible. Part of

---

[62] See Bersani, *Homos*, 48–9, for further critique of Butler's reading of *Paris is Burning*.

[63] Sandy Stone, 'The *Empire* Strikes Back: A Posttranssexual Manifesto', in Julia Epstein and Kristina Straub (eds.), *Body Guards: The Cultural Politics of Gender Ambiguity* (New York, 1991), 280–304: 286.

[64] Ibid.   [65] Ibid. 291.   [66] Ibid.

this process is known as *constructing a plausible history*—learning to lie effectively about one's past.'[67] Stone's main point is that 'authentic experience is replaced by a particular kind of story, one that supports the old constructed positions'.[68] In her manifesto, Stone criticizes this state of affairs very strongly, saying: 'this is expensive, and profoundly disempowering'.[69] There is seen to be power, instead, in the proclaiming of the refigured and reinscribed body. Ironically, this may well offer a more stable subject position for those who have put a trans-sex identification into material practice.

But what is of interest here is the seeming interrelation between fiction and identity. Stone defines a position where a fiction is allowed to conceal the 'reality' of experience, and indeed to supersede it. It might be argued that for transsexuals within the matrix of heterosexuality and binary gender, the concoction of a fictional identity and fictive past is (virtually) compulsory. Identification with a fiction may thus authenticate a gendered existence. The experience of the transsexual can be seen not so much to destabilize as re-enhance hierarchies of power and binary relations.

The same might be said of the experience of the hermaphrodite, whose dual gender might again be seen to trouble the regulatory matrix of heterosexuality. In his introduction to the memoirs of the nineteenth-century hermaphrodite Herculine Barbin, Foucault specifies how throughout history the possibility of identifying themselves as both sexes (or neither) was not open to hermaphrodites. Instead, up until the eighteenth century, they were free to determine the gender they would adopt on the threshold of adulthood. Foucault makes clear that 'changes of option, not the anatomical mixture of the sexes, were what gave rise to most of the condemnations of hermaphrodites in the records that survive in France for the period of the Middle Ages and the Renaissance'.[70] This code of practice suggesting that a singular gender identity must be

---

[67] Sandy Stone, 295.   [68] Ibid.   [69] Ibid.

[70] Michel Foucault, introduction to *Herculine Barbin: Being the Recently Discovered Memoirs of a Nineteenth-Century French Hermaphrodite* (Brighton, 1980), pp. vii–xvii: p. viii. Foucault's introduction only appears in the English translation of this work. The memoirs themselves appear in French as *Herculine Barbin dite Alexina B.* (Paris, 1978). The memoirs have also been made into a film by René Féret entitled *Mystère Alexina*.

performed coherently gives way to the even more regulatory notion that the hermaphrodite was only ever a pseudo-hermaphrodite whose sex could be correctly determined by an expert. Foucault stresses that despite advances in medicine in the nineteenth and twentieth centuries, the idea that one must have a true sex is far from dispelled. And this is a point which has its own bearing on the possibilities of transgressive gender identifications.

I would argue, then, that the material gender transgressions (adopted or given) of the transsexual or the hermaphrodite may be seen sometimes to produce such an acute instability in identity that the individual subject finds him/herself compelled to enact a fiction of singular and unified gender identification which works to uphold rather than undermine the regulatory matrix of heterosexuality and binary gender. Instability *is* interesting, but it still needs to be viewed in a context of cultural violence and social oppression which, as Foucault, Livingston, and Stone remind us in their different ways, are still social and political realities in the post-modern era.

This being said, unlike Rodowick, I do not wish to rule out the possibility of making use of the image of trans-sex identification in order to theorize reading relations, but it needs to be stressed that this experience of reading as another can be shattering as well as pleasurable, and is fraught with a complex nexus of power relations. The role of the queer reader is no easy one to adopt. S/he may find him/herself like Alexandre, Tournier's 'gay deconstructor', the victim of his/her decoding practice.

• *She must be Seeing Things*

It might be said that one implication of the framework of the argument I am creating here is that a conflictual reading encounter takes place necessarily between a reader who identifies as in some way queer and a text which upholds and reinscribes the social patterns of heterosexuality. Of course, films and texts have themselves worked manifestly not only to represent the social realities of homosexual experience, but also to challenge the regulatory matrix of heterosexuality, of binary gender and stable subject positions. Those films and texts which fall into the latter category can be seen, not infrequently, to call into question the very act of viewing or reading on which their existence may be seen to depend. This might be said, for example, as Rodowick shows, of Jacques Rivette's film *Céline et Julie vont en bateau*.

Rodowick reveals how the narrative trajectory of *Céline et Julie vont en bateau* 'stages a parable of reading that desires to transform spectators of the narrative into performers of the text'.[71] Rodowick perceives a close paralleling between the viewing scenario and the scenario enacted by Céline and Julie. He most aptly quotes Rivette himself in an interview from *Cahiers du cinéma*, saying: 'a film must be, if not an ordeal, at least an experience, something which makes the film transform the viewer, who has undergone something through the film, who is no longer the same after having seen the film'.[72] For Rivette, the film is seen as (trans) formative, and the experience of identification, one of the film's major subjects, is seen to be replayed on the stage of the viewer's own identity. *Céline et Julie vont en bateau* is both radical and playful in its questioning of gender, of the female homoerotic, of role play, of performance and viewing positions. In this way it differs particularly strikingly from many films which, as Rodowick puts it, 'encourage and perpetuate positions of identification aligned with the dominant definitions of sexual difference'.[73]

It is noticeable that as a film, *Céline et Julie vont en bateau* puts much emphasis on the performance of identity, and not on the gender specificity of identity. Rivette explores the potential of crossed identities and masquerade: Céline and Julie dress up as each other and play out each other's roles, Céline going to meet Julie's childhood fiancé, Julie performing Céline's magic act. The performance of alternative identities does not necessarily depend on crossing gender borders, simply on troubling the division between self and Other. Rivette would appear to stress how far identity is dependent on identification with the Other. *Céline et Julie vont en bateau* is ultimately a disorientating and unsettling film which at once maintains the privileged position

---

[71] Rodowick, *The Difficulty of Difference*, 109.
[72] Ibid.   [73] Ibid. 21.

of the male desiring viewer in its erotic presentation of the female–female double act, yet undermines this also through showing how far Céline and Julie may adopt the role of both subject and object of each other's gaze.

Céline et Julie vont en bateau fights shy, however, of overtly eroticizing the relation between the two women, limiting itself to troubling the binaries of sexual difference, and undoing divisions between dream and reality. Where the instability of gender positions is seen as a source of pleasure and play in this film, the pain concomitant with a transgressive identification is shown more readily in Sheila McLaughlin's controversial film *She must be Seeing Things*.

In *She must be Seeing Things* McLaughlin explores the pleasurable possibilities of Jo (Lois Weaver) as object of desire performing in silk camisole for Agatha (Sheila Dabney), her cross-dressing lover. The film takes spectatorship as a central subject. It works to show the imperfection implicit in Agatha's assumption of the male gaze: she is shown to be prey to jealous fantasies staged as scenarios where Jo is desired by a male lover. These might testify to the very insecurity of her adoption of the male gaze, where she sees herself only ever as the imperfect, and therefore less desirable, replica of the male desiring subject. The fantasies are themselves shown to be entirely continuous with the narrative of the film and in no way framed as 'unreal'. McLaughlin encourages her viewer to question borderlines between reality and fantasy. These borders are further troubled by the fact that the 'femme' protagonist, Jo, is herself a film-maker, deliberately staging reality and giving a visual dimension to desire. She stands as a double to McLaughlin herself, who, as Teresa de Lauretis suggests, may be seen as 'voyeur and exhibitionist, the "she" who must be seeing things, and the desiring subject of the film as a whole'.[74] McLaughlin encodes multiple viewing positions which parody and subvert the norms of spectatorship and the adoption of gender positions. Her practice of film-making, and the sexual practices she chooses to represent, are respectively self-conscious and parodic. Yet in her parody of a scenario of voyeurism she depends also on the troubled involvement of her own spectator, who in watching the

---

[74] Teresa de Lauretis, 'Film and the Visible', in Bad Object-Choices (ed.), *How do I Look?: Queer Film and Video* (Seattle, 1991), 223–64: 264.

film's erotic images of Lois Weaver and in questioning the truth or fiction of the film's paranoid fantasies finds him/herself complicit with Agatha and implicated in a specific economy of desire.

She must be Seeing Things may be said to subvert as well as reinscribe the power relations of viewing and desire, in its remapping of a scenario of voyeurism on to a lesbian couple, and in its framing of the representation of desire in a film which takes film-making as its subject. Like *Céline et Julie vont en bateau* the film offers a radical questioning of gendered viewing positions, by means of a self-conscious emphasis on performance and on the contingency of identity.

In this sense, it might be argued that films and texts which are most effective in challenging the regulatory matrix of heterosexuality, and in encouraging us to rethink viewing positions and gendered readings, are not those which create an alternative yet fixed viewing or reading position, but those which work to undo any certainty or any illusion of stable subjectivity. Their power might be said to come indeed from the emphasis placed on the very difficulty of adopting any transgressive or culturally unintelligible viewing or reading position. The texts I will examine in this study will be seen in different ways to question and represent reading practices which may work to undo the fiction of unified identity. It is in this sense that they may be seen to challenge the regulatory matrix of heterosexuality and its required reading positions. These may be seen to be texts which eschew their normative role by refusing to offer the reader a seductively unified subject position with which to identify. Yet they deliberately draw attention to the formative potential of fiction by representing identity as tenuous, fictive, and constructed through identification.

What all these texts testify to also, and this is telling, is the trauma and pain inherent in the performance of a culturally unintelligible identity. It is not enough, I think, to suggest that Proust or Duras, say, subscribe to a sado-masochistic economy of desire in order to explain the dissociation of the self effected in desiring relations in their texts. Their protagonists are tortured by imperfections and impossibilities: the impossibility of (re-)enacting fictions, and the impossibility of performing a stable identity when it is lived as a fiction imperfectly (re-)enacted; the impossibility of ever knowing or possessing an Other, and again the impossibility of performing a stable identity when it is inescapably dependent on that elusive or unknowable Other. Their texts come to act, in a way, as cautionary tales to the reader who finds his/her own deluded and uncertain practice of decoding disturbingly reflected in the text s/he consumes.

As I have tried to show, the denial of authorial control and the apparent declaration of interpretative freedom may be seen to effect, among other things, the compulsory imposition of a hierarchy of gendered reading and viewing positions. If the reader is free to interpret the text as s/he chooses, s/he may seemingly read as s/he desires. Yet this is entirely to ignore the function of texts in representing, replicating, or even creating the cultural and social matrix within and against which we are more or less obliged to live. By this token the reader is considerably less free than the death of the author might lead us to suppose.

What our reading of Barthes in the last chapter has led us to suggest is that the death of the author has not simply effected his absence from the text; it has resulted instead in a refiguring of relations between writer and reader. The apparent stability of paternal–filial relations is replaced by a far more unstable model of tenuous desires. The reading encounter is seen not (only) as contest for mastery but, in Freudian terms, as erotic conflict. And it is in this sense that fictions of desire take on their self-referential force, reflecting as they frequently do the desiring relations inherent in their production and consumption.

It has been my aim here to test these desiring relations against the cultural matrices which may be seen to determine the construction of sexual identity. My concern has been largely with the queer reader, the reader whose patterns of identification and sexual identity may be seen to be culturally unintelligible within the regulatory matrix of heterosexuality. I have attempted to show how far the freedom of the queer reader may be constrained as s/he reads texts which may form his/her identity differently. I have tried to stress the trauma as well as the pleasure of dissident identifications. Unlike Butler and Fuss, I am still uneasy about the possibilities of any forceful challenge to the social construction of identity posed by dissident reading patterns or parodic practices which may, in my terms, reveal the denaturalized and constructed status of binary genders and compulsory heterosexuality, but do not undo the lamentable seduction of these regulatory fictions. In this sense, I would argue that the regulatory fictions themselves need to be changed in order to affect cultural practice. My claims relate indeed to the formative power of fictions themselves.

I would argue that it is no coincidence that Proust draws on the experiences of an imagined queer reader in order to expound at some length then on the ways in which engagement with a fiction can change the self. In the context of fictions which (re)produce a heterosexual libidinal economy, the queer reader offers the spectre of reading differently. The conflict, even the trauma, of reading a text which does not replicate, which undoes the reader's own position as desiring subject, becomes infinitely desirable to the author intent on exploring relations between pain and pleasure in fiction, and on destabilizing the fiction of mirroring relations between text and reality. It might be said that Proust finds in the queer reader the reader his texts seek both to reflect and to produce. His texts, like those of Duras, Cixous, and Tournier, form a necessarily self-questioning and self-conscious reader who recognizes the alienating imperfections of identification and the fictive construction of identity. Of course it may be said that there are such self-conscious and self-questioning readers who identify themselves as heterosexual. We might ask whether any link can really be made between reading practice and sexual identity?

Butler's rethinking of the construction of sexual identity is important here. Rather than think of heterosexuality and homosexuality as equal but opposite, we may think of heterosexuality as the 'norm' regulated by a cultural matrix. Those identifications which fall outside that norm are in this sense culturally unintelligible, diverse, and different. The queer reader is thus one who identifies as other than heterosexual. His/her relation to the heterosexual matrix may be seen as challenging or conflictual, his/her experience of social existence within this matrix potentially traumatic. The same might be said of his/her experience of reading (heterosexual) fictions of desire, where the formative power of the text may lead him/her to fetishize and replicate heterosexual identifications, yet necessarily be traumatized by the imperfection of his/her possible identification.

The texts I will study here each in their own way pose a challenge to the regulatory matrix of heterosexuality. This is effected not specifically by the representation of gay and lesbian relationships and sex acts. Instead these texts undermine the stability of reading and viewing positions, by the use of textual strategies which work to deny the unity of identity, and the security of authorial control. The reader is in some senses constrained to adopt a dizzying freedom of interpretation and identification, of whose dangers the texts are only too ready to remind him/her. Thus the queer reader created by these texts is not one who necessarily puts his/her identification into sexual and cultural practice, but one who is led to recognize the traumatic instabilities of identification and desire. S/he is denied a seductive mirroring relation with the text: it is the experience of alienation and dislocated desire in the reading encounter that is ultimately formative.

Texts which construct the reading encounter as erotic, conflictual, and formative may create their own queer readers. Thus I suggest that it is not the reader's choice of reading position, but the sexual identity constructed in the reading encounter, which may pose a challenge to the regulatory matrix of heterosexuality. In the readings that follow I will attempt to reveal how texts of desire may themselves destabilize our fictions of identity.

3

Reading Albertine's Sexuality; or, 'Why not Think of Marcel Simply as a Lesbian?'

> Can sexuality even remain sexuality once it submits to a criterion of transparency and disclosure?
>
> (Judith Butler, 'Imitation and Gender Insubordination)

> Gomorrhe est infiniment plus troublante, noire, détournée, que Sodome.[1]
>
> (Philippe Sollers, 'Proust et Gomorrhe')

• *Reading Albertine*

I began the previous chapter by alluding at some length to the model of reading differently offered by Proust in *Le Temps retrouvé*. In the chapter that follows I will question how far Proust may be seen to engage his own reader in a reading practice which becomes necessarily a performance of destabilized desire. If, in dramatizing the narrator's deluded quest for knowledge of Albertine, Proust may be seen both to form and reflect the experience of his external reader, what effect may this be said to have on our own construction of desire? What, indeed, are the effects of the proximity posited by Proust between reading and desire? And what is the possible effect of a desiring reader on the text?

In a recent study of sexuality in Proust's *A la recherche du temps perdu*, Kaja Silverman asks the leading question: 'Why not think of Marcel simply as a lesbian?'[2] This seems effectively

---

[1] 'Gomorrah is infinitely more disturbing, dark, and twisted than Sodom.'
[2] Kaja Silverman, *Male Subjectivity at the Margins* (New York, 1992), 386.

a new turn in analyses of desire in Proust. Albertine, the character whose name appears most frequently in Proust's novel,[3] has
long been the focus of intense critical debate where Proust's
analysts seek to answer questions which Proust's own narrator
appears to find insoluble. The questions which lie at the heart of
the narrator's relationship with Albertine, and which are formu-
lated so neatly by Malcolm Bowie, 'has she had lesbian relationships in the past? is she having, or contriving to have, such
relationships now? how can truth be distinguished from falsehood in Albertine's reports on her actions and feelings?',[4] resur-
face in criticism which itself attempts to hold Albertine captive
and question her desires. Yet these readings have frequently
failed to perceive the challenge to (polarized) notions of homosexuality and heterosexuality that is posed by the relations
between Marcel and Albertine.

This chapter seeks to analyse some of the questions raised by
these rereadings of Albertine. My aim is to show how Proust's
text reveals that sexuality and gender identification occur in
performance, between two individuals. Moving away from any
notion of a search for knowledge of Albertine, I want instead to
reveal the importance of the fantasies which surround her. In
this sense the narrator's constructions of her sexual identity and
fantasies of her erotic practice are far more crucial to the text
than the 'truth' of her sexuality or her gender. Indeed it is
through the very indeterminacies of Albertine, and the necessary
instability of the narrator's position as desiring subject, that
Proust may be seen to explode the notion of fixed gender positions. This is sometimes denied in readings of Proust where
critics both undermine and evade the challenge to a fixed configuration of desire on which Proust's text manifestly insists.

I am interested in the way in which the construction of fantasies surrounding Albertine's sexuality is constitutive of the narrator's own identity category. Indeed the choice of Albertine as
object of desire may be seen to be motivated by the possibility it
affords the narrator for reliving a childhood drama. Albertine's
indeterminate sexuality may be alluring not only for its alterity,

---

[3] See Pierre-Edmond Robert, 'La Prisonnière: Notice', in Marcel Proust, A la
recherche du temps perdu (Paris, 1989), iii. 1628–93: 1628.
[4] Malcolm Bowie, Freud, Proust and Lacan: Theory as Fiction (Cambridge,
1987), 50.

as some critics have argued, but also, and more crucially, for its familiarity. Thus a reading of the last chapter of *Sodome et Gomorrhe*, and its telling revelation of the sudden return of the narrator's feelings for Albertine, may serve to demonstrate how far restaging past trauma determines present desire for the elusive Albertine.

If desire for Albertine is in part determined by the dictates of a text which examines the construction of identity in time, it is also directed by the text's obsession with interpretation. The narrator as lover embarks on a hermeneutic quest which will allow no blissful revelation of meaning or truth, but is itself evidently constitutive of his identity. In this sense we may wonder whether, in creating a hermeneut as hero whose decoding and remembering we as readers perhaps inevitably imitate, Proust demands that his readers question not only the validity of our interpretative method, but also the fragility and temporality of our identities and our desire.

• *Jealousy and Knowledge*

In the last chapter of *Sodome et Gomorrhe* the narrator uses a metaphor of himself as reader describing his 'grief' over Albertine as 'quelque chose comme celui que donne la lecture d'un roman'.[5] At this juncture in the text, before the reader has encountered the diffuse and tortured musings of *La Prisonnière* and *Albertine disparue*, the narrator fantasizes about closing the tale of Albertine and resolves 'et ne plus me soucier davantage de ce qu'avait fait Albertine que nous ne nous soucions des actions de l'héroïne imaginaire d'un roman après que nous en avons fini la lecture'.[6] The following voluminous sections of text work to thwart and deny this hesitant desire. It would seem indeed that in *A la recherche du temps perdu* Proust performs and proves the very impossibility of shutting the heroine within the text. In their readings of the text Proust's

---

[5] Proust, *A la recherche*, iii. 510: *In Search of Lost Time*, iv. 610 ('something like what we feel when we read a novel').

[6] *A la recherche*, iii. 511: *In Search of Lost Time*, iv. 610 ('to think no more about what Albertine had done than we think about the actions of the imaginary heroine of a novel after we have finished reading it').

critics appear themselves to have testified to this. With varying degrees of acuity and personal investment critics have contended with Albertine's challenge to the construal of meaning. What is often left aside is precisely the challenge Albertine poses to the construal of the meaning of the narrator's identity.

In this discussion of analyses of Albertine and of reading encounters with Proust's text, I shall begin with that of Malcolm Bowie, whose coruscating studies of Proust must necessarily define the parameters of my own. In his essay 'Proust, Jealousy, Knowledge', Bowie offers his readers an invitation to embark on his own account of 'a singular adventure of the moral imagination'.[7] In measured terms Bowie leads us into a certain understanding of the narrator's invention of 'a complete phantasy world of experimental observation'.[8] In a sense Bowie's revelations about Albertine are partly incidental in his argument: Bowie's scope is broader than my own, and his conclusions relate to the workings of the mind of the jealous lover rather than to his sexuality or that of his object of desire. Bowie expands our understanding of knowledge in Proust, as he specifies: 'by making the jealous lover, as he heeds his call to know, the main intermediary between the worlds of art and science, Proust has reminded us in the simplest possible way that all works of the mind—Lavoisier's as well as his own—are works of passion too'.[9] Bowie offers a new vision of Proust's novel as a portrayal of the theorizing mind and he reveals how it is in *La Prisonnière* in particular that Proust has created 'a dynamics of knowing, a portrait of the mind in process'.[10]

This recognition of a dynamics of knowing, of knowledge perceived as process, is derived from or perhaps proved by an analysis of Albertine. As Bowie comments: 'whereas "the truth" about Odette is eventually revealed to Swann and confirmed by fresh evidence from all directions, Albertine's sexuality remains an enigma'.[11] Bowie echoes the perpetuation of doubt over Albertine and draws attention to the narrator, who delights in his capacities as a 'modeller of nebulae', and for whom, as Bowie puts it, 'Albertine is one such nebula; each of his models

[7] Bowie, *Freud, Proust and Lacan*, 48.   [8] Ibid. 54.
[9] Ibid. 65.   [10] Ibid. 58.   [11] Ibid. 59.

accommodates some only of her features; features excluded from one model prompt the building of the next. But the process is unstoppable.'[12] Bowie's final word here on Albertine seems to be that 'Albertine cannot be known, unless this interminable passage from structure to structure is itself knowledge and our other notions of what it is to know are the products of a lingering infantile wish for comfort or mastery.'[13]

In his essay 'Freud and Proust' in the same volume, Bowie ingeniously perpetuates his thesis of the unknowability of Albertine whilst also coming closer to a revelation of his own diagnosis of her patterns of desire. Bowie writes for example: 'Albertine's mobile desires are the object of interminable speculation and analysis—of *albertinage*, as these irremediably anxious textual performances have been called.'[14] He continues to suggest that, for Proust's narrator, 'to answer the question that her sexuality poses would be to reach the blissful outcome of a tormented philosophical quest'.[15] Yet earlier in the same paragraph Bowie has suggested that 'for Proust's narrator in *La Prisonnière* and *La Fugitive*, bisexuality . . . figures as an epistemological outrage and moment by moment frustrates the search for intelligibility in his personal relationships'.[16] Bowie appears to suggest that it is Albertine's *bisexuality* which torments the narrator's desire for knowledge: it is implicit in Bowie's argument indeed that 'Albertine's obdurately ambiguous sexuality'[17] is shatteringly, disarmingly at odds with the narrator's pained question 'which does she *really* desire, men or women?'[18] What I shall suggest is that it is not Albertine's probable bisexuality which denies a blissful outcome to the philosophical quest; indeed I want to refute the very notion of this impossible and blissful discovery of the 'truth' of Albertine's sexuality; instead I will suggest here that it is the narrator's fantasy of Albertine's lesbianism which arouses his desire for her. In this sense, I will leave unanswered the question whether Albertine's sexual ident-

---

[12] Bowie, Freud, Proust and Lacan, 59.   [13] Ibid.   [14] Ibid. 77.

[15] Ibid. Bowie expresses this view again, all the more doubtfully it seems, in *The Morality of Proust*, his inaugural lecture delivered before the University of Oxford: 'To understand fully what Charlus in his vice, or Albertine in hers, does or feels or craves would be to find a key to the most difficult and fertile of enigmas' (Oxford, 1994), 9.

[16] Bowie, *Freud, Proust and Lacan*, 77.   [17] Ibid. 81.   [18] Ibid.

ity, as presented by Proust, is utterly unknowable, teasingly ambiguous, or ultimately bisexual. Instead I will look at how a fiction of Albertine's identity informs and arouses the narrator's desire.

• Homosexuality in the Other Sex

Now this position may appear rather close to that of Leo Bersani, who pursues Malcolm Bowie's questioning of the mobility of desire in his essay 'Death and Literary Authority: Marcel Proust and Melanie Klein'.[19] In drawing conclusions about Albertine's sexuality, and its place in the text, Bersani suggests that 'the most accurate sexual metaphor for a hopeless pursuit of one's own desire is undoubtedly the heterosexual's jealousy of homosexuality *in the other sex*'.[20] Bersani pursues this line stating: 'Albertine's lesbianism represents a nearly inconceivable yet inescapable identity of sameness and otherness in Marcel's desires; lesbianism is a relation of sameness that Marcel is condemned to see as an irreducibly unknowable otherness.'[21] It could be argued that the discussions presented by Bowie and Bersani converge at the point of unknowability: for Bowie it is the 'truth' of Albertine's sexual identity that is unknowable, for Bersani it is her erotic practice that is unknowable for the always excluded male desiring subject. As Bersani puts it: 'he shares Albertine's love for women, but not her point of view'.[22]

Bersani reveals how he finds in the closing pages of *Sodome et Gomorrhe* 'an extraordinary reflection on what might be called the necessity of homosexuality in a universal heterosexual relation of all human subjects to their own desires'.[23] Bersani's model is attactive here in the way it posits a continuum between homosexual and heterosexual desire, in the way in which it suggests that homosexuality and heterosexuality are not defined and bound as binary opposites, and, further, in the way it institutes a possible mobility in the adoption of gendered

---

[19] Leo Bersani, 'Death and Literary Authority: Marcel Proust and Melanie Klein', in *The Culture of Redemption* (Cambridge, Mass., 1990), 7–28.
[20] Ibid. 24.   [21] Ibid.   [22] Ibid.   [23] Ibid.

positions. There are, however, crucial points at which our arguments diverge.

In the first place, I would disagree in part with Bersani's suggestion that this is categorically 'a novel of *un*happy desire, a novel that depends . . . on Marcel's misreading of the otherness inherent in desire'.[24] It is perhaps not only Albertine's otherness but also her unknowability which is inherent in the narrator's desire for her. This unknowability is enticing and arousing for the narrator; it is the very pre-condition of his desire for Albertine. Her unknowability depends, as we have seen, on doubt as to her sexuality and erotic practice. Yet where her possible lesbianism constructs Albertine, for Bersani, as impenetrably other, I would argue that the issue is more complex. Where Bersani offers, as we have seen, an utterly persuasive theory that the heterosexual's jealousy of homosexuality in the other sex is the most accurate sexual metaphor for a hopeless pursuit of one's own desire, I am not convinced that this is the case as we find it in *Sodome et Gomorrhe*. Albertine's possible lesbianism may deny the narrator's happy fulfilment of his desire for her. His choice of her as object of desire may be fuelled in part by a latent masochism, or indeed by a recognition that her differing desires will allow his quest to be hopeless but thus exist in perpetuity. Yet it should be emphasized too that Albertine's lesbianism is a source of pleasure as much as pain. This pleasure may be seen to arise in part from the aura of exoticism sometimes surrounding lesbianism in the male imagination. It may be seen also that Albertine's lesbianism endorses her familiarity as much as her alterity. For the narrator, Albertine's erotic practices with women reveal her as emphatically familiar, holding the power to restore for him the involuntary memory of Montjouvain, and giving him access once more to the scopophilia which motivates his infant desires. The narrator here returns to a moment in his childhood when divisions between pain and pleasure are all but dissolved, when he experiences pleasure through exclusion and absence. Is this also, we might ask, a position which the text persuades the reader to adopt? Is the reader too poised between voyeurism and fantasized participation?

---

[24] *The Culture of Redemption*, 23.

One further way in which this analysis will diverge from Bersani's reading of Proust relates to the sexuality of the narrator. For Bersani, it appears that Proust's narrator is undeniably heterosexual; we are told that he shares Albertine's love of women; he is seen to experience 'the heterosexual's' jealousy of homosexuality in the other sex. For other critics, this assumption is, rightly or wrongly, less readily made as I will show below. Again it should be stressed that rather than to attempt to determine the 'truth' of the narrator's sexuality, however, my own aim is to study the processes and performances in which this is constructed.

- *Albertine 'as' a Man*

Drawing sometimes complacently on biographical material, critics have made an important challenge to the notion that the narrator is necessarily heterosexual. As Kristeva puts it in her recent study of Proust: 'Les amateurs de "clés" ont vite découvert, derrière "la fameuse Albertine", l'ami et chauffeur de Proust, Alfred Agostinelli, qui devint pilote et s'écrasa en monoplan pendant un vol d'entraînement le 13 mai 1914.'[25] While she briefly considers Albertine's 'transsexualisme', then taking up a position similar to that of Bersani, Kristeva is quick to add: 'c'est en connaisseur de femmes que se présente le narrateur d'*A la recherche*.[26] Bersani himself chooses to leave Proust's chauffeur, Alfred Agostinelli, undiscussed, but the temptation not to do so is too great for two later readers of Proust (and Bersani), Eve Kosofsky Sedgwick and Kaja Silverman. In her analysis of Proust in *Epistemology of the Closet*, Sedgwick returns to J. E. Rivers's book *Proust and the Art of Love: The Aesthetics of Sexuality in the Life, Times and Art of Marcel Proust*,[27] and his suggestion that the rereadings of

[25] Julia Kristeva, *Le Temps sensible: Proust et l'expérience littéraire* (Paris, 1994), 94 ('Readers who love finding hidden meanings have been quick to discover behind "the famous Albertine" Proust's friend and chauffeur Alfred Agostinelli, who became a pilot and crashed his monoplane on a training flight on 13 May 1914').

[26] Ibid. 95 ('the narrator of *A la recherche* presents himself as a connoisseur of women').

[27] J. E. Rivers, *Proust and the Art of Love: The Aesthetics of Sexuality in the Life, Times, and Art of Marcel Proust* (New York, 1980).

Proust based on the supposition that Albertine 'was really' a man, 'however vulgarizing, confused, and homophobic, however illegitimate as literary criticism or inadmissible in their assumptions about writing and loving, did nevertheless respond so strongly to a variety of unmistakable provocations in the text that the possibility of reading Albertine "as", in some radically to-be-negotiated sense, a man, is by now at least inalienably grafted onto the affordances of the text'.[28]

It seems difficult to perceive precisely at which point Sedgwick leaves her exposition of Rivers's point of view to pursue her own argument. She appears, at least to some degree, to follow Rivers's propositions about the transgendering of Albertine and the issue is certainly one that Proustian critics have not yet laid to rest. As Kaja Silverman puts it neatly: 'Proust's critics have found it difficult to know where to locate his homosexuality in the story of a man who is presented as loving only women. The classic solution has been to posit a concealed subtext to the novel.'[29] There is indeed a wealth of writing which aims to cross Albertine's gender and thus deny the narrator's heterosexuality. We might cite, for example, Monique Wittig, who, as Jonathan Dollimore reminds us, 'is inspired by Proust who, in *Remembrance of Things Past*, "made 'homosexual' the axis of categorization from which to universalize"'.[30] Wittig pursues her study of Proust in her article 'The Trojan Horse' where she develops the polemical theory that 'any work with a new form operates as a war machine, because its design and its goal is to pulverize the old forms and formal conventions'.[31] Wittig cites Proust's work as one of the best examples of 'a war machine with a delayed effect'[32] yet rather than citing the multiple formal innovations of Proust's text, she concentrates instead on issues of gender and sexuality suggesting that Proust succeeded 'in turning the "real" world into a homosexual-only

[28] Eve Kosofsky Sedgwick, *Epistemology of the Closet* (Hemel Hempstead, 1991), 233.

[29] Silverman, *Male Subjectivity at the Margins*, 373.

[30] Jonathan Dollimore, *Sexual Dissidence: Augustine to Wilde, Freud to Foucault* (Oxford, 1991), 60. See also Judith Butler's excellent critique of Wittig in *Gender Trouble: Feminism and the Subversion of Identity* (New York, 1990), 111–28.

[31] Monique Wittig, 'The Trojan Horse', in *The Straight Mind and Other Essays* (Hemel Hempstead, 1992), 68–75: 68–9.

[32] Ibid. 73–4.

world'.[33] Wittig claims that this transformation takes place since the reader in search of a *roman-à-clef* 'had to change around the women's and men's names, since most of the women in the book were in reality men'[34] and that the reader 'therefore had to take in the fact that a good many of the characters were homosexuals'.[35]

It seems, however, that even if the reader doesn't indulge in this rather peculiar activity of crossing the gender of Proust's characters, s/he will encounter a more than representative number of lesbians and gay men. Yet I would argue with Wittig's suggestion that 'homosexuality is *the* theme of the book'.[36] Although a fairly substantial number of characters do "discover" a homosexual orientation, it is noteworthy too that this transition between sexualities works in both directions. Alison Winton makes this point in her book *Proust's Additions* where she writes: 'if Proust is spreading inversion, he introduces too a topsy-turvy heterosexuality, now making Nissim Bernard's clerk, the lift-boy and Morel all turn away from homosexuality in insertions into *Le Temps retrouvé*'.[37] I would suggest indeed that Proust's Trojan horse discloses the instability and mobility of human desire and works in this way to destabilize categories of male and female, homosexual and heterosexual, gay and lesbian, in such a way that it should be seen as particularly limiting to read the narrator only as a closeted homosexual and Albertine as a mere man in drag. Yet readers seem impelled, perhaps in reaction to the very uncertainties of *A la recherche du temps perdu*, to stabilize the sexual identities revealed in the text's incompatible performances of desire.

The study of Albertine's male model is pursued by Pierre-Edmond Robert in his introduction to *La Prisonnière* in the recent Pléiade edition of *A la recherche du temps perdu*. Here he includes a section on Alfred Agostinelli, speaking of his role in the Albertine cycle.[38] Robert finds that *La Prisonnière* has at times the tone of an intimate journal,[39] yet he is also careful to distinguish between Agostinelli and Albertine. He ends his

---

[33] Ibid. 74.   [34] Ibid.   [35] Ibid.
[36] Wittig, 'The Point of View: Universal or Particular?', 59–67: 64.
[37] Alison Winton, *Proust's Additions* (Cambridge, 1977), 291.
[38] Robert, '*La Prisonnière*: Notice', 1632.   [39] Ibid. 1635.

comments on Agostinelli admitting that Proust chose to tell the tale of Albertine, rather than that of Agostinelli, which, in his view, would have been all the more *romanesque*.[40]

In his careful distinction between Agostinelli and Albertine, Robert avoids the insistence we find in Wittig's text on Albertine's cross-gendering, and in Rivers's text on her masculinity. This masculinity Sedgwick too finds problematic. She takes issue with the notion of transposition of gender and poses her reader the following list of questions:

For instance, if Albertine and the narrator are of the same gender, should the supposed outside loves of Albertine, which the narrator obsessively imagines as imaginatively inaccessible to himself, then, maintaining the female *gender* of their love object, be transposed in *orientation* into heterosexual desires? Or, maintaining the transgressive same-sex *orientation*, would they have to change the *gender* of their love object and be transposed into male homosexual desires? Or, in a homosexual framework, would the heterosexual orientation after all be more transgressive?[41]

Sedgwick's near exhaustive questioning is exhilarating for the reader yet it illustrates as well what she herself does not emphasize particularly strongly, namely the very problems involved in reading Albertine 'as' a man, in order to find a basis from which to deny the narrator's heterosexuality.

In this sense, however far Proust may have been influenced by his own possible (or impossible) love for Agostinelli, his text represents the narrator's love for Albertine, a love which, I would argue against Pierre-Edmond Robert, is every bit as *romanesque* as the tale of Proust's own passion. Here I would suggest that speculative questions about homophobia and disclosure are certainly relevant to an understanding of the conditions of production of Proust's text, yet should not necessarily cloud or transform our reading of the text and its own performance of desire, which may appear to transgress easy categorizations of male and female, homosexual and heterosexual identifications. Here it is necessary to specify one further way in which my reading will differ from those of Sedgwick and Silverman, and this is over the specific issue of Albertine's lesbianism.

---

[40] 'La Prisonnière: Notice', 1636.
[41] Sedgwick, *Epistemology of the Closet*, 233.

• *Oral Sex; or, 'Is Marcel a Lesbian?'*

After some discussion of the improbable possibilities of Albertine being a man, Sedgwick considers too what she describes as 'a gender-separatist emphasis on Albertine's female connections with women'[42] and she shows that these are seen as being 'in their very lesbianism, of the essence of the female—centrally and definingly located within femininity'.[43] However, this is also a model which is largely rejected in favour of the familiar view of Albertine's sexuality representing 'infinity, indeterminacy, contingency, play, etc. etc.'.[44] This is further nuanced by Sedgwick's proposition that, 'if a particular erotic localization is to be associated with her it must be the oral'.[45] This point of view Sedgwick substantiates with reference to Albertine's exquisite passion for ices and the narrator's delight in their kisses. On a far broader level, Sedgwick suggests compellingly that historians of sexuality will have to learn 'to think about something like a world-historical popularization of oral sex, sometime in the later nineteenth century'.[46]

The argument about oral sex is taken up by Kaja Silverman in the final section of her book *Male Subjectivity at the Margins*, to which she gives the title 'In Search of a Kissing Organ'. Here she formulates a further answer to the question she poses in the following terms: 'How are we to account for Albertine's presence within an erotic structure which seems to require precisely that "Albert" whom certain of Proust's critics have wanted to procure from his biography?'[47] Silverman's answer leads back to the question I have quoted in the title to this chapter and to which I wish to suggest some answers here. Silverman dwells at length on kissing as the 'preeminent synecdoche not only for sexual pleasure, but for desire and carnal "knowledge"'.[48] This investment in oral pleasure leads Silverman to the suggestion that there seems to be no place for the penis in the pursuit of oral gratification undertaken by Albertine and the narrator, and to the conclusion that 'it is consequently difficult to conceptualize their relationship as one involving two "men", however

---

[42] Ibid. 234. [43] Ibid. [44] Ibid. 236.
[45] Ibid. 235. [46] Ibid. 237.
[47] Silverman, *Male Subjectivity at the Margins*, 377.
[48] Ibid. 379–80.

deessentialized the definition of masculinity'.[49] I would certainly agree with this proposition as it stands, though not necessarily with the conceptual framework which constructs it. There appear to be more problems, however, with the next stage in Silverman's argument, and this she herself acknowledges as she begins: 'disquieting as the thought may be to many readers of *A la recherche*, however, Proust *does* encourage us to conceive of Marcel's affair with Albertine as one between two "women"'.[50] Silverman's inverted answer appears to be that it is not Albertine, but Marcel, who 'cross-dresses'. And Silverman comes to her next conclusion saying: 'it is thus only through lesbianism that we are finally able to locate the homosexuality which so clearly structures authorial subjectivity in *A la recherche*'.[51]

Silverman's discussion is grounded, as is my own, in the recognition that, for the narrator (and this is important), 'Albertine's lesbianism is not so much a difficulty within their relationship as its precondition.'[52] This leads Silverman to substantiate her suggestion that Proust's central character is 'psychically female, but corporeally male'[53] and thus she adds a further facet to the altogether fascinating argument she develops in *Male Subjectivity at the Margins* where she stresses that 'femininity inhabits male homosexuality in all kinds of interesting, enabling and politically productive ways'.[54] While not in any sense intending to detract from this argument, which I find in itself challenging and convincing, in the analysis of the last chapter of *Sodome et Gomorrhe* which follows, I will discuss certain issues which may in fact encourage us *not* to think of Marcel simply as a lesbian.

• *Space and Sexuality*

To pursue this reading of Proust I will refer to Foucault, and particularly to the first volume of his *Histoire de la sexualité*.[55] Following the theorization of proximities between the stage

---

[49] Silverman, *Male Subjectivity at the Margins*, 383.
[50] Ibid.   [51] Ibid.   [52] Ibid.   [53] Ibid. 386.   [54] Ibid. 387.
[55] Michel Foucault, *Histoire de la sexualité*, i: *La Volonté de savoir* (Paris, 1976): *The History of Sexuality*, i: *An Introduction*, trans. Robert Hurley (London, 1981).

where sexual identities are performed, and the space in which the reading encounter takes place, as discussed in the previous chapter, my discussion here will explore the relations between space and sexuality, between the enclosed world of the imagination and the literal interior where the narrator attempts to entrap the Albertine of his fantasies. I will be concerned with the ways in which the narrator's fantasies of Albertine, and his formative readings of her behaviour, direct and inform his erotic relations with her, and with the way in which her possible infidelities perversely structure the confines of *his* desire. In this sense, the narrator's sexual identification may be seen to depend on hermeneutic activity. His desire for Albertine is aroused by the impossible conundrum to which she allows him to return. He can only ever remain reader or viewer of her (lesbian) desiring relations, yet this position of exclusion is seen to be constitutive of his identity. The role of excluded voyeur and desiring reader is one constantly performed in the spaces of his fantasies.

In the second section of *La Volonté de savoir*, entitled 'L'Hypothèse répressive', Foucault draws out the contours of a world of perversions. His concern is with control and surveillance, with the power of the forbidden and the peculiar erotic charge created precisely as a product of the regulatory structure and punitive system. Foucault suggests that modern society has encouraged the proliferation of 'des proximités qui se donnent comme procédés de surveillance, et qui fonctionnent comme des mécanismes d'intensification; des contacts inducteurs'.[56] He gives the example of the nineteenth-century family house which becomes an instrument of the regulatory system, which institutes both the separation of adults and children, and the segregation of boys and girls, both of which, in Foucault's terms, belie 'l'attention éveillée sur la sexualité infantile'.[57] Foucault sees the family entrapped in its self-created web of hidden secrets and fears; he delineates 'un réseau de plaisirs-pouvoirs articulés selon des points multiples et avec des relations

---

[56] *Histoire de la sexualité*, i. 63: *History of Sexuality*, i. 46 ('proximities that serve as surveillance procedures, and function as mechanisms of intensification; contacts that operate as inductors').

[57] *Histoire de la sexualité*, i. 63: *History of Sexuality*, i. 46 ('attention focused on infantile sexuality').

transformables'.[58] This argument is then extended to apply, appropriately, to other 'régions de haute saturation sexuelle, avec des espaces ou des rites privilégiés comme la salle de classe, le dortoir, la visite ou la consultation'.[59] In his concern with space, Foucault has provided us with a map of the 'sexualité du foyer, de l'école, de la prison'.[60] What I want to study here is the way in which the rules of the game of power and pleasure outlined by Foucault relate to Proust's narrator's desire for Albertine. In the architecture of *A la recherche du temps perdu*, the reader may appear to find 'jamais plus de foyers où s'allument, pour se disséminer plus loin, l'intensité des plaisirs et l'obstination des pouvoirs'.[61]

- *L'Amie de Mlle Vinteuil*

The third chapter of *Sodome et Gomorrhe* ends with the narrator's resolve to break with Albertine. As the fourth chapter opens he is simply awaiting the appropriate moment for a definitive rupture. Yet in the next twenty or so pages his resolve itself is dramatically broken, and the course of the novel irrevocably changed. The ephemeral remark which catalyses this swift reversal in the narrator's passions comes as Albertine comments on her association with the infamous friend of Mlle Vinteuil. When the narrator speaks to Albertine of Vinteuil, of whom he assumes Albertine to be completely ignorant, she surprises him as she replies:

Vous vous rappelez que je vous ai parlé d'une amie plus âgée que moi, qui m'a servi de mère, de sœur, avec qui j'ai passé à Trieste mes meilleures années ... hé bien! cette amie (oh! pas du tout le genre de femmes que vous pourriez croire!), regardez comme c'est

---

[58] *Histoire de la sexualité*, i. 63: *History of Sexuality*, i. 46 ('a complicated network, saturated with multiple, fragmentary, and mobile sexualities').

[59] *Histoire de la sexualité*, i. 64: *History of Sexuality* i. 46 ('areas of extreme sexual saturation, with privileged spaces or rituals such as the classroom, the dormitory, the visit, and the consultation').

[60] *Histoire de la sexualité*, i. 65: (*History of Sexuality*, i. 47 ('sexuality of the home, the school, the prison').

[61] *Histoire de la sexualité*, i. 67: *History of Sexuality*, i. 49 ('never more sites where the intensity of pleasures and the persistency of power catch hold, only to spread elsewhere').

extraordinaire, est justement la meilleure amie de la fille de ce Vinteuil, et je connais presque autant la fille de Vinteuil.[62]

This revelation discloses to the narrator Albertine's unhoped for, uncanny familiarity, and precipitates him into remembering his voyeuristic vision at Montjouvain: 'une image s'agitait dans mon cœur, une image tenue en réserve pendant tant d'années que, même si j'avais pu deviner, en l'emmagasinant jadis, qu'elle avait un pouvoir nocif, j'eusse cru qu'à la longue elle l'avait entièrement perdu'.[63] Proust's narrator refers back in his memory, as Proust himself refers his reader back, to the formative evening at Montjouvain where he views Mlle Vinteuil and her lover. This scene is itself marked out as formative within the text where the narrator comments, firstly, 'C'est peut-être d'une impression ressentie aussi auprès de Montjouvain, quelques années plus tard, impression restée obscure alors, qu'est sortie, bien après, l'idée que je me suis faite du sadisme',[64] and he adds, secondly, 'On verra plus tard que, pour de tout autres raisons, le souvenir de cette impression devait jouer un rôle important dans ma vie'.[65] We may note that it is not as it is experienced, but only when it is remembered that the episode at Montjouvain takes on its revelatory power. The impression which remained 'obscure' as Proust puts it, using the optical imagery which resurfaces in the analysis of reading in *Le Temps retrouvé*, is now seen clearly as it is re-viewed and reread in the piercing light of Albertine's revelation.

In *Combray*, then, the narrator has already referred to the

---

[62] Proust, *A la recherche*, iii. 499: *In Search of Lost Time*, iv. 596 ('You remember my telling you about a friend, older than me, who had been a mother, a sister to me, with whom I spent the happiest years of my life, at Trieste . . . well, this friend (oh! not at all the type of woman you might suppose!), isn't this extraordinary, is the best friend of your Vinteuil's daughter, and I know Vinteuil's daughter almost as well as I know her').

[63] *A la recherche*, iii. 499: *In Search of Lost Time*, iv. 596 ('an image stirred in my heart, an image which I had kept in reserve for so many years that even if I had been able to guess, when I stored it up long ago, that it had a noxious power, I should have supposed that in the course of time it had entirely lost it').

[64] *A la recherche*, i. 157: *In Search of Lost Time*, i. 190 ('it is perhaps from [an] impression that I received at Montjouvain, some years later, an impression which at the time remained obscure to me, that there arose, long afterwards, the notion I was to form of sadism').

[65] *A la recherche*, i. 157: *In Search of Lost Time*, i. 190 ('we shall see, in due course, that for quite other reasons the memory of this impression was to play an important part in my life').

way in which the memory of Montjouvain will occur at the moment of his discovery of Albertine's association with the lover of Mlle Vinteuil, which is itself the first moment when he finds proof for his suspicions that Albertine is a 'pratiquante professionnelle du Saphisme'.[66] What I would suggest is that the memory of the episode at Montjouvain plays such an important role for the narrator since, in entirely spatial terms, it offers a structure for his later patterns of desire. And in this sense it may in part supersede the bedtime drama in disclosing the formation of the narrator's sexuality as it is discovered little by little as the text develops. Thus desire for Albertine is constitutive of the narrator's identity not simply for what it is but, in more complex terms, for what it recalls. This is itself a game of recollection in which Proust also engages the reader.

• *Montjouvain*

How, then, can the scenario at Montjouvain be seen to determine the narrator's sexuality? Here we might pause to re-examine the familiar details of the scene. At Montjouvain, as a child, the narrator falls asleep in the bushes surrounding Vinteuil's house. He wakes when it is almost dark, and he sees Mlle Vinteuil in the room immediately in front of him; she is described by the narrator as 'en face de moi, à quelques centimètres de moi'.[67] The child is in an ideal position to see without being seen; as the narrator comments: 'La fenêtre était entr'ouverte, la lampe était allumée, je voyais tous ses mouvements sans qu'elle me vît'.[68] Here the half-open window is placed perfectly ambiguously neither entirely to exclude nor to include the narrator in the diegetic space of the drama he will witness. Outside he watches the women's kisses and their desecration of Vinteuil's portrait through a screen of glass which is

[66] *A la recherche*, iii. 500: *In Search of Lost Time*, iv. 597 ('practising and professional Sapphist').

[67] *A la recherche*, i. 157: *In Search of Lost Time*, i. 191 ('in front of me, and only a few feet away').

[68] *A la recherche*, i. 157: *In Search of Lost Time*, i. 191 ('the window was partly open; the lamp was lighted, I could watch her every movement without her being able to see me').

itself seductively open. 'Laisse donc tout ouvert,'[69] cries Mlle
Vinteuil's lover, leaving their passion open to the gaze of the
unseen child.

It is this illicit vision which, in the persuasively complex
teleology of the novel, defines the narrator's desire for Albertine.
He places her possible affairs with women behind the glass of
his imagination. He places himself always outside the 'room'
where her love is consummated; and he loves her precisely
because her mobile desires can place him in this tortured position of exclusion. In his attempt to hold Albertine captive, to
prevent her lesbian liaisons, the narrator confines her, paradoxically, in a prison whose very presence testifies to his desire for
her inevitable betrayal.

• *Departure at Parville*

Like so much else in the novel, lesbianism is linked implicitly in
A la recherche du temps perdu to space and location. As the
narrator awakens to the realization of the seeming truth of
Cottard's diagnosis in the casino of Parville he reveals: 'C'était
une *terra incognita* terrible où je venais d'atterrir, une phase
nouvelle de souffrances insoupçonnées qui s'ouvrait'.[70] This
realm of suffering has been presaged earlier in the text when the
narrator has listened to Cottard's comments on Albertine and
Andrée as they dance. His suffering is realized, rarefied, and
extended as Albertine offers fire to his fantasies and the narrator
comments: 'C'est souvent seulement par manque d'esprit
créateur qu'on ne va pas assez loin dans la souffrance'.[71]

Two points should be raised here. The first relates to the
perceived intermeshing of fantasy and reality. The narrator
analyses his situation and his suffering thus, saying: 'la réalité
la plus terrible donne, en même temps que la souffrance, la
joie d'une belle découverte, parce qu'elle ne fait que donner

---

[69] *A la recherche*, i. 159: *In Search of Lost Time*, i. 193 ('Leave them open').

[70] *A la recherche*, iii. 500: *In Search of Lost Time*, iv. 597 ('It was a terrible *terra incognita* on which I had just landed, a new phase of undreamed-of sufferings that was opening before me').

[71] *A la recherche*, iii. 500: *In Search of Lost Time*, iv. 598 ('it is often simply from lack of creative imagination that we do not go far enough in suffering').

une forme neuve et claire à ce que nous remâchions depuis longtemps sans nous en douter'.[72] Suffering brings the joy of discovery. Reality, in Proust's terms, is seen to offer a form and a contour to the world of the imagination. The narrator is seen to be intent on a project of recognition whereby reality may be read to reflect and refigure his fears and desires. We might note too the implications of this for the external reader of Proust's text. The discovery the narrator describes is also that of the reader who begins to perceive how far the novel verifies the narrator's solipsistic vision, how far the places described offer a disturbingly convincing spatial correlative for the inner realm of fantasy and fiction.

A recognition of this coincidence of thought and space leads me to a second point which relates also to location. The reader will probably note that Albertine's revelation of her knowledge of Mlle Vinteuil and her lover comes, as the narrator specifies, 'comme nous entrions en gare de Parville'.[73] In lavishly symbolic terms Parville becomes the location of discovery. Now Parville is described as Albertine's *destination*; as she gets up to get out, the narrator says: 'ce mouvement qu'elle accomplissait ainsi pour descendre me déchirait intolérablement le cœur'.[74] It is the spatial separation which so tortures the narrator and he writes: 'Elle me faisait si mal en s'éloignant que, la rattrapant, je la tirai désespérément par le bras'.[75] The narrator resolves that he can no longer bear to know that Albertine is at a distance. Her presence is necessary not only to the security and seeming stability of his knowledge of her, but also to the illusory integrity of his identity. The narrator seeks to deny the evident alterity of Albertine. In his efforts to internalize her, he attempts also her interment.

[72] *A la recherche*, iii. 500: *In Search of Lost Time*, iv. 598 ('And the most terrible reality brings us, at the same time as suffering, the joy of a great discovery, because it merely gives a new and clear form to what we have long been ruminating without suspecting it').

[73] *A la recherche*, iii. 499: *In Search of Lost Time*, iv. 596 ('as we were entering the station of Parville').

[74] *A la recherche*, iii. 501: *In Search of Lost Time*, iv. 598 ('but this movement which she thus made to get off the train tore my heart unendurably').

[75] *A la recherche*, iii. 501: *In Search of Lost Time*, iv. 598 ('she gave me such pain by her withdrawal that, reaching after her, I caught her desperately by the arm').

• *Localization*

Albertine becomes necessarily entrapped within the narrator's thoughts as a ricocheting series of suspicions intensifies both his suffering and his desire. These suspicions dictate the anxious measures he will now take to divide Albertine from her desire and to retain her within his field of vision. Firstly the narrator persuades Albertine to return with him to spend the night at Balbec, thus preventing her symbolic departure at Parville. At Balbec, Albertine doesn't sleep with the narrator, but separated from him, in another room, on another floor. He is left in solitude, prey to insomniac fantasies, revelling in the very lucidity of his suspicions and probing the open lesion his love for Albertine has become.

Albertine becomes thus the catalyst for the reliving and reperforming of the narrator's childhood desires. He is again caught in the space of Montjouvain, as he admits: 'Derrière Albertine je ne voyais plus les montagnes bleues de la mer, mais la chambre de Montjouvain où elle tombait dans les bras de Mlle Vinteuil'.[76] Albertine has been transposed in the space of his imagination: it is she who is now viewed through the half-open window. As the narrator admits later, in an image seemingly drawn from sexual fantasy: 'A Mlle Vinteuil maintenant, tandis que son amie la chatouillait avant de s'abattre sur elle, je donnais le visage enflammé d'Albertine'.[77] The narrator generates the belief that this enclosed stage where he has first viewed lesbian passion is the very stage where Albertine herself has learnt the performance of her desires. The scene viewed in childhood is replayed in an adult fantasy which is shown to be formative in the construction of the narrator's sexual identity.

As the narrator rehearses his fantasies of Albertine's desires he sits by a window open to the night: 'Je m'assis près de la

---

[76] *A la recherche*, iii. 501: *In Search of Lost Time*, iv. 599 ('behind Albertine I no longer saw the blue mountains of the sea, but the room at Montjouvain where she was falling into the arms of Mlle Vinteuil').

[77] *A la recherche*, iii. 504: *In Search of Lost Time*, iv. 602 ('To Mlle Vinteuil, while her friend titillated her desires before flinging herself upon her, I now gave the inflamed face of Albertine').

fenêtre . . . je n'avais même pas pensé à fermer les volets'.[78] The literal location copies in its structure the fantasized and remembered location of Montjouvain. Yet, now, the narrator places himself within the room of his fantasy. He attempts also to retain Albertine within this fantasy space. While his aim is to eradicate any possibility of her meeting Mlle Vinteuil's lover, what he does instead is lock her into the house of his imagination, and its architectural correlatives, where she is always necessarily the errant lesbian viewed by the excluded child.

The narrator's desire to possess Albertine becomes concentrated, in displaced terms, on the desire to limit her movements in space. Her location and her lesbianism become inextricably linked as the narrator presumes in tortured terms: 'Mais je pensais qu'elle allait bientôt partir de Balbec pour Cherbourg et de là pour Trieste.'[79] And Trieste, where Albertine has suggested that her affair with Mlle Vinteuil's lover took place, necessarily holds a sinister signification for the narrator, who surmises immediately that 'ses habitudes d'autrefois allaient renaître',[80] and who thus admits, 'Ce que je voulais avant tout, c'était empêcher Albertine de prendre le bateau, tâcher de l'emmener à Paris'.[81]

The narrator himself recognizes how far this desire to trap Albertine in space is illogical and he says, indeed: 'Certes j'aurais pu me dire qu'à Paris, si Albertine avait ces goûts, elle trouverait bien d'autres personnes avec qui les assouvir'.[82] He admits, further, in terms of self-justification, 'Je savais bien que cette localisation de ma jalousie était arbitraire',[83] and he comes close to repeating himself in the space of a few pages, recognizing again that 'si Albertine avait ces goûts elle pouvait les assouvir

[78] *A la recherche*, iii. 501: *In Search of Lost Time*, iv. 599 ('I sat by the window . . . I had not even remembered to close the shutters').

[79] *A la recherche*, iii. 503: *In Search of Lost Time*, iv. 601 ('But I reflected that she would presently be leaving Balbec for Cherbourg, and from there going to Trieste').

[80] *A la recherche*, iii. 503: *In Search of Lost Time*, iv. 601 ('her old habits would be reviving').

[81] *A la recherche*, iii. 503: *In Search of Lost Time*, iv. 601 ('what I wished above everything else was to prevent Albertine from taking the boat, to make an attempt to carry her off to Paris').

[82] *A la recherche*, iii. 503: *In Search of Lost Time*, iv. 601 ('of course I might have reminded myself that in Paris, if Albertine had those tastes, she would find many other people with whom to gratify them').

[83] *A la recherche*, iii. 505: *In Search of Lost Time*, iv. 603 ('I knew quite well that this localization of my jealousy was arbitrary').

avec d'autres'.[84] Yet this so aptly named localization is an inescapable focus of the text, and a phenomenon Proust explores in
multiple dimensions.

Here, for example, in the first place it is Trieste which is
located as city of unknown desires, and as capital of Gomorrah.
The narrator describes Trieste as 'ce monde inconnu',[85] recalling
thus the *terra incognita* where he finds himself as a result of
Albertine's revelation. He reveals how Trieste has become a
dread location in the map of his imagination, undergoing
indeed a particularly insidious *inversion maligne*: 'ce n'était
plus comme vers un pays délicieux où la race est pensive,
les couchants dorés, les carillons tristes, que je pensais
maintenant à Trieste, mais comme à une cité maudite que
j'aurais voulu faire brûler sur-le-champ et supprimer du monde
réel'.[86] In a sense the narrator achieves this desire to remove
Trieste from the real world, yet he does this only by rebuilding
the city in the world of his imagination. He admits: 'Cette
ville était enfoncée dans mon cœur comme une pointe
permanente'.[87]

The localization of his jealousy takes its second form in his
behaviour towards Albertine. In the desperate attempt to prevent her return to Trieste (and by analogy to lesbian pleasure)
the narrator proposes that she should accompany him to Paris,
and live there alone with him. He rationalizes the proposition in
the following terms: 'A tout prix il fallait l'empêcher d'être
seule, au moins quelques jours, la garder près de moi pour être
sûr qu'elle ne pût voir l'amie de Mlle Vinteuil'.[88] In seemingly
Foucauldian terms, the necessity of localization masks the need
for surveillance. The narrator desires to control Albertine and to
contain his knowledge of her. He meditates on the desperate

---

[84] *A la recherche*, iii. 505: *In Search of Lost Time*, iv. 603 ('if Albertine had these
tastes, she could gratify them with others').

[85] *A la recherche*, iii. 505: *In Search of Lost Time*, iv. 603 ('that unknown world').

[86] *A la recherche*, iii. 505: *In Search of Lost Time*, iv. 604 ('it was no longer as of
a delightful place where the people were pensive, the sunsets golden, the church bells
melancholy, that I thought now of Trieste, but as of an accursed city which I should
have liked to see instantaneously burned down and eliminated from the real world').

[87] *A la recherche*, iii. 505: *In Search of Lost Time*, iv. 604 ('this city was
embedded in my heart as a fixed and permanent point').

[88] *A la recherche*, iii. 506: *In Search of Lost Time*, iv. 604 ('At all costs I must
prevent her from being alone, for some days at any rate, must keep her with me so
as to be certain that she could not meet Mlle Vinteuil's friend').

lengths to which this desire might lead him, concentrating first on the possibility of his suffering and then, more disturbingly, on hers: 'pour qu'Albertine n'allât pas à Trieste, j'aurais supporté toutes les souffrances, et si c'eût été insuffisant, je lui en aurais infligé, je l'aurais isolée, enfermée, je lui eusse pris le peu d'argent qu'elle avait pour que le dénûment l'empêchât matériellement de faire le voyage'.[89]

This sado-masochistic desire to command and survey Albertine is provoked not so much by the narrator's wish literally to control her activities and inflict on her the suffering he feels as a result of her imagined sexual liberties; it is, I would argue, more properly the result of the narrator's need to retain Albertine within his imagination. In this internalized position she serves both to deny and to define the performance of the narrator's sexuality. She is located as object of desire, yet the specificity of her sexual definition allows the narrator to be always already excluded from the scenario of passion, yet always also its pained observer.

• *'Journées de lecture'*

Near the resolution of the last chapter of *Sodome et Gomorrhe* the narrator attempts to synthesize his protracted musings on his desire for Albertine; here he expresses himself revealingly in the following terms: 'Mais les mots: "Cette amie, c'est Mlle Vinteuil" avaient été le Sésame, que j'eusse été incapable de trouver moi-même, qui avait fait entrer Albertine dans la profondeur de mon cœur déchiré'.[90] And he continues: 'et la porte qui s'était renfermée sur elle, j'aurais pu chercher pendant cent ans sans savoir comment on pourrait la rouvrir'.[91] Where

[89] *A la recherche*, iii. 505: *In Search of Lost Time*, iv. 603 ('in order that Albertine might not go to Trieste, I would have endured every possible torment, and if that proved insufficient, would have inflicted torments on her, would have isolated her, kept her under lock and key, would have taken from her the little money that she had so that it should be physically impossible for her to make the journey').

[90] *A la recherche*, iii. 512: *In Search of Lost Time*, iv. 612 ('But the words: "That friend is Mlle Vinteuil" had been the *Open Sesame*, which I should have been incapable of discovering by myself, that had made Albertine penetrate to the depths of my lacerated heart').

[91] *A la recherche*, iii. 512: *In Search of Lost Time*, iv. 612 ('And I might search for a hundred years without discovering how to open the door that had closed behind her').

Albertine's words of revelation have, in the image Proust chooses, opened the space of the narrator's heart to her, paradoxically this is a space where she must dwell enclosed, yet never possessed. Albertine remains the narrator's coveted prisoner, languishing it seems like Persephone in the Underworld. The narrator's heart serves here as his space of surveillance, as he is constructed himself as paranoid prison guard.

In his use of the imagery of the key and the door Proust evidently perpetuates the motifs of space, location, enclosure, and confinement we have found proliferating in this part of *A la recherche du temps perdu*. What Proust does here as well, which is particularly relevant to the purposes of this argument, is to draw on imagery he has used previously with specific reference to the reading process.

In his text 'Journées de lecture' Proust meditates, in terms which will inform the studies of reading within *A la recherche du temps perdu*, on the pleasures of the reading scenario. He opens with the statement: 'Il n'y a peut-être pas de jours de notre enfance que nous ayons si pleinement vécus que ceux que nous avons cru laisser sans les vivre, ceux que nous avons passés avec un livre préféré'.[92] He locates these formative childhood days in their specific time and space, dramatizing the act of reading and setting its scene, as we have seen also to be the case in *Combray*. Proust writes of the pleasures of reading in bed, deftly eliding any difference between the enclosed space of the bedroom and the diegetic space of the text in which the reader is captivated. Proust specifies: 'alors, cette vie secrète, on a le sentiment de l'enfermer avec soi quand on va, tout tremblant, tirer le verrou'.[93] As the reader literally locks the door, in the slippage Proust's imagery effects, he appears to enclose himself within the treasured solipsistic realm of the text.

In this erotic exegesis of reading pleasures Proust's concern, as with gentle irony he gives voice to the child's emotions, is precisely with the seeming vanity and ephemerality of the reading encounter:

[92] Marcel Proust, 'Journées de lecture', in *Contre Sainte-Beuve* (Paris, 1971), 160–94: 160: *Against Sainte-Beuve*, 195–226: 195 ('There are no days of my childhood which I lived so fully perhaps as those I thought I had left behind without living them, those I spent with a favourite book').

[93] 'Journées de lecture', 167: *Against Saint-Beuve*, 202 ('then you have the sense of locking this secret life in with you, as you go, trembling all over, to bolt the door').

Alors, quoi? ce livre, ce n'était que cela? Ces êtres à qui on avait donné plus de son attention et de sa tendresse qu'aux gens de la vie, n'osant pas toujours avouer à quel point on les aimait, et même quand nos parents nous trouvaient en train de lire et avaient l'air de sourire de notre émotion, fermant le livre, avec une indifférence affectée ou un ennui feint; ces gens pour qui on avait haleté et sangloté, on ne les verrait plus jamais, on ne saurait plus rien d'eux.[94]

This elegy to the finished book and the inevitably forgotten character is hardly in keeping with the sober sentiments voiced in *Sodome et Gomorrhe* where Proust's narrator envisages so apparently optimistically the possibility of closing the book on Albertine with no regrets. In 'Journées de lecture' Proust continues: 'On aurait tant voulu ... ne pas avoir aimé en vain, pour une heure, des êtres qui demain ne seraient plus qu'un nom sur une page oubliée, dans un livre sans rapport avec la vie.'[95] These lines intermingling regret and desire come closer, it seems, to elucidating the narrator's desire for Albertine in the later text.

In this sense I would argue that the tortured fantasies evolving out of Albertine's ever uncertain sexuality are the result of the narrator's (and Proust's) attempt to retain interest in Albertine and to stress that the text created in the encounter between the narrator's imagination and Albertine's seeming lesbian passions is one which opens ever into new dimensions, thus denying the reader's desire to master the text in the reading encounter. And here we witness a possible irony further disrupting the impossible relationship between the narrator and Albertine. In 'Journées de lecture' Proust writes of the desire not to have loved in vain. Yet in inventing, or perceiving, Albertine's lesbianism, the narrator comes inevitably to designate his love of Albertine as, precisely, vain and hopeless. Indeed it is the love

[94] 'Journées de lecture', 170: *Against Saint-Beuve*, 204 ('Was there no more to the book than this, then? These creatures on whom one had bestowed more attention and affection than on those in real life, not always daring to admit to what extent you loved them, and even, when my parents found me reading and seemed to smile at my emotion, closing the book with studied indifference or a pretence of boredom; never again would one see these people for whom one had sobbed and yearned, never again hear of them').

[95] 'Journées de lecture', 171: *Against Sainte-Beuve*, 206 ('One would have so much liked ... not to have loved in vain, for an hour, human beings who tomorrow will be no more than a name on a forgotten page, in a book unrelated to our lives').

that so manifestly excludes him that is his perpetual erotic obsession, as we have seen. The narrator only desires Albertine because he suspects that she is a lesbian: this is proved specifically in the episode of his 'revirement' towards her. Yet this suspicion feeds into the very vanity of his passion, which is, in the masochistic economy of Proust's analysis of desire, cherished for its very impossibility and for its capacity to cause pain.

Proust's narrator appears then, in this formulation of his sexual identity, to seek a love which is as solipsistic, as intense, and as impossible as the child's initiatory encounters with love in fictions. This is the love which dominates the jealous narrative, the suspicions, and interrogations of *La Prisonnière* and of *Albertine disparue*. The perpetuation of fantasies of Albertine and the continual, insistent lack of any resolution or discovery of truth, reveal a double bind in which Proust places his suffering narrator. In his passion for Albertine it would seem that the impossible has been achieved and that the imaginary heroine has been allowed to exist beyond her prescribed text, yet the irony is that the narrator's love for Albertine throughout all her ricocheting real and imagined adventures is necessarily vain and illusory since he knows her only as a fiction. Yet as a fiction upon which his identity is dependent.

In the narrator's relationship with Albertine, Proust appears to play out on a grand scale a drama which enacts the dangers of reading he warns against in 'Journées de lecture'. This the reader may construe, indeed, as cautionary tale. We may notice that Proust speaks first of the salutary effects of reading, writing: 'Tant que la lecture est pour nous l'incitatrice dont les clefs magiques nous ouvrent au fond de nous-même la porte des demeures où nous n'aurions pas su pénétrer, son rôle dans notre vie est salutaire'.[96] Here, noticeably, the imagination is seen again in spatial terms: reading is seen to open doors to an inner realm and to reveal (or create?) previously unknown dimensions of the self. This passage uses imagery which, deliberately or not, is picked up, as we have seen, in *Sodome et Gomorrhe*. Yet,

---

[96] 'Journées de lecture', 180: *Against Sainte-Beuve*, 213 ('For as long as reading is for us the instigator whose magic keys have opened the door to those dwelling places deep within us that we would not have known how to enter, its role in our lives is salutory').

here, Proust leads us quickly from an image of opening to one of closure: Albertine is confined so irrevocably in the narrator's imagination, and the door closed so firmly behind her, that he suggests that he could search for years and years without finding the key to release her.

In 'Journées de lecture' equally, the consideration of the salutary effects of reading is transformed rapidly into a more cautious reckoning, where Proust specifies: 'Il devient dangereux au contraire quand, au lieu de nous éveiller à la vie personnelle de l'esprit, la lecture tend à se substituer à elle'.[97] And it is to this very danger, I am arguing, that Proust's narrator falls victim in his love of Albertine. Firstly, he substitutes fantasies for his possible knowledge of Albertine, and allows these fantasies to dictate and exacerbate his desire. Secondly, he allows these fantasies of Albertine to be formed and staged in the space of Montjouvain, the location of lesbianism now indestructibly present in his imagination. Indeed this placing of Albertine on the stage of Montjouvain is reiterated in various formulations in the last chapter of *Sodome et Gomorrhe* and Proust stresses particularly how this jealous vision supersedes the narrator's sensory impressions and obliterates his view of 'reality'. As the narrator reveals, in plaintive tones: 'mais derrière la plage de Balbec, la mer, le lever du soleil, que maman me montrait, je voyais, avec des mouvements de désespoir qui ne lui échappaient pas, la chambre de Montjouvain où Albertine, rose, pelotonnée comme une grosse chatte, le nez mutin, avait pris la place de l'amie de Mlle Vinteuil'.[98]

This passage is particularly rich in terms of its play of substitution. Where the narrator's mother is the prime female focus of the passage at its opening, just as the bedtime drama has been seen as the primary focus of *Combray*, the maternal and marine landscape the mother reveals is entirely screened by the vision of the enclosed space of Montjouvain. A new stage opens out for

[97] 'Journées de lecture', 180: *Against Sainte-Beuve*, 213 ('It becomes dangerous on the other hand, when, instead of awakening us to the personal life of the mind, reading tends to take its place').

[98] Proust, *A la recherche*, iii. 513–14: *In Search of Lost Time*, iv. 614 ('But beyond the beach at Balbec, the sea, the sunrise, which Mamma was pointing out to me, I saw, with a gesture of despair which did not escape her notice, the room at Montjouvain where Albertine, curled up like a great cat, with her mischievous pink nose, had taken the place of Mlle Vinteuil's friend').

the performance of the narrator's sexual identity, a stage where Albertine enacts the role of Mlle Vinteuil's friend, and in her feminine and feline eroticism entirely supplants the narrator's mother as object of desire.

The narrator may be seen as the obsessed victim of his fictive passions, ever restaging an elusive fantasy and witnessing this supplant and screen his affective relations. If he succumbs thus to the dangers of reading, is this the fate also of the external reader?

• La Prisonnière

The fourth chapter of *Sodome et Gomorrhe*, in its brief, brusque movement from the desire to leave to the need to marry Albertine, has its own polished internal structure. Proust's text dwells in ever extending concentric circles on the impact of Albertine's revelation of her knowledge of Mlle Vinteuil. Proust's reader has entered a space of repetition and recurrence where s/he is forever unsure of what is real and what imagined. And it is of course important that no easy solutions to this uncertainty should be found. In this sense Proust gives his reader few privileges over the narrator: our view is no more panoramic than his own, and although we may wish to come to some reckoning with the 'truth' or otherwise of the experiences imagined, we are necessarily in no position to do so. Thus the challenge to interpretation posed by Albertine is the delight and torment of the reader as much as the narrator. Through the figure of Albertine the narrator may come to reread his childhood and his tortured desires, while the reader is him/herself drawn to reflect on the very construction of sexuality through interpretative process.

La Prisonnière opens with the realization of the narrator's desire to hold Albertine captive in Paris. The space where they live is structured as one at once of separation and of intimacy. The narrator's confinement of Albertine also, importantly, would seem to exclude his own possession of her. Indeed while he is confident in the security of his prison-house he loses interest in her (in a further repeating pattern). He notes: 'Sa séparation d'avec ses amies réussissait à épargner à mon cœur de nouvelles souffrances'.[99] Yet without suffering the narrator's desire dies, as he specifies: 'Mais enfin ce calme que me procurait mon amie était apaisement de la souffrance plutôt que joie'.[100] He admits to no longer finding Albertine attractive, and, plainly, to being bored. Instability is evidently necessary to the construction of the narrator's sexual identity. As he reveals lucidly: 'Je n'aimais plus Albertine, car il ne me restait plus rien de la souffrance, guérie, maintenant, que j'avais eue dans le tram, à Balbec, en apprenant quelle avait été l'adolescence d'Albertine, avec des visites peut-être à Montjouvain'.[101] The narrator is allowed, briefly, the expression of the belief: 'Tout cela, j'y avais trop longtemps pensé, c'était guéri'.[102] Yet the Proustian reader will inevitably look forward to the next exacerbation of passion and the discovery that infidelity cannot be locked in time and space.

The narrator's attempt to dissipate his anxiety and his jealous passion has taken the form of separation and flight. These measures have in a sense achieved their aim, as the narrator states: 'J'avais pu séparer Albertine de ses complices et par là exorciser mes hallucinations'.[103] Yet in the depths of his new-found lack of interest in Albertine, he comes to the realization that 'si on pouvait lui faire oublier les personnes, rendre brefs ses attachements, son goût du plaisir était, lui aussi, chronique et n'attendait peut-être qu'une occasion pour se donner cours',[104] and he proceeds to the shattering revelation, 'or, Paris en fournit autant que Balbec'.[105]

[99]   *A la recherche*, iii. 522: *In Search of Lost Time*, v. 4 ('her separation from her girlfriends had succeeded in sparing my heart any fresh anguish').

[100]   *A la recherche*, iii. 522: *In Search of Lost Time*, v. 4 ('but this calm which my mistress procured for me was an assuagement of suffering rather than a joy').

[101]   *A la recherche*, iii. 530: *In Search of Lost Time*, v. 14 ('I no longer loved Albertine, for I no longer felt anything of the pain I had felt in the train at Balbec on learning how Albertine had spent her adolescence, with visits perhaps to Montjouvain').

[102]   *A la recherche*, iii. 530: *In Search of Lost Time*, v. 14 ('I had thought about all this for long enough, and it was now healed').

[103]   *A la recherche*, iii. 532: *In Search of Lost Time*, v. 16 ('I had managed to separate Albertine from her accomplices, and, by so doing, to exorcise my hallucinations').

[104]   *A la recherche*, iii. 532: *In Search of Lost Time*, v. 16 ('if it was possible to make her forget people, to cut short her attachments, her taste for sensual pleasure was chronic too, and was perhaps only waiting for an opportunity to be given its head').

[105]   *A la recherche*, iii. 532: *In Search of Lost Time*, v. 16 ('now Paris provided just as many opportunities as Balbec').

The locating of Gomorrah has proved to be an impossibility, the mapping of the imagination on to a specific place to be radically unstable and liable to an unceasing series of displacements. The narrator writes: 'En réalité, en quittant Balbec, j'avais cru quitter Gomorrhe, en arracher Albertine; hélas! Gomorrhe était dispersée aux quatre coins du monde'.[106] The narrator's jealous itineraries begin again in his imagination. He appears at this point in the text to resign himself indeed to a state of perpetual unknowing, anxiety, and desire: it is of course he who is the true prisoner of his passion for Albertine. His questions are open-ended; in his expectation of knowledge of Albertine and her pleasures he appears resigned to failure. He suggests in a moment of revelatory synthesis: 'Et, moitié par ma jalousie, moitié par ignorance de ces joies (cas qui est fort rare), j'avais réglé à mon insu cette partie de cache-cache où Albertine m'échapperait toujours'.[107]

- *Reading Proust*

It is this game of hide-and-seek in which the text also strategically engages its reader. This can be understood in quite literal terms if we draw again on the revelations made by Alison Winton in her *Proust's Additions*. Winton notes: 'Proust also evidently wished, in his expansion of *A la recherche*, to amplify characteristics or situations marked by ambiguity and uncertainty, ranging from mistaken identity to proliferation of rumour, or from Albertine's lies to manifestations of bisexuality.'[108] Winton stresses that Proust adds discoveries which both absolve and condemn Albertine on the charge of lesbianism and she suggests that 'the principal intention is to generate more uncertainty around her actions, and to show the effect this has on Marcel'.[109] Winton's text appears clear in its evidence that

---

[106] *A la recherche*, iii. 533: *In Search of Lost Time*, v. 17 ('in leaving Balbec, I had imagined that I was leaving Gomorrah, plucking Albertine from it; in reality, alas, Gomorrah was disseminated all over the world').

[107] *A la recherche*, iii. 533: *In Search of Lost Time*, v. 17 ('and partly out of jealousy, partly out of ignorance of such joys (a case which is extremely rare), I had arranged unawares this game of hide and seek in which Albertine would always elude me').

[108] Winton, *Proust's Additions*, 254.

[109] Ibid. 272–3.

even the 'last additions about Albertine's lesbianism perhaps provide no firmer ground for conclusions than did the incidents already in the MS, often amounting to a chain of nervous deductions based merely on Albertine's stares'.[110]

As recent criticism has shown, in its emphasis on the indeterminacies of both the narrator's and Albertine's desires, *A la recherche du temps perdu* may be seen to create a representation of sexuality which endorses the gender trouble effected by recent queer theory. I have attempted here to emphasize the instability of identity categories as they are performed in this text, but the implications this has for the reading encounter need to be thought through further. This instability has its own emphatically unsettling effect on the reader. I would argue that in the accumulation of uncertain evidence Proust tests the effect his text has on the reader, as well as showing the effect of uncertainty on the narrator. The reader also is engaged in this alluring yet fruitless quest; his/her passions are aroused in the discovery of knowledge about Albertine; s/he is encouraged to question his/her hermeneutic desires with the rigour and with the lack of resolution of the pained narrator. And it is here that the text persuades us to perceive the patterns of reflection between the desiring process within the text and the reading process of the text.

While the reader may find his/her reading practice reflected in distressingly seductive terms within the text, *A la recherche du temps perdu* works effectively to deny any fixed patterns of identification in which the reader might recognize, or by which s/he might determine, his/her sexuality. The text might be seen to uphold the position of the male desiring subject, yet the narrator's control over his gaze, or indeed his object of desire, is revealed to be disarmingly precarious. Security of mirroring identity is not ensured for the reader who identifies as male, either straight or gay. Heterosexual desiring relations may apparently be mimicked in the relations between Marcel and Albertine, but these depend on her lesbianism, which is the necessary and impossible pre-condition for her status as object of desire. Heterosexual desire is undercut by the necessity for exclusion.

[110] Winton, *Proust's Additions*, 283.

The reader who identifies as male and gay may be tantalized by the phantom presence of an elusive Agostinelli, and by the very ambiguities of the independent and androgynous Albertine. Yet secure identification is once more undermined by virtue of the sexual differences upon which desire between the narrator and Albertine necessarily depends. The reader who identifies as lesbian may find Albertine an alluring object of desire, yet is doubtless troubled by the transgender position identification with the narrator requires, not only because this may itself be unsettling, but because this also implies subscribing to an economy which presents lesbianism as erotic fantasy for heterosexual men. But the position of the female reader who identifies as heterosexual is perhaps the most unsettling of all. And each of these desiring positions is only relative and contingent, depending not only on the performance of the reader's identity, but also on the ever uncertain assumption that Albertine does indeed entertain lesbian desires.

The security of the desiring position of the reader is alarmingly undermined in the represented passions circling around the elusive centre Albertine creates. The relationship between the narrator and Albertine exists between homosexual and heterosexual, between memory and desire, between inside and out. Proust's achievement here is in the very destabilizing of desiring reading positions. It is thus that his text makes its challenge to the regulatory matrix of heterosexuality, exploding as it does any normative function it might hold.

Further, in retaining supposedly 'straight' desiring relations as the centre of his focus, yet showing these relations to be dependent on an obsession with lesbian passion, Proust posits a continuum between homosexual and heterosexual relations, and a resurgent similarity and instability in libidinal power structures. In this sense, through the narrator's love of Albertine, Proust explores an impossible passion and imaginary desire which is dependent on the interplay of similarity and difference. By concentrating on an impossible and supposedly heterosexual desiring relation he takes apart the notion of a dichotomy between the allowed and the illicit in heterosexual and homosexual desire. Proust's obsession is with passions of the imagination, of confinement and constriction which cut across any of the common axes used to define desiring relations.

Attempts to define Albertine as male (in drag) or the narrator as (clandestine) lesbian work in some ways to obliterate the desired yet torturous distance and space between them. However closely the narrator guards Albertine within the confines of his Parisian apartment, she inevitably escapes his grasp, and thus, contrarily, arouses his desire. Her allure is manifestly dependent on her lack of definition. In this sense the narrator seeks and needs a love-object who will necessarily exclude him from an engaged desiring position.

A la recherche du temps perdu works to undo perceived notions of sexuality. The text enacts paradoxical and polyvalent desires in such a way as to necessitate a re-evaluation of representations of desire, and, further, a rethinking of the desiring relations inherent in the act of reading. Mobility, trans-gendering, and cross-identification are necessary for a reader who attempts to engage with the multiple possibilities of Albertine's identity, and who will, in the quest for knowledge of the text, perform the drama of desire for Albertine. What I want to suggest is that it is through our patterns of desiring engagement with the text, through our enactment of the text and our involvement in its mirroring projections of our acts of decoding, rather than through the search for a single 'truth' or an occluded subtext, that we may come to a rereading of Albertine's sexuality. It is in this sense that Proust may come to create his own queer reader whose desiring position is forever destabilized, whose identity is unsettled as a result of his/her identification with a troubled fiction.

The text presents us with a character (Albertine) whose patterns of desire, as far as we may know them, are the imagined product of her lover's fantasies about her. Proust reveals how far desire is the product of a process of reading where the narrator fits his 'reality' into the contours of his imagination. For the narrator, indeed, the imaginary supersedes reality to such an extent that it displaces and even radically effaces any distinction between what is true and what is false. As I have argued, the narrator can be seen to succumb to the dangers of reading described in 'Journées de lecture'. What I would suggest too is that this is the (pleasurable?) fate of the reader for whom reading is formative when it supersedes and takes the place of 'la vie personnelle de l'esprit'. Like Charlus reading Musset, we are in some senses free to fit the relations between the narrator and Albertine into our own structures of desire; this critics have done as they derive differing yet definite readings from the text. Yet the text ceaselessly denies the desperate narrator and his doubling reader any security, or hope in the search for proof. The text necessarily engages us in this search for knowledge, which is defined as much by its vanity as by its allure. It is this encounter which is at once familiar and formative, and it is thus that Proust undermines the regulatory matrix of heterosexuality.

A la recherche du temps perdu is a text of inescapable substitutions. Albertine displaces and replaces the narrator's mother as elusive object of desire, the scopic pleasures of Montjouvain screen and occlude the reading encounter of the bedtime drama. Proust may remind his reader that engagement with a fiction becomes dangerous when this heightened encounter displaces 'reality', yet he reveals in the ricocheting drama of decoding that the text may be seen to become that the narrator is in some senses the complicit victim of his reading encounter with 'reality' where he attempts to construct his identity in the compulsory performance of a text. The narrator's identity depends on a series of imperfect re-enactments which at once recall and occlude the previous roles he has performed. The text may testify to the dangers of reading, but, following Butler, we might say that these are dangers by and with which we are forced to live.

A la recherche du temps perdu offers its reader no seductive illusion of cohesive identity. Rather, taking the reading process as its obsessional subject, it mimics and re-presents the hazardous and tenuous progress of its desiring interpreter. Proust reveals how far identity is unstable, non-self-identical, and dependent on a series of fragile self-images created through identification. His text draws attention thus to the contagious effects of fictions which offer a contour to reality. Yet by virtue of the uncertainties of *A la recherche du temps perdu*, of an unwillingness to replicate or prescribe any singular or certain regulatory matrix, Proust undermines any normative function which might be assigned to his fiction.

Imagining Albertine is a compulsive activity, yet I hope here not to have enclosed her within further confines, but to have gone some way towards elucidating the mechanisms which work both within the text and without to avoid the definition of her elusive sexuality. For both the narrator and the reader she is the product of the reading encounter as her form is imagined, yet not contained, in the illumined space behind a half-open window.

4

'La Passion selon H.C.': Reading in the Feminine

Gloire du long désir, Idées
Tout en moi s'exaltait de voir
La famille des iridées
Surgir à ce nouveau devoir.[1]

(Stéphane Mallarmé, 'Prose pour des Esseintes')

C'est que l'écriture ne s'adresse pas d'abord au lecteur extérieur, elle commence par moi. J'écris; je m'écris, elle s'écrit.[2]

(Hélène Cixous and Mireille Calle-Gruber,
Hélène Cixous, photos de racines)

• Reading the Self

In her seminar series 'A la recherche de l'auteur inconnu' given at the Collège international de philosophie in Paris between 1989 and 1990, Hélène Cixous spoke once, for some minutes, of her love of exotic flowers. This strategy of reading the self as text, and reading through the self, is a not uncommon feature of her writing practice. Cixous tends her own life with intimate care, offering to her readers fragments of her dreams, her passions, moments of being, and measured recollections. Her work incessantly draws into question the identity of the writer and of the reader, and, further, the relations between the two. In one of

---

[1] 'Ideas, glory of long | Longing, my all leapt to see | The tribe of the iris throng | To fulfil this fresh duty.' (trans. Keith Bosley.)
[2] 'Writing doesn't address itself firstly to the exterior reader, it starts with me. I write; I write myself, it writes itself.'

her infinite analyses of Clarice Lispector, Cixous pauses over a sentence in the novel *Agua viva* where Lispector appears to address her reader, saying: 'Look at me and love me. No: look at yourself and love yourself.'[3] In her unravelling of Lispector's meaning, Cixous suggests: 'In fact, in the act of writing, the truth, let us say, of the first sentence is in the second: "Look at yourself and love yourself". That is to say, you think you read me, but what you do is look at yourself and love yourself.'[4] Her account of the act of reading comes close to that of Proust we have examined in *Le Temps retrouvé*. In the chapter that follows I will look in detail at Cixous's reinscription and metamorphosis of the act of reading, and at her creation of a practice of reading in the feminine and at how this may be formative for the reader. Cixous's work appears to pre-empt and desire a performative reading; her texts reverberate with the drama of their own reception. Indeed Cixous creates an enclosed world of mirrors, and specular desires, where the reader's activity is in fact closely directed by the text s/he encounters. What I will seek here are the necessary blind spots in this seductive play of reflections, and in this search I am guided by the Lacanian concept of the 'pas tout', which Jacqueline Rose sums up as 'the idea that there is no [system of representation], however elaborated or elevated it may be, in which there is not some point of impossibility, its other face which it endlessly seeks to refuse—which could be called the vanishing-point of its attempt to construct itself as a system'.[5] The vanishing-point in Cixous's system of representation may be located, as I will argue, in her desire to control the Other, her reader, and her desire to construct herself as Other, as Clarice, through the looking-glass. In this sense I want to challenge the notion that *lecture féminine* offers an enfranchised alternative to the contest of mastery we have seen to be implicit in accounts of the reading encounter.

---

[3] Hélène Cixous, *Reading with Clarice Lispector* (London, 1990), 24. This collection of transcriptions of Cixous's seminars is edited, translated, and introduced by Verena Andermatt Conley. No equivalent volume exists in French and for this reason quotations here are in English.

[4] Ibid.

[5] Jacqueline Rose, *Sexuality in the Field of Vision* (London, 1986), 219.

• *Inside*

As a point of departure in this study of Cixous I will make a reading of one of her earliest novels, *Dedans*, a text which in its concern with relations between interior and exterior, between self and Other, and writer and reader, may be framed as an ideal entrance into the space of Cixous's writing.

In *Dedans*, Cixous begins in the interior, yet this is a text which incessantly troubles borders between inside and outside: it is a text of initiation, transformation, and rereading, which opens in paradox as Cixous writes: 'Le soleil se couchait à notre commencement et se lève à notre fin.'[6] *Dedans* is a novel about the death of the father, about the realization of his absence and the attempt to deny it. As such it will be seen to meditate on the charged relations between loss, mourning, and identification.

Verena Andermatt Conley writes that in *Dedans*, 'présent et passé se confondent dans une remémoration onirique'.[7] She claims that, unlike Proust, who recovers the past through writing, Cixous deliberately brings together the present moment and eternity. In the opening passages of *Dedans*, which combine opening and closure, beginning and end, Cixous speaks of both birth and death. She sets out the relations between love, death, and life which will be rewoven throughout the text. She writes: 'On dit que l'amour est aussi fort que la mort. Mais la mort est aussi forte que l'amour et je suis dedans. Et la vie est plus forte que la mort, et je suis dedans.'[8] Her style is familiarly repetitive and incantatory; she begins in imaginative language to create a complex structure of metaphors which enclose her text in its own mesmeric realm. Emblematic of her lavishly poetic discourse and of her desire to fuse the spatial and the textual is the revelation that 'dans mon jardin d'enfer les mots sont mes fous'.[9]

[6] Hélène Cixous, *Dedans* (Paris, 1986; first pub. Paris, 1969), 7 ('The sun was setting at our beginning and rises at our end').

[7] Verena Andermatt Conley, 'Délivrance', in Françoise van Rossum-Guyon and Myriam Diaz-Diocaretz (eds.), *Hélène Cixous: Chemins d'une écriture* (Amsterdam, 1990), 35–44: 36 ('present and past mingle in a dreamlike act of recollection').

[8] Cixous, *Dedans*, 7 ('They say that love is as strong as death. But death is as strong as love and I am inside. And life is stronger than death, and I am inside').

[9] Ibid. ('in my garden of Hell words are my madmen').

Her garden of hell is an inverted paradise garden, the garden of the writer's mind, or of her own text, where words, estranged, seem to dwell like madmen. Cixous signals early on in her text how far language and the transformation of language are essential to the thematics of her work.

Perpetuating her imagery of the inferno she writes: 'Je suis assise sur un trône de feu et j'écoute ma langue.'[10] *Dedans* is a quest for language, within language. Cixous writes at one point in the text: 'j'ai peu de mots'.[11] She encourages us to hear her narrator's fear, as well as her deprivation. She continues, 'mon père qui les avait tous, est parti si précipitamment, qu'il n'a pas eu le temps de me les donner'.[12] Language is, of course, the possession of the father. It is stolen, reappropriated, and, to use one of Cixous's most recurrent metaphors, reborn in the text of the daughter, in her coming to writing.

- *Lecture féminine*

Much has been written by Cixous and others about women's stealing of language and their flight into language. The body of *écriture féminine* has been variously celebrated, challenged, and dissected by readers and critics alike. It is my intention here to suggest that essential to our understanding of Cixous's work as a whole is, not so much a reckoning with the elusive specificities of *writing* in the feminine, but rather a recognition of the crucial and even coercive centrality of a thematics and a practice of reading. In her sibylline image of the writing subject seated on a throne of fire, Cixous emphasizes not the act of giving voice, but the act of listening. I will argue here that Cixous's work as a whole forms a study of receptivity which is in itself paradoxically directive. Cixous's texts seek thus to exercise their own formative power.

The possibilities of *lecture féminine* have already been examined in some detail by Cixous's critics. The last section of *The Body and the Text: Hélène Cixous, Reading and Teaching*, a

---

[10] Cixous, *Dedans*, 7 ('I am sitting on a throne of fire and I am listening to my tongue'). [11] Ibid. 52 ('I have few words').
[12] Ibid. 52 ('my father who had them all has left so quickly that he has not had time to give them to me').

volume which presents the collected proceedings of the colloquium on *Études féminines* held at Liverpool in 1989, contains very positive accounts of the influence Cixous has had and possibly will continue to have on feminist pedagogy. The approaches to reading and textuality which are revealed to derive from Cixous are themselves close to the concerns of the present study in so far as they are seen to lay stress on 'the collaborative role of the reader'.[13] However, as I shall go on to discuss, it seems that there are in fact some serious problems with a reading practice which, in some senses, and paradoxically, we might whole-heartedly endorse.

In 'Teaching after Cixous' the editors comment on the discovery, in Cixous's seminar, of 'a non-judgemental, non-competitive approach to texts in which the reader opens herself to what may have motivated the writer to produce a particular text as well as to the sorts of life-experiences with which the text deals'.[14] This implies necessarily both a receptivity and an expansive generosity towards the text. As Verena Andermatt Conley suggests: 'à un monde de domination, [Cixous] substitue celui de l'amour, et d'un échange non restreint'.[15] In these terms Cixous would appear both to create and to call for an economy of giving and exchange. The type of reading practice this implies is defined by Judith Still as 'reading in a motherly, creative fashion'.[16] In her essay 'A Feminine Economy: Some Preliminary Thoughts' Still is herself cautious in her suggestions and conscious, it seems, of the dangers of an entirely enthusiastic embracing of a practice of reading dependent on openness and creativity. She ends her essay, however, with the comment: 'a search for feminines in texts can be a celebration of what we find as well as an analysis of the interplay of all the various differences'.[17] It is, in effect, the possible failure to bring into play the

[13] Helen Wilcox, Keith McWatters, Ann Thompson, and Linda R. Williams (eds.), *The Body and the Text: Hélène Cixous, Reading and Teaching* (London, 1990), 187.

[14] Ibid.

[15] Verena Andermatt Conley, 'Féminin et écologie', in Mireille Calle (ed.), *Du féminin* (Grenoble, 1992), 53–64: 58 ('[Cixous] substitutes a world of love , of non-restricted exchange, for a world of domination').

[16] Judith Still, 'A Feminine Economy: Some Preliminary Thoughts', in Wilcox *et al.* (eds.), *The Body and the Text*, 49–60: 57.

[17] Ibid. 58.

differences produced in the reading encounter which I will caution against in the following sections of this chapter.

Mireille Calle suggests that one of the most unnecessary and
useless questions in (Cixous) criticism relates to the issue of
distance from the text. Thus she eschews the necessity of an-
swering the question she formulates in the following terms: 'à
quelle distance en parler, en écrire?'[18] Yet I would suggest that
one might be too hasty in rejecting this question and that it
might be reformulated to enquire what distance Cixous allows
her reader from her texts.

Susan Sellers has written an instructive paper entitled 'Learning to Read the Feminine' where she details the discovery of Cixous's work and reading practice within her own
autobiography as reader. This confessional practice is fairly
common amongst Cixous's critics and only endorses the intimacy between Cixous and her readers: just as she foregrounds
the way she writes through the self, reading the self and
making the self her fiction, so her critics are peculiarly willing to
emulate this process of self-creation, constructing themselves
precisely as readers of Cixous. Lynn Kettler Penrod, for example, not only relates her first textual encounter with Cixous at
a moment when, significantly, she was in a period of personal
distress, she also elaborates the importance of her reading
of Cixous to her work and her practice of teaching, saying: 'je
tiens à encourager un engagement émotionnel . . . on essaie
de faire une lecture ouverte, sans interprétation formaliste'.[19]
There is in criticism an emphasis on the fact that Cixous's
work has been and is still seen as transformative. Nicole Ward
Jouve goes so far as to comment: ' "It changed my life, it so
moved me", I have heard people say of "The Laugh of the
Medusa".'[20]

Susan Sellers suggests that she found in Cixous's seminar

---

[18] Mireille Calle, 'L'Écrire-penser d'Hélène Cixous', in Calle (ed.), Du féminin,
97–111: 98 ('at what distance should one speak about it, write about it?').

[19] Lynn Kettler Penrod, 'Hélène Cixous: Lectures initiatiques, lectures centrifuges', in Calle (ed.), Du féminin, 83–95: 94 ('I am anxious to encourage an
emotional engagement . . . we try to make an open reading, without a formalist
interpretation').

[20] Nicole Ward Jouve, 'To Fly/to Steal: No More? Translating French Feminisms
into English', in White Woman Speaks with Forked Tongue: Criticism as Autobiography (London, 1991), 46–58: 49.

a place where texts were read not to demolish another's theory in order to replace it with one's own, nor to appropriate the text by listing all its flower or blood metaphors—nor even to explore all the various ways in which men and women are represented—but which focused on the text itself, on the author's motivations for writing and our own role in reading, on the processes by which meaning is created and the life-experiences with which the text deals.[21]

Sellers appears to find a space where, in collective terms, what I have called the reading encounter comes to take place. Cixous has created around herself a conceptual space and a tightly woven seminar group whose responses and papers reflect and enhance Cixous's own reading practice.

Sellers suggests that the best way to describe a ' "feminine" reading is to say that it implies "opening" the self to what it is the text is saying, even if this is puzzling or painful or problematic'.[22] She specifies further: 'it means acknowledging that I as reader participate in the ongoing process of the text's creation';[23] and, finally, she adds: 'it means recognizing that my reading is itself a product of certain questions, blind-spots, needs and desires, and that these motivations are constantly changing'.[24]

In writing about gender, for example, Sellers stresses the evident importance of Cixous's work on the fluctuating nature of gender, and that this work 'on the way we all take up different "gender" positions, of mastery or openness, when confronted by different attitudes or situations, offers a useful context in which to explore the various ways we as readers collude with, merge with, resist or appropriate the "gender" positions proposed by a text'.[25] Now these are the very issues which head my agenda in this study, yet I am not as confident as Susan Sellers appears to be that the writing and reading practice of Cixous can so effectively solve the problems which dwell in this domain. And I would suggest that one major problem that Cixous's reader faces is the disconcerting fact that her texts appear precisely to *resist* resistant readings. It is telling that criticism frequently centres on the issue of resisting or differing from Cixous herself rather than on the resistant reading of her

[21] Susan Sellers, 'Learning to Read the Feminine', in Wilcox *et al.* (eds.), *The Body and the Text*, 190–5: 191.
[22] Ibid. 192.   [23] Ibid.   [24] Ibid.   [25] Ibid. 193.

texts. In this sense, when Gayatri Spivak makes a fairly critical reading of Cixous in her paper 'Cixous sans frontières', read, admittedly, in the presence of Cixous, she prefaces it with the statement: 'je sais que Cixous est assez généreuse pour me laisser être voleuse de son écrit (ure)'.[26] In this chapter I am not so much questioning Cixous's apparently exemplary generosity to her less adoring critics as seeking to elucidate the ways in which Cixous's texts, consciously or otherwise, prefigure and direct our reading of them. My argument rests on the contention that her texts and practice of reading necessarily attempt to engage the reader in a seductively specular encounter. And I will suggest that it is to this end that Cixous makes use of her imagery of lesbian eroticism (which will be discussed further below).

In her own contribution to the colloquium at Liverpool, Cixous proposes: 'there is no writing without reading. Writing is actually a kind of alliance between writer and reader. The reader within myself and the reader outside'.[27] What I want to suggest here is that, using the most subtle and delicate tactics, Cixous contrives to create the reader outside as a mirror image of the reader within.

• *Collage*

Dedans is a text which prefigures and brings into existence many of the intertwined concerns of Cixous's later texts on reading and writing. As Morag Shiach suggests, 'intertextual collage of allusion, theory and autobiographical exploration'[28] is an important element in Cixous's primarily fictional works which 'transform, reshape, and re-invent the narratives, myths and philosophical discourse that shape our identities'.[29] Cixous herself can be seen, in this way, to be intent on transforming the reader him/herself, and on creating a narrative which in its

---

[26] Gayatri Spivak, 'Cixous sans frontières', in Calle (ed.), *Du féminin*, 65–81: 67 ('I know Cixous is generous enough to let me be a thief of her writing').

[27] Hélène Cixous, 'Difficult Joys', in Wilcox *et al.* (eds.), *The Body and the Text*, 5–30: 26.

[28] Morag Shiach, *Hélène Cixous: A Politics of Writing* (London, 1991), 69.

[29] Ibid.

innermost recesses, and in constantly reiterated forms, reflects the activity of the reader it desires.

In her description of the texture and layers of Cixous's writing Shiach's use of the metaphor of a 'collage' appears to foreground the associations between Cixous and other experimental modernist writers who privilege fragmentation and dislocation of the textual surface. This strategy Verena Andermatt Conley sees as directed specifically towards the reader. She suggests: 'From a generalised belief that narrative represses and establishes a continuity of passivity, a circuit—or complicity—between reader and writer, Cixous, like many writers and film makers of the period, strove to break down continuity that comes with the telling of a tale.'[30] She continues: 'The "author" frustrates the readers who, made uneasy, need to question themselves, their values, beliefs and reactions.'[31] What I want to question here is how this possibility of self-analysis relates to the identity of the reader and to the challenge to the regulatory matrix of heterosexuality Cixous may perhaps be seen to effect.

Dedans is itself a text in pieces. It is made up of two defined parts which are each formed by a series of fragments of differing lengths. While there is still some loose sense of narrative flow, Cixous also indulges in a mercurial versatility and mutability, allowing her text to function through a method dependent on juxtaposition and association. The first sentence or couple of sentences of each section is highlighted, in upper-case letters, allowing Cixous to create emphasized, fetishized statements which stand out from the text, differ from it, yet frame its parts, and form a thread running through the fabric of the narrative. (Here my use of imagery is indebted to Judith Still's recognition that '*écriture féminine* . . . should be a writing shot through (like shot silk) with otherness'.[32]) Cixous renders the reading process strange: her tactics are those of violence and re-creation; she seeks thus to seduce and illuminate her reader.

Yet I would choose here in some senses to argue against Andermatt Conley's notion of the frustration of the reader. While Cixous may attempt to undermine our notions of

---

[30] Verena Andermatt Conley, *Hélène Cixous* (London, 1992), 10.
[31] Ibid.
[32] Still, 'A Feminine Economy: Some Preliminary Thoughts', 57.

narrative, of linearity, and of the art of decoding, her texts work not so much to alienate and frustrate as to draw the reader within their confines, calling us to take up a privileged relation inside the text. And it is in this sense that the very title of the novel *Dedans* and its repeated reference to the spatial relations of interior and exterior themselves appear to refer insistently to the notions of the reading encounter Cixous develops in her later texts.

• *'Un Jardin de deuil'*

'MA MAISON EST ENCERCLÉE. ELLE EST ENTOURÉE PAR LE GRIL-LAGE. DEDANS, nous vivons.'[33] These words begin the first full chapter of *Dedans*. Cixous starts with a literal image of a house which not only encloses its own interior, but is itself surrounded and encircled. The house is posited as a location of enclosure and containment, yet also of protection. The character created to speak as the 'je' of the text dwells within these walls of security, yet she herself initiates the transition between interior and exterior, between inner and outer, upon which the novel as a whole depends. As she shows, this movement is entirely necessary: 'il faut bien que je sorte tous les jours. Je n'ai pas peur, j'ai l'habitude.'[34] This novel of the interior is defined paradoxically by its movement outwards, its creation and re-peated transgression of boundaries or limits.

As Morag Shiach argues 'spatial metaphor is a crucial element of [*Dedans*]'.[35] In her discussion of the novel she suggests a multiplicity of referents for this central metaphor. She argues, for example, that ' "Inside" represents an enclosure: in the past the house had been open, but her father had enclosed it. This is the "inside" from which the narrator needs to escape, a space which is entirely defined by the father.'[36] I would argue that the father's death has in the first place defined the interior as the space of the coffin and the place of the corpse. Equally, death is

---

[33] Cixous, *Dedans*, 11 ('My house is encircled. It is surrounded by the wire fencing. Inside, we live').

[34] Ibid. ('I have to leave everyday. I am not afraid, I am used to it').

[35] Shiach, *Hélène Cixous*, 72.

[36] Ibid. 73.

seen to be within the self; Cixous describes 'la mort autour et dedans nous'.[37] Death forms the interior of the narrator's identity, shadowing and shaping the text she creates. Within the text of *Dedans* Cixous restages and re-presents the death of the father.

This novel of the interior is contrarily one of exteriorization and, specifically, of expiation. The final lines of *Dedans* are indeed: 'mais dedans nous aurons cessé de mourir'.[38] In *Dedans* Cixous is writing within death, and with death within, yet also she writes emphatically against death. She rejects the fantasy of the daughter as Electra mourning a dead father as her narrator admits: 'et bien que je sois la princesse des avant-temps, et la fille d'un dieu mort, et la maîtresse des inscriptions tombales, des livres de pierre, des robes de mer, je ne suis pas contente'.[39] Cixous rejects the death within; *Dedans* is a text of harrowing, and one of transgression and discovery. And this is a discovery through the body, of the body.

Shiach suggests that 'the body offers no security of identity in this novel, with its images of bodily fragmentation and carnal destruction'.[40] Cixous certainly writes about the death of the father in graphically corporeal terms. Her narrator states emphatically at the head of one section: 'ET MON PERE POURRIT'.[41] The rotting and disintegration of the body is also disturbingly taken into the self, as the narrator suggests: 'dans ma peau j'étais déjà prête à pourrir, mon épiderme s'effritait, chaque sortie hors de la maison se soldait par la perte d'un morceau plus ou moins important'.[42] Yet this interiorization of the body of the father serves a more positive purpose in the text. The narrator writes within *Dedans* of 'la découverte de [s]on anatomie'.[43] This discovery of anatomy links and underlies the text's themes and its very texture.

This is highlighted in a scene in *Dedans* where the narrator

[37] Cixous, *Dedans*, 150 ('death around and inside us').

[38] Ibid. 209 ('but inside we will have stopped dying').

[39] Ibid. 208 ('and although I am the princess of antiquity, and the daughter of a dead god, and the mistress of funerary inscriptions, of books of stone, of sea robes, I am not content').

[40] Shiach, *Hélène Cixous*, 74.

[41] Cixous, *Dedans*, 26 ('And my father rots').

[42] Ibid. 53 ('in my skin I was already ready to rot, my epidermis was peeling away, every time I left the house I ended up losing a more or less significant part of myself').

[43] Ibid. 24 ('the discovery of [her] anatomy').

and her mother look together at a textbook where they see a body laid out in coloured diagrams. The placing of the anatomy book within the text serves to negotiate the exchange between corporeality and textuality which is an obsession for Cixous. The narrator describes the coloured page where she sees an image of a flayed athlete whose red and white muscles resemble tulip petals.[44] She associates this delineated, defined body with that of her father, admitting, for example, that she is anxious to get to the heart: 'pour voir comment battait le petit cœur de mon père'.[45] The image of the flayed body also, however, creates a mirror image of the self for the narrator: she perceives her own body as dislocated, as alien and dispossessed. The narrator reveals: 'mes doigts étaient hachés en phalanges, ma main, que je trouvais belle et vive, était découpée, articulée, lointaine'.[46] The narrator finds her body in pieces; she writes of its 'cinquante mille morceaux'.[47] Cixous appears to allude to Lacan's images of the *corps morcelé* in her own attempt to explore the breaking down of identity and the dislocation of the self.[48] She images the body in pieces as the self decomposing; the death of the father is internalized in the very disintegration of the self. The body of the daughter becomes the father's phantasmatic mirror image, as his death is inscribed in her flesh.

The association of the body entirely with carnal destruction and disintegration (in Shiach's terms) appears only a part of Cixous's project as a whole where the body is more commonly valorized and even idealized. As Sarah Cornell specifies: '[in Cixous] the body is linked to the unconscious. It is not separated from the soul. It is dreamed and spoken. It produces signs. When one speaks, or writes, or sings, one does so from the body. The body feels and expresses joy, anxiety, suffering and sexual

[44] Cixous, *Dedans*, 48.

[45] Ibid. ('so that I can see how my father's little heart used to beat').

[46] Ibid. 53 ('my fingers were cut to pieces, my hand which I used to think was fine and alive, was carved up, jointed, and far away').

[47] Ibid. ('fifty thousand pieces').

[48] See Jacques Lacan, 'Le Stade du miroir comme formateur de la fonction du Je', in *Écrits* (Paris, 1966), 93–100: 97: 'The Mirror Stage as Formative of the Function of the I', in *Écrits: A Selection*, 1–7: 4. For further discussion of the *corps morcelé*, see also 'L'Agressivité en psychanalyse', in *Écrits*, 101–24: 104: 'Aggressivity in Psychoanalysis', in *Écrits: A Selection*, 8–29: 11, and *Les Complexes familiaux dans la formation de l'individu* (Paris, 1984), 60.

desire.'[49] The body is seen as a locus of sensation and imagination. In *Dedans* it is also the site of rebirth and reintegration of the self. It is only after she has delved *within* the body of the father, uncovering his flesh and sinew, that the narrator can come to an absolved sense of herself and her own corporeal identity.

In a scene of healing, Cixous's narrator discovers a new and positive relation to her body. Cixous images this in terms of an exchange between self and Other. A hand reaches out to the surface of the shattered body and traces, caresses, its contours. Cixous creates a scene of tactile, hesitant eroticism: 'la main bleue hésite ou plutôt flotte, posée sur la surface mouvante de moi, ou plutôt glisse sur ma surface figée, jusqu'où?'[50] The scene is such that distinctions between self and Other are all but broken down; the hand slides: 'glisse main les longs doigts bleus fins jusqu'où je suis puis ne suis plus'.[51] The Other reintegrates the radically fractured relation between self and body image. The narrator admits that there has been progress: 'je suis extensible, et sans doute préhensible, je distingue grand et petit, noir et bleu, forme et moi. S'il y avait de la lumière je me verrais peut-être.'[52] The specular image is gradually restored, the mutilated body healed, and the self reborn. This restoration of a relation to the body allows Cixous to pursue the text's differing thematics of the interior and its positive affects.

- ### 'Toucher du dedans'

In her essay 'Délivrance', Verena Andermatt Conley argues: '"dedans" se réfère à la fois à une angoisse, à un enfermement et à un paradis, là où le plaisir du vécu serait aussi proche que possible du mot écrit'.[53] She makes the point that Cixous's

[49] Sarah Cornell, 'Hélène Cixous and *les Études Féminines*', in Wilcox *et al.* (eds.), *The Body and the Text*, 31–40: 39.

[50] Cixous, *Dedans*, 98 ('the blue hand wavers or rather floats, placed on my moving surface, or rather slides over my fixed surface, where?').

[51] Ibid. ('hand slides long fine blue fingers to where I am then am no longer').

[52] Ibid. 99 ('I am extendable, and no doubt prehensile, I can make out large and small, black and blue, form and me. If there was light I would perhaps see myself').

[53] Conley, 'Délivrance', 36 ('"inside" refers at once to an anxiety, to an enclosure, and to a paradise where the pleasure of lived experience would be as close as possible to the written word').

interior 'jardin de deuil' is also, necessarily, and conversely, an enclosed paradise garden and, particularly, a realm of reading and writing. Conley pursues her reading of the paradise garden in Cixous's writing in her essay 'Féminin et écologie'. She suggests that Cixous's work is guided by the search to re-create a lost paradise. She states specifically: 'au monde postmoderne qu'Hélène Cixous condamne, elle oppose un paradis (linguistique) qu' "elle" porte en soi'.[54] The emphasis on the existence of this paradise *within* the self is of particular relevance to *Dedans*; as Conley states succinctly: 'le paradis est perdu, mais il est encore en "je"'.[55]

The realm of paradise within is more or less defined in Cixous's work as the domain of dream, of language, and of writing. In this sense, in its title, *Dedans* may be seen to refer to the space of the imagination; Cixous writes: 'il y la tête avec ce qu'il y a dedans',[56] and her narrator suggests: 'ma vie avait l'immensité de l'imaginable'.[57] The imagination is revealed to have the power to expand and extend the interior, to deny its enclosure, and to create spatial freedom. This notion of extensibility appears deliberately linked with the image of the extendable body which feels and transcends its own limits. Where previous readers of Cixous have largely emphasized the fragmented, alienating quality of her text, my aim is to shed light on the smooth, compelling aspects of the text which seemingly work their seduction over the reader, revealing how this seduction is dependent on a sensuous and positive relation to the body, its surface, and its interiority.

The association of the interior with the imagination is significant to this argument, further, since, in Cixous's writing, it is in the *interior* that the reading encounter takes place. This reading within, and inside, is a practice defined by Cixous herself as a practice of *lecture féminine*. She takes up the notion of 'dedans' in an essay on Clarice Lispector entitled 'L'Auteur en vérité'. Here she elaborates some of the ideas which have inspired in

[54] Conley, 'Féminin et écologie', ('to the post-modern world she condemns, Hélène Cixous sets in contrast a (linguistic) paradise which "she" carries within herself').

[55] Ibid. 63 ('paradise is lost, but it is still in "I"').

[56] Cixous, *Dedans*, 21 ('there is the head with what there is inside').

[57] Ibid. 20 ('my life was as large as all that can be imagined').

various readers the charge of biological essentialism.[58] Yet in her writing on the (female) body Cixous maintains a peculiar and elusive relation between the metaphorical and the real, never quite allowing her statements to depend entirely on anatomy, yet never quite severing her argument from questions of corporeal sexual difference.

In 'L'Auteur en vérité' Cixous creates a tale of the paradise garden, of good and evil, of Adam and Eve. In her retelling Cixous shows Eve tempted by the apple and specifically by its secret interior and its hidden flesh of knowledge: 'la pomme est visible, est promesse, est appel'.[59] Cixous continues: 'ce que Eve va découvrir, dans son rapport à la réalité concrète, c'est l'intérieur de la pomme, et cet intérieur est bon'.[60] Eve's capacity to appreciate the interior is seen to be dependent, in the spirals of Cixous's logic, on her own capacious body. Cixous states simply: 'Eve n'a pas peur de l'intérieur, ni du sien, ni de l'autre. Le rapport à l'intérieur, à la pénétration, au toucher du dedans est positif.'[61] Cixous's statements here are then expanded as she continues to elaborate her contentious, yet in some senses compelling, argument; she suggests: 'Car virtuellement ou réellement mères, toutes les femmes ont quand même une expérience de l'intérieur, une expérience de la capacité d'autre, une expérience de l'altération non négative par de l'autre, de la bonne réceptivité. N'est-ce pas vrai?'[62] The more tentative, interrogative note added to the end of this statement is, I would argue, in itself revealing. I do not intend here to debate the truth or otherwise of Cixous's literal association of identity and anatomy. Her writings on pregnancy, engendering, and creativity are extensive and recurrent; in a recent lecture given at the University of California, for example, she pursues her line,

---

[58] See e.g. the critique of Cixous made by Toril Moi in 'Hélène Cixous: An Imaginary Utopia', *Sexual/Textual Politics* (London, 1985), 102–26.

[59] Hélène Cixous, 'L'Auteur en vérité', in *L'Heure de Clarice Lispector* (Paris, 1989), 121–68: 138 ('the apple is visible, is a promise, an appeal').

[60] Ibid. ('what Eve will find in her relation to material reality is the apple's interior, and this interior is good').

[61] Ibid. 139 ('Eve is not afraid of the interior, neither her own, nor the other's. Her relation to the interior, to penetration, to touching inside, is positive').

[62] Ibid. 142 ('For, potentially or really mothers, all women have even so an experience of the interior, an experience of the capacity to hold the other, an experience of non-negative transformation by the other, of good receptivity. Isn't this true?').

saying: 'a woman who writes is a woman who dreams about children. Our dream children are innumerable.'[63] The problems surrounding the possible materiality of the maternal metaphor in Cixous's work have been answered in part by Spivak's gloss on Cixous's use of 'la paléonymie de "mère" '.[64] Spivak instructs us, writing: 'notez que les essentialismes dèterminatifs n'ont pas de pertinence ici. Il importe peu que je n'aie pas d'enfant, pas d' "expérience" à "donner la mère à l'autre femme". C'est un sens général du maternel.'[65] What I intend to do instead is to reveal how far the belief in the positive relation to interiority defines, yet entirely undermines, Cixous's (textual accounts of) reading practice.

When 'L'Auteur en vérité' was published in 1989 in the volume *L'Heure de Clarice Lispector*, it was preceded by the text *Vivre l'orange*, which Cixous had published in 1979. This grouping of the two texts appears to draw together some of Cixous's disparate meditations on Lispector, but also to corroborate Cixous's theories of reading practice. Indeed in writing about reading Lispector, Cixous may in fact be (c)overtly giving her readers and students a lesson in reading her own texts. The problem that this causes the reader arises from the realization that Cixous herself can be seen to be more and more manifestly present within her texts, choreographing the performance of reading her texts demand.

- *'Clarice, son pas d'ange dans ma chambre'*

Vivre l'orange is, more explicitly perhaps than any of the other texts I am treating here, the tale of a reading encounter. Annette Kuhn remarks that Cixous's earlier essays constitute a 'yearning toward, rather than a grasping of, an alternative practice'.[66] She continues: 'her more recent writings seem to pose something of

---

[63] Hélène Cixous, *Three Steps on the Ladder of Writing* (New York, 1993), 74. These lectures have, so far, only been published in English.

[64] Spivak, 'Cixous sans frontières', 73 ('the paleonymy of "mother" ').

[65] Ibid. ('note that determinist essentialism has no relevance here. It matters little that I don't have a child, that I have no "experience" of "being a mother to the other woman". This is a general sense of the maternal').

[66] Annette Kuhn, 'Introduction to Hélène Cixous's "Castration or Decapitation?" ', *Signs*, 7/1 (1981), 36–40: 38.

a break in this respect'[67] and as a specific example she cites *Vivre l'orange*. In this text Cixous writes in language that is lavishly sensual, calling up a series of surreal images, echoes, and associations. She reveals the arrival of Clarice in her life as a form of apparition or annunciation: 'une voix de femme est venue à moi de très loin . . . cette voix m'était inconnue, elle m'est parvenue le douze octobre 1978, cette voix ne me cherchait pas, elle écrivait à personne, à toutes, à l'écriture, dans une langue étrangère, je ne la parle pas, mais mon cœur la comprend, et ses paroles silencieuses dans toutes les veines de ma vie se sont traduites en sang fou, en sang-joie'.[68] Her imagery of flesh and blood immediately draws attention to the carnal nature of this encounter. In the eroticizing of a reading encounter between female writer and female reader, Cixous offers the spectre of a lesbian desiring relation. She looks towards a complete interpenetration of the thematics of sexuality and textuality. Her text enacts a reading encounter in terms of sexual desire, and of the intimate mingling of self and Other. But what are we to make of the impossible specularity and circularity of the libidinal economy Cixous creates?

Cixous shows the encounter with Clarice to take place at night. She writes: 'cette nuit l'écriture est venue à moi'.[69] She creates a scene of complete intimacy and complete privacy where Clarice is imaged as an angel: 'mon ange a lutté avec moi; mon ange de pauvreté m'a appelée, sa voix Clarice'.[70] Cixous begins a series of aural images which will run through the passage, where receptivity is linked with the ability to *hear* language. The ear indeed becomes a fetishized sensory organ; Cixous writes: 'j'écoutais mes oreilles s'ouvrir, se dilater, se tendre'.[71] Equally, Cixous calls on her own reader to hear her

---

[67] Ibid.

[68] Hélène Cixous, *Vivre l'orange*, repr. in *L'Heure de Clarice Lispector*, 7–113: 11: 10. This is a bilingual edition. ('A woman's voice came to me from far away . . . this voice was unknown to me, it reached me on the twelfth of October 1978, this voice was not searching for me, it was writing to no one, to all women, to writing, in a foreign tongue, I do not speak it, but my heart understands it, and its silent words in all the veins of my life have translated themselves into mad blood, into joy-blood').

[69] Ibid. 43: 42 ('This night the writing came to me').

[70] Ibid. ('My angel struggled with me; my angel of poverty called me, its voice Clarice').

[71] Ibid. 45: 44 ('I listened to my ears opening, dilating, straining').

text, which resonates with echoes between words, with puns, and with alliteration which suggests the very amorphous, meta-morphosing quality of Cixous's language where the sounds of one word are quickly subsumed into those of another.

Cixous writes of the reading encounter: 'j'ai lutté, elle m'a lue, dans le feu de son écriture, je l'ai laissée me lire, elle s'est lue en moi'.[72] She makes play between activity and passivity, between choosing and reading. Commenting on her own play of signifiers, she points out in her lecture 'The School of Dreams': 'when we read: "je l'élus" . . . in French we also hear something else, i.e., "I read it"—"je l'ai lu". This is typical dream writing.'[73] In the dream writing of *Vivre l'orange* the encounter between Cixous and Clarice is seen as a struggle, a battle. (We might recall that Cixous's most explicit work of lesbian desire is itself entitled *La Bataille d'Arcachon*.) The use of battle imagery is in keeping with the sensations of pain and pleasure which run throughout *Vivre l'orange*. For Cixous this reading encounter with Lispector is one of *ravissement* in both senses of the word. In a coda to *Vivre l'orange* which begins, 'lire femme? Écoutez: Clarice Lispector'[74] Cixous describes Lipector as powerful and predatory: 'Clarice arrive premièrement comme ceci; en nous sautant dessus, au-devant de nous, flêche, vit vole, panthère et se pose'.[75]

Cixous appears to desire to deconstruct the distinction between pain and pleasure as she writes: 'Peur? Peut-être: une peur exaltante, comme une joie. Peur dans la Joie. Une peur sans crainte. Seulement le tremblement de la Joie.'[76] Fear and joy are seen entirely to inhabit each other; fear is to be found *within* joy. And this itself is corroborated in Cixous's writing elsewhere on both her desire in reading and on the intensities of love between women. In her lecture 'The School of the Dead', she quotes Kafka writing: 'but we need the books that affect us like a disaster, that grieve us deeply, like the death of someone we

[72] Hélène Cixous, 43: 42 ('I struggled, she read me, in the fire of her writing, I let her read me, she read herself into me').

[73] Cixous, *Three Steps on the Ladder of Writing*, 81.

[74] Cixous, *Vivre l'orange*, 113 ('to read a woman? Listen: Clarice Lispector').

[75] Ibid. 113 ('Clarice arrives firstly like this; in leaping upon us, in front of us, aims, lives, flies, as a panther and comes to rest').

[76] Ibid. 61: 60 ('Fear? Perhaps: an exalting fear, like a joy. Fear in the Joy. A fear without fright, only the trembling of the Joy').

loved more than ourselves'.[77] This search for an absolute of pain
and pleasure, for a violent relationship in both textual and
sexual terms, is enacted also in *La Bataille d'Arcachon*. The
desire described between the unnamed H and her lover
Promethea is at once desperate and devastating, and also dependent on the possibilities of entering the Other and of feeling
within. As Cixous writes: 'H a caché son visage entre les seins de
Promethea, elle a voulu entrer dans Promethea pour cesser de la
voir. Elle a été terrifiée.'[78]

Cixous seeks and describes experiences which privilege relations between inside and out, between internalization and movement within. In the quoted letter from Kafka, a fragment
incorporated into the text, grief is felt inside and mourning is
internalized; likewise we have seen the narrator in *Dedans* take
the body of the father into herself. In *La Bataille d'Arcachon* H
responds to grief by desiring to withdraw within the body of
Promethea; as in *Dedans* the body inside forms both sarcopha-
gus and refuge. I would suggest that the reading encounter with
Clarice is poised between incorporation and the erotic entering
of the body. Imaging (the words of) the author entering the body
of the reader, Cixous writes: 'elle s'est lue à moi, jusqu'à moi, à
travers mon absence jusqu'à la présence. Elle est entrée, elle s'est
posée devant moi.'[79] In this erotic entrance, the Other is seen to
bring the self into existence, to create identity in desire.

Vivre l'orange is thus apparently, as I have been demonstrating, a text of discovery, of the birth of the Other within the self.
Yet I would suggest that behind this narrative of revelation lies
a more puzzling and resistant subtext. In one passage Cixous
describes the time before her writing, and before the arrival of
Clarice, when she was herself 'à l'intérieur de l'écriture'.[80] She
says specifically: 'j'étais en je alors. Et ainsi Clarice-je en son
je.'[81] And she continues: 'demeurer était la joie la plus naturelle

---

[77] Cixous, *Three Steps on the Ladder of Writing*, 17. The inset quotation from
Kafka comes from his *Letters to Friends, Family, and Editors* (New York, 1978), 16.

[78] Hélène Cixous, *La Bataille d'Arcachon* (Laval, 1986), 65 ('H has hidden her
face between Promethea's breasts, she has wanted to enter Promethea to stop seeing
her. She has been terrified').

[79] Cixous, *Vivre l'orange*, 49: 48 ('she read herself to me, through my absence up
to the presence. She came in, she alighted in front of me').

[80] Ibid. 47: 46 ('inside of writing').

[81] Ibid. ('I was in I then. Angeling and thus Clarice-I in her I').

quand je vivais encore à l'intérieur, tout était jardin et je n'avais pas perdu l'entrée'.[82] Mireille Calle makes a compelling reading of the primordiality of the 'en-je' of Cixous's writing and she argues: 'l'écriture d'Hélène Cixous passe nécessairement par la mise en *je*: le pronom'.[83] She suggests that, 'l'en-je est lieu d'intuitions, de rôles, de représentations'.[84] One element of the 'mise en je' which does not draw comment from Calle, however, is a further evident play of words motivating Cixous's choice and abundant use of the expression. In her description of herself 'en je' Cixous echoes the appelation 'ange' she has chosen for Clarice. I would see this as more than an indulgence in aural similarities. This play of words may be seen to suggest a reflexive equivalence between the self within ('en je') and the exterior Other ('ange'). *Vivre l'orange* signals how in the dream writing of her text, and in her dreams ('en son je'), Cixous takes on the specular identity of Clarice, constructing the writer she reads as her own doubling Other.

We might note also that at this point in the text Cixous alludes to a world of the interior, to the garden to which she has not yet lost the key (and the reader is likely here to hear the echoes of *Alice in Wonderland*). This interior world, with its paradise garden is, I would argue, that created and enclosed already, ten years earlier in the novel *Dedans*. What *Vivre l'orange* alludes to only obliquely, and in passing, is the fact that 'Clarice en son je' is in fact present within Cixous's writing in a manner and in a text which entirely pre-dates Cixous's first reading of Lispector in 1978.

• *Flower Poetics*

In her coda to *Vivre l'orange* Cixous expands on the echoes she hears in the name Clarice Lispector, allowing the syllables to stand alone and take on their disparate multiple meanings. She ends with an invocation: 'O Clarice tu es toi-même les voix de la

---

[82] Cixous, *Vivre l'orange*, 49: 48 ('Abiding was the most natural joy when I was still living inside, all was garden and I had not lost the way in').

[83] Calle, 'L'Écrire-penser d'Hélène Cixous', 105 ('Hélène Cixous's writing comes through the bringing into play of the "I": the pronoun').

[84] Ibid. 106 ('In the I is the place of intuitions, of roles, of representations').

lumière, l'iris, le regard, l'éclair, l'éclaris orange autour de notre fenêtre.'[85] Amongst these associations I want to pause over the iris, the last in a series of flower images which interweave throughout *Vivre l'orange*. Cixous has been recognized as an author who makes a highly personal use of sensory motifs; her choice of citrus fruit, and the ubiquitous orange in particular, has been studied variously, and most notably by Nicole Ward Jouve in her essay 'Oranges et sources: Colette et Hélène Cixous'.[86] Ward Jouve also offers her own version of citrus writing in an autobiographical homage to Cixous entitled '*Ananas*/Pineapple'.[87] However, Cixous's flower poetics have tended to be left to one side with critics perhaps more cautious about suggestions of floral and florid sensuality in Cixous's work. Yet flowers abound and their use is frequently, with metonymic precision, to designate feminine eroticism and female desire. In her essay 'Structures du silence/du délire: Marguerite Duras/Hélène Cixous', Christiane Makward cites a passage from the novel *LA* as an example of Cixous's use of a 'poétique "style saphique"': 'et sur ses hanches de Liban une ceinture d'anémones. Son ventre écharpé de safrans. Mon petit jour, mon grand jour. Mon ultra rouge . . . Que boirons-nous? A genoux dans ta garance de temps à autre goutte à goutte une gorgée de ta mer mêlée de miel.'[88] In this analysis of 'style cixolien' Makward leaves in silence the image of oral eroticism and the suggestive flowers with which it is encircled.

In *Vivre l'orange*, Cixous writes:

Toucher le cœur des roses: c'est la manière-femme de travailler: toucher le cœur vivant des choses, être touchée, aller vivre dans le tout près, se rendre par de tendres attentives lenteurs jusqu'à la région du toucher, lentement se laisser porter, par la force d'attraction d'une

[85] Cixous, *Vivre l'orange*, 113 ('Oh Clarice you are yourself the voice of light, the iris, the gaze, the lightning, the orange Claricelight, around our window').

[86] Nicole Ward Jouve, 'Oranges et sources: Colette et Hélène Cixous', in Françoise van Rossum-Guyon and Myriam Diaz-Diocaretz (eds.), in *Hélène Cixous: Chemins d'une écriture* (Amsterdam, 1990), 55–73.

[87] Nicole Ward Jouve, '*Ananas*/Pineapple', in *White Woman Speaks with Forked Tongue*, 37–45.

[88] Christiane Makward, 'Structures du silence/du délire: Marguerite Duras/Hélène Cixous', *Poétique*, 35 (Sept. 1978), 314–24: 321 ('and a belt of anemones around her hips of Lebanon. Her belly sashed in saffron. My little daylight, my great day. My ultra red . . . What shall we drink? On my knees in your rose madder once in a while drop by drop a mouthful of your honeyed sea').

rose, attirée jusqu'au sein de la région des roses, rester longtemps dans l'espace du parfum, apprendre à se laisser donner par les choses ce qu'elles sont au plus vivant d'elles-mêmes.[89]

In her rather lush writing Cixous creates a multilayered metaphor for her own advocated practice of reading. In both her seminars and her written texts she exhorts her readers to proceed with patience, with intimacy and desire. She elaborates on this in her seminars on Lispector, calling for an 'approach . . . always on the side of touching, tasting'[90] and she even works to draw associations between flowers and Clarice's texts saying: 'each flower can give pleasure separately. Each paragraph can also please.'[91]

In *Vivre l'orange* the rose is the gift of Clarice Lispector. *Vivre l'orange* works indeed to create Clarice as the flower which opens in Cixous's life, opening up for her a tender and cultivating textual practice. Yet this notion of a new flowering in Cixous's writing and reading is in itself illusory as a simple glance at the chronology of her texts will reveal. In 1979, in *Vivre l'orange*, Cixous writes: 'j'ai envie de rayonner Clarice, l'art-clarice à mes amies, j'ai besoin de l'exhaler, son parfum, l'iris'.[92] This iris is to be found already, implanted as an emblem of textual practice in *Dedans*.

• *White Iris*

Dedans is a novel embellished with images of flowers, decorating the necropolis of the father. Cixous transposes her images of petals and flesh where, formerly, muscles in the anatomy book have been seen striped like tulips and, latterly, flowers are described in the following visceral terms: 'couleur sang de cadavre,

---

[89] Cixous, *Vivre l'orange*, 107: 106 ('Touching the hearts of roses is the womanly-way of working: touching the living hearts of things, being touched, going to live in the nigh, making one's way with tender, attentive slowness to the region of touching, slowly letting oneself be borne, by the force of attraction of a rose, attracted unto the bosom of the region of roses, staying long in the space of the perfume, learning to let oneself be gifted by things, giving what they are at their most alive').

[90] Cixous, *Reading with Clarice Lispector*, 31.

[91] Ibid. 27.

[92] Cixous, *Vivre l'orange*, 63: 62 ('I feel like radiating Clarice, the Clarice-art to my amies, I need to exhale it , her perfume, the iris').

violacés, cicatrisés sont les pieds de coq, fleurs, lèvres coriaces et plates'.[93] Cixous's narrator observes: 'il ne faut pas que les fleurs des morts meurent trop vite'.[94] The flowers of the dead become a fetish against death, their petals recalling and commemorating the flesh of the lost body, their flowering and life both representing and denying loss and disintegration. The white iris within *Dedans* is a flower which is used to denote precisely the loss of death and the end of the corpse's tyranny over his daughter's body. Although relatively little attention is drawn to its importance in the text of *Dedans* itself, it should be recognized that the narrator's discovery of 'un iris blanc, seule fleur née d'un février, haut perchée hors de portée de [s]a main qui brûle de l'arracher'[95] opens out in the text a scenario which is readily comparable with Cixous's later descriptions of a feminine practice of reading and crucial to our understanding of them.

In *Dedans* the narrator is irresistibly drawn to the iris; she confesses that the iris has become indispensable to her.[96] Her passion for the flower is caught between obsession and desire; she admits to getting up before dawn to see the iris in the first light of day and she says that she watches it with violence.[97] She appears intent on knowing the iris in its every detail: 'mes yeux le dévoraient, le caressaient, le photographiaient, le radiographiaient, l'inventoriaient. J'aurais voulu compter chaque poil sur son corps et le nommer pour l'adorer.'[98] Cixous describes here precisely the strategies of her own reading practice, as developed later, apparently in homage to her discovery of Clarice Lispector.

In this sense, the metaphoric activities which Cixous alludes to in order to describe her narrator's observation of the flower are themselves appropriately evocative of the tactics Cixous calls on her reader to use. She writes of caressing the flower,

[93] Cixous, *Dedans*, 88 ('the colour of blood from a corpse, deep purple, the cockspur are scarred, flowers with thick and flat lips').

[94] Ibid. ('the flowers of the dead must not die too quickly').

[95] Ibid. 151 ('a white iris, the only flower born one February, perched high out of the reach of [her] hand which burns to pick it').

[96] Ibid. 152.

[97] Ibid.

[98] Ibid. ('my eyes devoured it, caressed it, photographed it, took its X-ray, took its inventory. I would have wanted to count every hair on its body and name it to adore it').

which recalls for the reader the tactile eroticism privileged repeatedly in her writing on reading and receptivity as we have seen above. Yet we are reminded here that Cixous's practice is not one merely of passive appreciation, but, in more active terms, one of predatory appropriation. Her narrator will take a photograph or an X-ray of her iris, she will make an inventory of its attributes, absorbing it and describing it in her own textual system. These highlighted practices of appreciation and appropriation have their own reflexive relevance to the text *Dedans* itself.

Notable here are the references to the visual senses. Throughout Cixous's work there is a concern with portraits, or rather with the impossibility of making a portrait of the Other, or indeed of the self as Other.[99] In *Dedans* where the narrator attempts to photograph the iris (in her mind's eye) the act is already undermined by the text's meditations on the impossible invisibility of images.

The narrator describes a photograph she has of her father's mother saying that this photo of his mother in 1935 is dearer to her than anything in a museum.[100] The face is revealed as 'ce visage invisible',[101] only the smile is visible yet this image has effaced, for the narrator, the passion that she had for painting: 'mes Rembrandt, mes Greco, mes Ingres ont disparu dans ce sourire'.[102] Cixous's text works to replace these pictures with images from an interior museum. Indeed *Dedans* becomes a hallucinatory museum of the narrator's interior. Embedded in the text is description of a gallery as if seen in a dream: 'tous les tableaux flottent, leurs couleurs diluées déversent dans le blanc des formes mortes'.[103] In this museum of dreams the narrator stops, as one might expect her to do, before a still life, saying: 'dans le musée il n'y a de joie que dans la coupe de fruits'.[104] The naming of the genre of painting draws comment; the narrator

[99] See Calle, 'L'Écrire-penser d'Hélène Cixous', 110 for a reading of Cixous which makes reference to the visual arts.

[100] Cixous, *Dedans*, 155.

[101] Ibid. ('this invisible face').

[102] Ibid. 156 ('my Rembrandt's, my El Greco's, my Ingres's have disappeared in this smile').

[103] Ibid. 47 ('all the paintings float, their diluted colours spill out dead forms into the blankness').

[104] Ibid. ('in the museum there is only joy in the bowl of fruit').

reveals: 'ma mère dit que c'est une nature morte puis elle le dit en anglais, pour m'apprendre un mot. C'est une still life.'[105] Cixous's text is placed between these two appelations; her subject is both the *nature morte* and the stilled life surrounding and surpassing the death of the father. While the death of the father is her subject, Cixous's means of evoking and describing this death is by detailing the still life led by the daughter as she mourns, inhabited by the death of her father.

In her concern with images in *Dedans*, Cixous reflects the thematics of her novel and, also, the action of her text which displaces the signifiers and icons of European culture with images drawn from an interior and personal past which are themselves displaced and dispossessed. Cixous frames her subject-matter from within, setting up a mirror to the practice of writing in which she engages.

This might be illustrated equally with reference to the further images of taking an X-ray or making an inventory. The image of the X-ray recalls the obsession within the text with the search beneath the skin, within the body. *Dedans* is rich in images of flaying and in a penetrating vision within. This relates not only to the possible sado-masochistic element of Cixous's writing, where, as we have seen, pain and pleasure are not polarized but intimately interdependent. It also testifies to Cixous's commitment to a vision of the writer as a scientist of the imagination, charting, codifying, defining its vicissitudes and invisible images. This practice is reflected in part in the activities in which the narrator of *Dedans* engages. She describes her attempts, even as a child, at impossible enumeration, in an image of herself and her father: 'nous sommes heureux, nous ne faisons rien la nuit, sauf moi qui compte tous les astres que je peux voir'.[106] In her image of an inventory Cixous appears to signal how her text bears witness to its own impossible aims, how it enacts the impossibility of making an inventory of the stars, of the iris, or of the death of the father. *Dedans* both attempts and refutes the task of making death decorative. The text acts as ceremony, celebrating the funeral of the father and decorating it in images

---

[105] Ibid. ('my mother told me that it is a *nature morte* then she says it in English to teach me a word. It's a still life').

[106] Ibid. 75 ('we are happy, we do nothing at night, except that I count all the stars that I can see').

of funerary inscriptions and a necropolis, yet it reveals also the impossibility of definitively burying death.

The relation between death, incorporation, and identity is also integral to the element of the narrator's appreciation of the iris which remains to be discussed: that of devouring. The desire to devour figures first in Cixous's list and its importance to Cixous's work as a whole is striking. In the image of devouring Cixous would appear to refer implicitly to the desire to take the Other into the self. It has been seen how this desire is constructed in her writings on reading as one of positive receptivity, yet I would hazard the suggestion that this receptivity masks the desire to possess and appropriate wholly and completely.

The arrival of Clarice Lispector in Cixous's texts is constructed as an epiphany, an entrance of the Other into the self. What this insistence on the entrance of the Other hides is the fact that Cixous emphatically seeks in the Other an affirming reflection of what is already present within her text. In this sense the Clarice Cixous reads and allows to enter her texts serves to reflect rather than deflect Cixous's own textual practice, leading to an intense specularity. A remaining question which needs to be examined here relates precisely to the effect this reflexive practice has on the constructed identity of both the writer and the reader.

• *Reading and Melancholia*

As the reader might wholly expect, the death of the father is not satisfactorily contained in *Dedans*. His phantoms haunt Cixous's later texts also; notably in the recent *Jours de l'an* Cixous writes: 'l'auteur est la fille des pères-morts'.[107] *Jours de l'an* is in some senses a return to the internal territory of *Dedans*. Cixous justifies this return to an earlier text and to a primary scene in her own (imagined) childhood in a comment she makes on Thomas Bernhard where she states: 'l'enfance nous y arrivons à la fin'.[108] *Jours de l'an* is a further attempt to reach into childhood, to record the day and date of its traumatic death. In this later text Cixous attempts not only to delve further

---

[107] Hélène Cixous, *Jours de l'an* (Paris, 1990), 154 ('the author is the daughter of the dead fathers').

[108] Ibid. 85 ('we reach childhood in the end').

within the death of the father, but also to examine the creation of the self as 'l'héroïne de l'apocalypse'.[109] She resurrects the language of interiority and blindness, writing, 'je suis dedans, je ne vois rien';[110] and draws further, pained attention to the splitting in the self at the moment of loss: 'le douze février 1948, c'est à cette date que j'ai été mise en douze, le monde a sauté comme un seul soldat sur une mine, il a été déchiqueté'.[111]

One of the elements in *Jours de l'an* to which we might draw particular attention is this association of the splitting of the self in grief with the multiplying of identity in writing. Cixous's concern, repeatedly, in *Jours de l'an*, is with the creation of identities who will perform her experiences in her writing. There is, tellingly, a splitting in the narrating subject whose identity appears to be changing and contingent. One of the central questions which is rehearsed in the text is, precisely, 'en quoi suis-je moi?'[112] Cixous stresses progression and dispossession in writing as her narrating persona explains: 'la personne que nous avons été, est maintenant un "j'étais", le personnage de notre passé. Elle nous suit, mais à distance. Et parfois elle peut même devenir le personnage d'un de nos livres.'[113] *Jours de l'an* signals explicitly Cixous's recognition of the self's alterity and artificiality. What I want to suggest is that this is linked crucially to the thematics of death explored in both *Dedans* and *Jours de l'an*. Where *Jours de l'an* marks a new departure in Cixous's writing is the way in which the text openly heralds the dramatic entrance of death.

This forms the major epiphany of *Jours de l'an*. The second section of the novel is entitled 'Le Personnage principal de ce livre c'est . . .',[114] and Cixous leaves the statement unfinished until the last page of the section when she writes: 'Mais oui, c'est la mort.'[115] Death is described as 'cette présence en moi qui ne voulait pas et qui m'empêchait, et qui était assise sur mon cœur

[109] Ibid. 66 ('the heroine of the apocalypse').

[110] Ibid. ('I am inside, I see nothing').

[111] Ibid. ('the twelfth of February 1948, it was on the date that I was split in twelve parts, the world was hit like a single soldier on a mine, it was blown to pieces').

[112] Ibid. 30 ('in what am I myself?').

[113] Ibid. 45 ('the person we have been is now an "I was", the figure from our past. She follows us, but at a distance. And sometimes she can even become the character of one of our books').

[114] Ibid. 35–49 ('The main character of this book is . . .').

[115] Ibid. 49 ('Yes, it's death').

comme un oiseau de pierre essayant de couver une pierre'.[116] It
is possible to perceive certain similarities between this image of
death and those of the very opening of *Dedans*, yet now death
is seen to be within the self where, formerly, the self was within
death. In taking death within the text in *Jours de l'an* and
attempting to revivify the thematics of death Cixous comes to
undo any stability of thought or definition. In *Jours de l'an* she
writes significantly: 'la mort n'est pas ce que nous pensons'.[117]
This line she repeats at the opening of the next section of the
text, and here she continues:

Penser n'est pas ce que nous pensons.
   Nos pensées sont des étrangères. Elles viennent à nous sous des
formes fantasques qui leur ressemblent. Nous ne les reconnaissons
pas.[118]

The misconception of death leads to a rethinking of thought
precipitating a prolonged meditation on hazard, chance, and
unknowability where Cixous comes completely to dispossess the
writing self. The text comes to a close, indeed, with lines which
render its very writing hypothetical and which serve to divorce
the text we have read from the one discussed and described by
its narrating persona who undoes her very ending with a vision
of a new beginning:

Si j'écrivais un livre, je commencerais par un jardin à l'aube, rose, au
pied d'une montagne. Je ferais absolument tout pour que le livre ne se
retourne pas contre moi,
   pour qu'il aille vers le sud, vers la rose, vers la mer, qui sont mes
vraies directions, si jamais c'était moi qui écrivais.[119]

   Pursuing a discussion of this relation between mourning and
the splitting or dispossession of the self, to illuminate Cixous's
practice of writing and the reading it prescribes, I want to turn
now to a text by Judith Butler where she explores, briefly, the

---

[116] Hélène Cixous, *Jours de l'an* (Paris, 1990), 154 ('this presence in myself which
was not willing and which held me back, and was sitting on my heart like a stone
bird trying to hatch a stone egg').
[117] Ibid. ('death is not what we think').
[118] Ibid. 53 ('Thinking is not what we think. Our thoughts are foreigners. They
come to us in fantastic forms which are in their likeness. We do not recognize them').
[119] Ibid. 276 ('if I were to write a book, I would begin with a garden at dawn,
rosy, at the foot of a mountain. I would do absolutely everything for the book not
to turn back against me, for it to go to the south, to the rose, to the sea, which are
my true directions, if ever it were me who was writing').

concept of psychic mimesis. In her article 'Imitation and Gender Insubordination' Butler studies a set of psychic identifications which she herself claims are not simple to describe. She discusses specifically Freud's thesis in 'Mourning and Melancholia', asking her reader to consider that 'identifications are always made in reponse to loss of some kind, and that they involve a certain *mimetic practice* that seeks to incorporate the lost love within the very "identity" of the one who remains'.[120] She goes on to show how other psychoanalytic theorists, notably Mikkel Borch-Jacobsen and Ruth Leys, have put forward a theory of primary mimetism that differs from Freud's account of melancholic incorporation. In this theory of primary mimetism, identification is seen to precede identity and constitute identity as that which is fundamentally 'other to itself'.[121] As Butler demonstrates, mimetism is not motivated by a drama of loss and wishful recovery, but appears to precede and constitute desire itself. Butler chooses not to make a definitive choice between loss and mimetism; she states instead: 'whether loss or mimetism is primary (perhaps an undecidable problem), the psychic subject is nevertheless constituted internally by differentially gendered Others and is, therefore, never, as a gender, self-identical'.[122] Butler goes on to state, however, that, in her view, the self only becomes a self on condition that it has suffered a separation, which she describes as, 'a loss which is suspended and provisionally resolved through a melancholic incorporation of some "Other"'.[123] She sums up her argument by suggesting: 'that "Other" installed in the self thus establishes the permanent incapacity of that "self" to achieve self-identity; it is as it were always already disrupted by that Other; the disruption of the Other at the heart of the self is the very condition of that self's possibility'.[124]

This theory of the incapacity of the self to achieve self-identity, of the Other always disrupting the self, of the lack of singular gender identity, relates centrally to the view propounded by Butler, and adopted in my own study, of gender as performative and of identity as multiple, variable, or fractured.

---

[120] Judith Butler, 'Imitation and Gender Insubordination', in Diana Fuss (ed.), *Inside/Out: Lesbian Theories, Gay Theories* (New York, 1991), 26.
[121] Ibid.   [122] Ibid. 27.   [123] Ibid.
[124] Ibid.

But I will also argue that it has a specific relevance to this discussion of Cixous.

It may be fairly evident that in *Dedans* Cixous enacts a Freudian scenario where her narrator reacts to the death of her father by identifying with the lost object (of desire). Such a reading may be encouraged by Cixous herself in her use of the vocabulary and imagery of incorporation and identification. Yet it is only, I would argue, as one comes to reread this earlier text through the filter offered by Cixous's later fictions that we may come to perceive how far this drama of mourning and melancholia holds far-reaching implications for the notion of identity and for the relation to the Other in Cixous's works. Far more than forming an autobiographical or expiatory narrative of the death of the father, *Dedans* makes use of that death in fiction as a primary loss which predetermines the creation of her future repertoire of personae.

I have been arguing throughout this chapter that Cixous's texts implicitly deny the agency and identity of the Other. I have tried to reveal how she selects Clarice Lispector as Other, and how this choice is motivated by the possible patterns of identification between Cixous and Lispector which *do not* entail the acceptance of the radically other within the self. Lispector is appropriated so smoothly, indeed, into Cixous's textual system that the reader is left with the uncanny sense that she was always already present in Cixous's writing. This unconfessed rejection of alterity I see to relate also to the attitude towards the reader, who, through Cixous's seeming generosity and emphasis on the sensuality and subjectivity of reading, would seem to be given the freedom of the text, but whose response is in fact guided by a radiating structure of textual reflections of reading practice, written directives from Cixous, and a whole network of studies of reception, pedagogy, and feminine practice.

Yet I think it should be recognized, in conclusion, that in practice Cixolien textuality is more tentative, and the construction of the writing self more fragile than I have been tending to suggest. There may be a concerted rejection of the Other, but this does not come in the face of a display of the untroubled identity and stable selfhood of the psychic subject. Cixous's texts resonate with statements bearing witness to the displacement and disintegration of the self and identity; I have concentrated in particular on *Jours de l'an* since it offers a rewriting of the obsessions of *Dedans*, and appears one of Cixous's finest texts to date, yet it should be recognized that the theme and enactment of self-dispossession recur widely in her works. In *Le Livre de Promethea*, for example, she writes: 'je s'abandonne. Je m'abandonne. Je se rend, se perd, ne se comprend pas.'[125] In her recent paper 'En Octobre 1991 . . .', Cixous registers a split between herself and her writing persona(e) as she says, 'il est apparu, à travers les différentes lectures qui ont été proposées de ce que j'ai pu écrire—de ce qui *Cixous*, comme on dit, a pu écrire—que je suis—enfin, *elle* est—occupée souvent, peut-être principalement, de la perte et de ses paradoxes'.[126] And following this brief enactment of the self's alterity, I want to comment further on this statement concerning loss.

In *Jours de l'an* Cixous writes: 'vivre c'est avancer vers l'inconnu jusqu'à se perdre'.[127] She writes of the necessity of running the risk of losing the self, and she makes of her text a living memorial and a transposition into language of this loss of self. She writes, indeed, 'à la fin je perdrai aussi le mot "perdre"? Et je le retrouverai changé en perles dans une autre langue.'[128] In 'Difficult Joys' Cixous cites Shakespeare's Ariel's Song as 'one of the most important pieces of poetry in [her] life of writing'.[129] The transition she inscribes in her texts from *perdre* to *perles* inevitably, I think, reflects her love of the lines:

> Full fathom five thy father lies,
>   Of his bones are coral made;
> Those are pearls that were his eyes;[130]

Cixous's text attempts to enact its own sea-change with what she describes as 'the transposition of dead parent into beautiful metaphor'.[131]

---

[125] Hélène Cixous, *Le Livre de Promethea* (Paris, 1983), 28 ('I abandons herself. I abandon myself. I gives herself up, loses herself, doesn't understand herself').

[126] Hélène Cixous, 'En Octobre 1991 . . .', in Calle (ed.), *Du féminin*, 116 ('It has become apparent, through the different readings which have been put forward of what I have been able to write—of what *Cixous*, as they say, has been able to write—that I am —well *she* is—often, perhaps principally, preoccupied by loss and its paradoxes').

[127] Cixous, *Jours de l'an*, 53 ('living is going towards the unknown until one loses oneself').

[128] Ibid. 244 ('in the end will I also lose the word "lose"? And I will find it again changed into pearls in another language').

[129] Cixous, 'Difficult Joys', 19.

[130] From Shakespeare, *The Tempest*, quoted by Cixous, 'Difficult Joys', 19.

[131] Cixous, 'Difficult Joys', 19.

Cixous favours change and transition, her texts perpetually responding to loss by means of re-creation and reappropriation. The loss of the father, which is staged as essential to the creation of her identities as writer, precipitates the incorporation of the Other into the self. Incorporation leads to the identification of the self with the Other in a response to and refusal of loss. Cixous's texts maintain this ambivalent relation to the Other within the self and depend on reflection and identification between self and Other. This rejection of alterity leads in textual terms to the favouring of an intense specularity where the reader reflects the writer's desire. Yet this seeming security and refusal of loss are tempered in Cixous's texts by a disintegration and dispersion of the self such that identity becomes disparate and even diverse. Stable identity becomes a lost object of desire in texts which perpetually foreground yet undo their subjectivity and their mediation through a perceiving 'je'. Her texts become, indeed, dramas of the loss of self.

The primary importance of Cixous's texts lies in their revelation of possibilities of creation through the self, and their meditations on the construction of identity. Cixous foregrounds the Freudian notion, which we find reiterated in Butler, that loss is constitutive of identity, and it is this which motivates her tales of the death of the father. Cixous appears to display more anxiety than Judith Butler, however, over the possibility of an identity dependent on the disruption wrought by the Other at the very heart of the self. Cixous shows the Other to be unassimilable in its very alterity, and increasingly in her works shows the self to be displaced, dispossessed, and perhaps even destroyed. Her fictions become an attempt to precipitate and crystallize these errant and fragmented selves. She writes in *Jours de l'an*: 'nous ne pouvons pas vivre sans nos images, nous avons besoin d'être peints ou décrits ou représentés'.[132] It may be significant that Cixous's most recent text, *Hélène Cixous, photos de racines*, reveals to the reader some of the images which make up Cixous's own family album. Cixous may fulfil this need to be represented, to be constructed as visual image and verbal fiction for herself in her texts, but again the representation alone does not suffice. The narrator of *Jours de l'an* admits: 'il

[132] Cixous, *Jours de l'an*, 113 ('we cannot live without our images, we need to be painted or described or represented').

ne nous suffit pas d'être nés pour être en possession de notre existence, nous voulons être regardés, nous voulons jouir de notre éclat'.[133]

This need to be seen leads us back finally to the role of the reader, who, as I have been arguing, is desired in Cixous's texts in order to view the self and to offer a mirroring yet illusory image of the self. And appropriately Cixous herself alludes to this pattern of reflection and reflexive readings as she finishes her paper at Liverpool with the words: 'Let's not forget the mysterious, grave, humorous cycle, where we readers are authors of the writers, we writers are both engendering and engendered . . . à suivre'.[134]

• 'Mère sans Tain'

I would argue that it is this desire for a seductive reflection of the female author which motivates the engagement with lesbian eroticism in Cixous's writings on reading and reception. Indeed this mirroring complicity is itself a determining aspect of the representation of desire between women in Cixous's fictions. In LA the encounter with the object of desire is one of terrifying, seductive specularity; Cixous writes: 'La porte s'ouvre! Alarme! Effroi! Nous nous trouvons face à face! Double dame, Miroir des Seins, mère sans Tain, face à face nous trouvons.'[135] The Other becomes an illusory mirror, a fleshed reflection. The Other is seen to give access to an image of the self, to imaginary integrity, security, and repose: 'je me sens rentrer chez moi, ma flamme entre dans ta glace, déjà comme tu me calmes! je me regarde avec tes yeux.'[136] The division between 'je' and 'tu' which allows the images here of alterity and penetration is seemingly elided, where entering the Other 'je' finds herself chez elle. The erotic act is played out on the stage where identity is

[133] Ibid. ('it is not enough for us to be born to possess our own existence, we want to be watched, we want to enjoy our full radiance').

[134] Cixous, 'Difficult Joys', 26.

[135] Hélène Cixous, LA (Paris, 1976), 103 ('The door opens! Alarm! Terror! we find each other face to face! Double woman, Mirror of breasts, double-mirroring mother, face to face we find ourselves').

[136] Ibid. ('I feel myself return to my origins, my flame enters your glass, already you soothe me! I watch myself with your eyes').

performed, the lesbian m/other desired for the seductive images she offers 'je' of herself.

Cixous offers her readers charged and lavish representations of lesbian desire, creating a new mythology and resource of images of love between women. But I would argue that it is not thus that her texts pose their challenge to the regulatory matrix of heterosexuality and the fiction of stable identity. Cixous's representations of lesbian desire, like the relations imagined between writer and reader in *Vivre l'orange*, depend on specularity as a guarantor of identity. In desiring and reading relations Cixous would appear to seek to avoid the alterity which is necessarily both disruptive of and constitutive of identity. The reader of her texts is, it seems, desired in so far as s/he will replicate and mimic the reading process designated implicitly within the text. In ideal terms, the reader will perform the role of the Other always already present within the text.

Yet the reader's performance of desire and engagement with the text can, of course, in no way be controlled. Cixous creates a space in her texts where the reader is sought as accomplice, where the drama of desire enacted is that of the author for a reader. But we have seen, in the model adopted from Proust in Chapter 2, that fictions are formative when they offer the occasion for the rereading and creating of the self as the reader enacts the text's performance of desire. Where Cixous's texts amply eschew their normative function with their refusal of the coercive representation of culturally intelligible gender positions and sexual identities, this necessarily entails also the radical undermining of any stable desiring position as we have found in Proust.

Cixous's texts appear to perpetuate a latent nostalgia for the illusory security of desiring relations between m/other and child, which we have seen occluded in *A la recherche du temps perdu*. It might even be feared that lesbianism is idealized as erotic replication of this early intimacy, and thus is seen to exist prior to and excluded from the cultural and social construction of identity. There may be an implicit tendency within some of Cixous's texts to erect an alternative matrix of (female) homosexuality which would appear to regulate the reading encounter and its possibilities of identification and desire. This may be the conclusion we are inclined to draw as a result of our engagement in the seductive recesses of her fictions. It should be added too that this illusion of mirroring identity, of security through the replication of a reading practice, may offer its own pleasures. These specular textual relations may, for the reader, at once commemorate and deny the loss of relations with the m/other.

Yet it should be recognized also that mirroring security of identity is always sought, yet never achieved. In *Le Livre de Promethea* desire between Promethea and H is dependent always on 'la nouvelle ignorance'[137] and on forgetting. The self seeks yet never achieves integrity, and it is ultimately this position of tenuous, shattering desire that is sought by Cixous in both the desiring relations represented in her fictions and the reading position she affords for her interpreter. Cixous's are texts of prolonged and tantalizing seduction. They subscribe to an economy of desire which validates the possibility of security of identity, yet they emphatically deny the achievement of untroubled reflection.

The self created and negotiated in Cixous's texts is increasingly dissociated and dispossessed, traumatized yet seduced by the impossibility of stable identity. I would argue that it is, paradoxically, in these disparate images of the desiring self that the reader finds fragments of his/her own reflection. It is in their (unwilling?) avowal of the impossibility of secure identity that Cixous's texts undo the fictions of unified, intelligible identity upon which the regulatory matrix of heterosexuality depends. It is then the failure to replicate the desiring relations framed by the text which can be seen to be formative for the reader. The subversive impact of Cixous's texts derives thus from the distance and difference between the reading encounter desired and that which will necessarily be imperfectly enacted.

---

[137] Cixous, *Le Livre de Promethea*, 138 ('the new unknowing').

5

'La Chair ouverte, blessée': Tournier, the Body, and the Reader

Our sentence does not sound severe. The condemned man has the commandment that he has transgressed inscribed on his body

(Franz Kafka, 'In the Penal Colony')

Bâtir sur du sable, n'est-ce pas cultiver l'attente de l'inattendu?[1]

(Algirdas-Julien Greimas, *De l'Imperfection*)

- Leçon d'anatomie

In the summer of 1990 a colloquium was held at Cerisy about Michel Tournier. The author himself was invited and attended the seven-day gathering. Despite his enthusiastic participation, in the recently published *Actes du colloque*[2] there is a postface by Tournier where he describes his original response to the idea of 'une semaine Tournier'.[3] He writes: 'Surpris par cet honneur exorbitant, j'avais réagi par un refus paniqué. Je me voyais déjà en cadavre nu et disséqué entouré de funèbres personnages chapeautés de noir, comme dans la *Leçon d'anatomie* de Rembrandt.'[4] While Tournier's comment is amusing, and perhaps understandable, I would argue that it may also be read as a more serious revelation of the writer's attitude to his readers.

[1] 'Building on sand, isn't this fostering the expectation of the unexpected?'
[2] Arlette Bouloumié and Maurice de Gandillac (eds.), *Images et signes de Michel Tournier* (Paris, 1991).
[3] Ibid. 391 ('A Tournier week').
[4] Ibid. ('Surprised by this excessive honour, I had reacted with a panic-stricken refusal. I could already see myself as a corpse, naked and dissected, surrounded by funereal personages in black hats, as in Rembrandt's *Anatomy Lesson*').

Indeed, despite Tournier's amply justified reputation as (intellectual) aggressor,[5] his fear of the reader is surprisingly foregrounded in a number of accounts of reading and reception, as we have seen in Chapter 1.[6] It is my aim here to address further this seeming anomaly, seeking thus to deconstruct the figure of the author on the dissecting-table. It is my contention, indeed, that analysis of the double binds of fear and resistance in the writer–reader relation may lead to an elucidation of the troubling aggression and mutilation in Tournier's fiction. Tournier's reader is led inevitably, I think, to question the impact of the carnal violence of his texts. In the chapter that follows I will argue that this commitment to bodily disintegration in Tournier's texts is intimately and inextricably linked both to the thematics of signification integral to these fictions, and to the dramas of identity formation they seek to enact.

Tournier has alluded to Rembrandt's *Leçon d'anatomie* previously in a short text entitled 'Éloge de la chair dolente'.[7] Here he takes dissection as his subject and places Rembrandt's painting in a tradition of anatomical drawing dating from the Renaissance. Indeed Tournier goes on to analyse what he sees as the very necrophilia of the Renaissance where 'tous les artistes vont se ruer dans les cimetières, sous les gibets, dans les chambres de

---

[5] See particularly Colin Davis's fine paper 'Les Interprétations', in Bouloumié and Gandillac (eds.), *Images et Signes de Michel Tournier*, 191–206. Here Davis examines the antagonistic duplicity of Tournier's attitude towards the interpretation of his texts; Davis writes: 'Le texte littéraire ne cesse d'exercer une contrainte interprétative sur ses lecteurs; et Tournier se permet d'être le médiateur d'une vérité textuelle apparemment inentamée par ses affirmations quant à la liberté du lecteur' (p. 194) ('The literary text always exerts an interpretative constraint over its readers; and Tournier allows himself to be the mediator of a textual truth apparently unaffected by his assertions of the reader's freedom').

[6] As Tournier writes in a text entitled 'La Solitude des grands hommes': 'Un écrivain connu pourrait dire à l'un de ses lecteurs anonymes: "Ayant lu tous mes livres, vous savez tout de moi. Et moi en échange, que sais-je de vous? Rien. Vous me cernez, vous me dominez, vous me possédez".... Quiconque a publié une œuvre littéraire—littéraire, c'est-à-dire où il se livre—s'est senti devenir ventre mou étalé sous les pieds de la foule' (*Des Clefs et des serrures* (Paris, 1979), 150) ('A well-known writer could say to one of his anonymous readers: "Having read all my books you know all about me. And what do I know in return about you? Nothing. You work me out, you dominate me, you possess me".... Whoever has published a literary work—literary meaning literally that he delivers himself in book form—has felt himself spread out, his soft underbelly trampled under the feet of the crowd').

[7] Ibid. 77–9.

torture'.[8] This interest in dissection has been pursued similarly in Tournier's récit *Gilles et Jeanne*. The Florentine Prélat comments: 'Nos chirurgiens osent maintenant ouvrir les ventres et fouiller les entrailles';[9] and Prélat goes on to claim that the essence of Renaissance art is to be found in the 'réalité anatomique'[10] of images of the body. The specific interest here of 'Éloge de la chair dolente' and *Gilles et Jeanne* is not so much in their factual accounts of the Renaissance, as in Tournier's (clinical) analysis of the desire which lies behind dissection. This analysis is of specific relevance to a study of the thematics of the body in Tournier's fiction.

In 'Éloge de la chair dolente' Tournier describes 'le corps humain blessé, soigné, tué et mis en linceul' as a 'grand thème qui remue en chacun de nous des vertiges métaphysiques et des ivresses sadomasochistes'.[11] All readers may not be in accord with the inclusive nature of Tournier's statement; it reveals, however, how far Tournier is fascinated with precisely those themes which may stir and disturb the reader and may engage his/her more distressing desires. Tournier's interest in this 'grand thème' is displayed repeatedly in his texts and most obtrusively perhaps in the novel *Le Roi des Aulnes*, which takes almost as its motto the clever and compelling comment: 'la chair ouverte, blessée est plus chair que la chair intacte'.[12] While I intend to make a detailed examination of the thematics of wounded flesh in Tournier's fiction, this exploration will be related to the image of the writer's flesh dissected. In this way I want to question how precisely the terror, fear, and violent fragilization of the body which haunt Tournier's fictions relate to questions of the creation and the reception of a text. How does the primordiality of pain relate to the sensitiz-

[8] 'La Solitude des grands hommes', 77 ('all the artists will rush to the cemeteries, under the gibbets and into the torture chambers').

[9] Michel Tournier, *Gilles et Jeanne* (Paris, 1983), 68: *Gilles and Jeanne*, trans. Alan Sheridan (London, 1989), 59 ('Our surgeons are now daring to open up bellies and rummage among the entrails').

[10] Ibid. 70: 61 ('anatomical reality').

[11] Tournier, *Des Clefs et des serrures*, 79 ('The human body wounded, nursed, or killed and wrapped in a shroud . . . grand theme which stirs in each of us a metaphysical fever and a sado-masochistic ecstasy').

[12] Michel Tournier, *Le Roi des Aulnes* (Paris, 1970), 369: *The Erl-King*, no translator named (London, 1983), 298 ('Flesh open and wounded is more flesh than flesh intact').

ing of the reading process? What may take place in the performance of desire in which Tournier's reader is (compulsively?)
engaged?

- *'La Blessure de Pelsenaire'*

Le Roi de Aulnes is a novel which takes mutilated flesh as a
central obsession. Tournier presents his readers with almost
an anatomy of abrasions. His hero, Abel Tiffauges, nurtures a
queasy passion for wounded flesh which is seen to date from
a sado-masochistic scenario in his childhood where he cleans a
wound with his tongue. Tiffauges, in his journal, sets out
his vision of the wound with a mania for detail: 'La plaie d'où
le sang continuait à sourdre étalait tout près de mes yeux sa
géographie capricieuse avec sa pulpe gonflée, ses élevures
blanchâtres de peau excoriée et ses lèvres roulées en dedans.'[13]
The exquisite precision of the text is overlaid by a minute
analysis of Tiffauges's emotions and sensations as he places
his lips on the broken flesh. Near the end of the novel, remembrance of this scene leads Tiffauges, like Proust's narrator,
to a realization of the specificity of his pleasure in pain; he
admits: 'ce qui m'a dévasté au moment où mes lèvres ont
rencontré les lèvres de la blessure de Pelsenaire, ce n'est
rien d'autre qu'un excès de joie, une joie d'une insupportable
violence'.[14]

Tiffauges's 'ivresses sadomasochistes' derive not merely
from the wound itself, or indeed from the oral eroticism of the
displaced act. As he goes on to expound, he draws pleasure
from the very poignant layering of flesh, skin, and dressing.
Peeling away the dressing of a wound becomes an act of discovery and decoding as Tiffauges admits to 'la curiosité avide
avec laquelle je suivais l'enlèvement successif de la bande, du
tampon d'ouate et de la gaze, pour surprendre, au centre de la

[13] *Le Roi des Aulnes*, 23: *The Erl-King*, 20 ('Blood went on welling out of the
wound. My eyes were right up against its whimsical geography—swollen pulp,
whitish wheals of abrased skin, in-turned edges').
[14] *Le Roi des Aulnes*, 370: *The Erl-King*, 298 ('What ravaged me when my lips
encountered those of Pelsenaire's wound was nothing but an excess of joy, a joy of
unbearable violence').

peau blanchie et gauffrée, le visage de la plaie'.[15] Tournier comments indeed on the value of the dressing in his 'Éloge de la chair dolente', saying: 'le pansement prend la relève du drapé classique, plus intime, plus équivoque, puisqu'il habille non la nudité, mais la plaie'.[16] In exploring Tiffauges's obsession, Tournier appears to bear in mind his own reference to Valéry's statement: 'La vérité est nue, mais sous le nu, il y a l'écorché.'[17] The desire to reveal and analyse is taken beneath the skin, as the text moves beyond interest in nudity into a fascination with fragilization, in quest, it might seem, of a deeper, more painful truth about sado-masochistic desires. Tiffauges himself comments: 'Quant à la plaie elle-même, son dessin, sa profondeur, et même les étapes de sa cicatrisation fournissaient à mon désir un aliment combien plus riche et plus inattendu que la simple nudité d'un corps.'[18]

The figurative language Tournier uses here is itself revelatory of a certain desire within his texts. Tiffauges has described the 'dessin' of the wound; it is imaged in terms of an anatomical drawing. This is also the case with the image of the headless corpse of the child Hellmut von Bibersee. Tiffauges details his 'observation de ce corps maigre et comme dessiné à l'encre de Chine sur le drap blanc où il était posé, structure osseuse chargée çà et là de masses musculaires'.[19] Tournier effects a certain distancing from the emotive horror of the scene he describes. His language is coolly clinical as he lists 'les tendons, les nerfs, les viscères, les vaisseaux';[20] employing anatomical terminology, he displays a constant desire to detail and define.

---

[15] *Le Roi des Aulnes*, 370: *The Erl-King*, 299 ('The avid curiosity with which I followed the removal of first the bandage, then the wadding, then the gauze, to come at last, in the middle of the white puckered skin, upon the visage of the wound itself').

[16] Tournier, *Des Clefs et des serrures*, 79 ('the dressing takes over from the classical drape, but it is more intimate, more ambiguous, covering not nudity, but the wound').

[17] Ibid. ('Truth is naked, but beneath the naked, there is the flayed').

[18] Tournier, *Le Roi des Aulnes*, 370: *The Erl-King*, 299 ('As for the wound itself, its shape, depth, and even the stages of cicatrization fed my desire more richly and strangely than a mere naked body').

[19] *Le Roi des Aulnes*, 364: *The Erl-King*, 294 ('contemplating the thin body, outlined as if in Indian ink on its white sheet, a bony structure covered here and there with round masses of muscle').

[20] *Le Roi des Aulnes*, 364: *The Erl-King*, 294 ('the tendons, the nerves, the viscera, the blood-vessels').

An obsession with anatomy and the diagram reflects, therefore, both the subject-matter of Tournier's texts and the scientific style he favours.

The scene where Tiffauges spends the night with the headless child is exemplary of the brutality and pathos of Tournier's texts. The decapitation of Hellmut may itself be seen to recall the beheading of the serial killer Weidmann, which Tournier has described earlier in the novel.[21] Hellmut is the victim of 'la flamme arrière d'un Panzerfaust'.[22] His body, 'cette dépouille décapitéc',[23] is laid out in a chapel and Tiffauges watches over him as night moves into day. He recounts the scene in his journal with poignant tranquillity: Tournier makes of the vigil an interlude of peculiar delicacy in the apocalyptic last section of the novel.[24] Watching the child, Tiffauges wonders about death and flesh, pursuing the solipsistic theorizing which obsesses his *Écrits sinistres*.

Tiffauges is fascinated by the relation between mind and body; he states: 'Par la tête, le corps est spiritualisé, désincarné, éludé.'[25] He is interested in the body at its most carnal and for him this explains his strong feelings towards Hellmut's corpse; as he says: 'décapité au contraire, [le corps] tombe sur le sol, soudain rendu à une incarnation formidable, doué d'une pesanteur inouïe'.[26] The night with Hellmut fires Tiffauges's latent necrophilia, leading him to question: 'Se pourrait-il que ma veillée auprès de la dépouille d'Hellmut m'eût donné à tout jamais le goût d'une chair plus grave, plus marmoréenne que

---

[21] In one of Tournier's games of intertextual inversion, Gilles de Rais, in *Gilles et Jeanne*, decapitates children and keeps their heads rather than their bodies. See *Gilles et Jeanne*, p. 132.

[22] Tournier, *Le Roi des Aulnes*, 363: *The Erl-King*, 294 ('the rear flame of a *Panzerfaust*').

[23] *Le Roi des Aulnes*, 364: *The Erl-King*, 294 ('that decapitated body').

[24] In this last part of *Le Roi des Aulnes* the reader may hear 'la pulsation des canons de l'Apocalypse' (p. 365) signalling that the Revelation of Saint John the Divine is a conscious intertext ('[the] pulsating . . . cannons of the Apocalypse', *The Erl-King*, 295). The decapitated child is therefore prefigured, since in Revelation 20: 4 St John writes: 'and I *saw* the souls of them that were beheaded for the witness of Jesus'.

[25] Tournier, *Le Roi des Aulnes*, 364: *The Erl-King*, 294 ('By the head the body is spiritualized, disincarnated, dodged').

[26] *Le Roi des Aulnes*, 364: *The Erl-King*, 294–5 ('But when the body is decapitated it falls to the ground, suddenly restored to terrific incarnation and endorsed with incredible weight').

celle qui ronflote et s'ébroue gentiment sur l'hypnodrome?'[27] Sleeping boys are now superseded by infinitely more desirable, and forbidden, dead flesh. Yet this newly acquired appetite is seen as a further manifestation of a former passion. As Tiffauges himself states: 'La gémellité, qui s'accompagne d'une partition de l'esprit et d'un alourdissement proportionné de la chair, m'avait fourni une version *relative* de ce phénomène que la mort restitue dans son *absolu*.'[28]

Tiffauges has previously shown himself to be an ardent (and sinister) theorist of twinship.[29] In Kaltenborn, his *napola*,[30] there are identical twins named Haïo and Haro, whom Tiffauges studies with intense interest. Again the passion for twins is inspired by the very 'déspiritualisation de la chair'.[31] Tiffauges comments that 'ces deux corps n'ont qu'un seul concept pour s'habiller intelligemment, pour se pénétrer d'esprit'[32] and, as a consequence of this, according to the contortions of his persuasive logic, 'ils s'épanouissent donc avec une tranquille indécence, étalant leur carnation crémeuse, leur duvet rose, leur pulpe musculaire ou adipeuse dans une nudité animale *insur-*

---

[27] *Le Roi des Aulnes*, 365: *The Erl-King*, 295 ('Could it be that my vigil by Hellmut's body has given me for ever a taste for flesh more solemn, more marmoreal than that which is snorting and snoring sweetly on the hypnodrome?').

[28] *Le Roi des Aulnes*, 364–5: *The Erl-King*, 295 ('The phenomenon of twins, which is accompanied by a dividing up of the mind and a proportionate increase in the weight of the flesh, had given me a relative instance of this; death now gave me an absolute example').

[29] Tiffauges's experiments with twins closely echo those of Mengele in Auschwitz. See Gerald L. Posner and John Ware, *Mengele: The Complete Story* (London, 1986), 29–40, for a distressing account of Mengele's atrocities. Posner and Ware detail the taking of measurements of skulls, ears, noses, and other external features (see *Le Roi des Aulnes*, 305); they go on to state: 'These in vivo tests furnished Mengele only with superficial and incomplete information. In his passion to learn everything about the similarities and differences between twins, it was the next and final stage of his experiments that was the most important: the dissection of their bodies so that their organs and general development would be compared' (*Mengele*, 38).

[30] As Tournier reminds us, the *napolas* (*National-politische Erziehungsanstalten*) were 'ces prytannées militaires S.S. où une élite d'enfants très sévèrement sélectionnés étaient élevés pour devenir la fine fleur du futur Reich' (*Le Vent Paraclet* (Paris, 1977), 104: *The Wind Spirit*, 87: 'the SS's military training schools, where a hand-picked elite was raised to become the cream of the future Reich').

[31] Tournier, *Le Roi des Aulnes*, 304: *The Erl-King*, 247 ('the despiritualization of the flesh').

[32] *Le Roi des Aulnes*, 304: *The Erl-King*, 247 ('The two bodies really have only one concept between them with which to clothe themselves in intelligence and fill themselves with spirit').

passable'.[33] They are seen to be exemplary in their nudity.[34] Tiffauges provides a loving inventory of the twins' physical characteristics. The final confirmation that the twins form an incarnation of Tiffauges's personal obsession with inversion comes in the realization that 'la moitié gauche de Haro correspond à la moitié droite de Haïo, de même que sa moité droite reproduit exactement la moitié gauche de son frère'.[35] The discovery that these are mirroring twins leads Tiffauges, who has been obsessed with the very concept of inversion, to conclude with passionate satisfaction: 'Voici que je retrouve inscrit en pleine chair d'enfant ce thème qui n'a cessé de me hanter.'[36]

- *'Les Frères-pareils'*

Inscription *in* flesh is a primary theme within *Le Roi des Aulnes*.[37] This drama of signification in the flesh is played out further in the novel *Les Météores* where again twinship is a repeating compulsion. It is this novel which I shall look at in some detail in this chapter, since above all in Tournier's fiction it serves to reflect on relations between identity, decoding, and impossible desire. Paul Surin, narrator of large sections of *Les Météores* and eloquent theorist of geminate relations, suffers a mutilation which may be read as the inscription of his personal tragedy in his flesh.

[33] *Le Roi des Aulnes*, 304: *The Erl-King*, 247 ('So they develop with calm indecency, exhibiting their creamy complexion, their pink down, their muscular or adipose tissue in an animal nudity which is unsurpassable').

[34] *Le Roi des Aulnes*, 304: *The Erl-King*, 247. Tournier's Gaspard meditates further on rereadings of the concept of nudity; he comments: 'Avec Biltine, il me semblait que je découvrais la chair pour la première fois. Sa blancheur, sa roseur lui donnaient une capacité de nudité incomparable . . . Biltine était toujours nue, même couverte jusqu'aux yeux' (*Gaspard, Melchior et Balthazar* (Paris, 1980), 23: *The Four Wise Men*, no translator named (London, 1983), 17: 'With Biltine I felt that I was discovering flesh for the first time. Her whiteness, her pinkness, gave her an incomparable aptitude for nudity. . . . Even with every inch of her covered, Biltine was always nude').

[35] Tournier, *Le Roi des Aulnes*, 306: *The Erl-King*, 248–9 ('Haro's left half corresponds to the right half of Haïo, and Haro's right to Haïo's left').

[36] *Le Roi des Aulnes*, 307: *The Erl-King*, 249 ('And now here I find the theme that has always haunted me actually written out in children's flesh').

[37] See *Le Roi des Aulnes*, 109: *The Erl-King*, 89.

Paul is a twin who relishes the intimacy and the plenitude of the geminate bond. He writes with docile pleasure: 'je dispose d'une image vivante et absolument vérace de moi-même, d'une grille de déchiffrement qui élucide toutes mes énigmes, d'une clé qui ouvre sans résistance ma tête, mon cœur et mon sexe. Cette image, cette grille, cette clé, c'est toi, mon frère-pareil.'[38] He contrasts his position with that of the singleton, saying 'l'homme sans-pareil à la recherche de lui-même ne trouve que des bribes de sa personnalité, des lambeaux de son moi, des fragments informes de cet être énigmatique, centre obscur et impénétrable du monde'.[39] The novel's central irony lies in the fact that Paul will be rendered a dispaired and despairing single-ton; despite their physical similarity, the twins are in fact harrowed by the very differences in their needs and desires. In the patterns of Tournier's 'literalizing of the figurative'[40] this harrowing is rendered carnal in an escape tunnel beneath the Berlin Wall.

Images of the wound begin to multiply in the novel after Jean's final departure from his brother. Paul makes a journey to follow in his brother's footsteps, embarking on a deluded quest to mirror his brother's trajectory. He attempts to move from following to being Jean, and Tournier marks this with a play on words when Paul comments: 'ces trois mots *Je suis Jean* me calment, me rassurent'.[41] On this obsessive journey, Paul is, inevitably, (mis)recognized not as himself but as his brother and he describes this experience as 'l'aliénation'. The experience of being rendered other is, at first, painful and Paul describes it in figurative terms as 'le coup de lance de l'*aliénation*, cette blessure qui n'a pas cessé . . . de se rouvrir, mois après mois, de

---

[38] Michel Tournier, *Les Météores* (Paris, 1975), 247: *Gemini*, trans. Anne Carter (London, 1981), 205 ('I have a living image of myself of absolute veracity, a decoding machine to unravel all my riddles, a key to which my head, my heart and my genitals open unresistingly. That image, that decoder, that key is you, my twin brother').

[39] *Les Météores*, 247: *Gemini*, 204 ('The twinless man in search of himself finds only shreds of his personality, rags of his self, shapeless fragments of that enigmatic being, the dark, impenetrable centre of the world').

[40] Michael Worton, 'Use and Abuse of Metaphor in Tournier's "Le Vol du vampire"', *Paragraph*, 10 (Oct. 1987), 13–28: 18.

[41] Tournier, *Les Météores*, 426: *Gemini*, 353 ('those three words *I am Jean* are soothing and reassuring').

saigner, encore et encore, récompense et châtiment à la fois de ma quête de mon frère-pareil'.[42] The image of the lance becomes a literalization of Paul's surname, Surin (knife, dagger), the sign he bears. It also commemorates the literal impaling of the red-haired twins near the end of *Le Roi des Aulnes*, where they are seen 'percés d'oméga en alpha, les yeux grands ouverts sur le néant'.[43] Here the mutilation of the twins' flesh becomes the distressingly apt culmination of a text obsessed with excess, distortion, and signification.[44]

Paul's own laceration is seen as a form of crucifixion. The trauma is described in measured terms: 'lorsque la mâchoire molle et ruisselante se referme lentement sur son corps crucifié, il sent ces pièces dures le broyer comme des dents d'acier'.[45] Paul experiences a real cleaving and fragmentation of his body; he resembles precisely his own description of the singleton's dissociated, fractured self. In the scene of dislocation, Paul loses the left side of his body, which he has associated with his twin brother. Tournier appears to call his reader to refer to Plato's *Symposium* where, according to Aristophanes, Zeus says of the human race: 'I will cut each of them in two; in this way they will be weaker, and at the same time more profitable to us by being more numerous. They shall walk upright on two legs. If there is any sign of wantonness in them after that, and they will not keep quiet, I will bisect them again, and they shall hop on one leg.'[46] Paul would seem to receive this punishment, yet it becomes, potentially, the source of his salvation. The impact this may be seen to have for the reading encounter will be discussed below. What is of immediate interest to this

[42] *Les Météores*, 339: *Gemini*, 281 ('the spear thrust of *alienation*, the wound which has never since healed but has bled, month after month, on and on, at once the reward and the punishment of my quest for my twin brother').

[43] Tournier, *Le Roi des Aulnes*, 390: *The Erl-King*, 314 ('pierced from omega to alpha, their eyes staring into space').

[44] In the patterns of reflection within the text, the death of the twins serves to commemorate the impaling of Tiffauges's beloved pigeons (*Le Roi des Aulnes*, 162: *The Erl-King*, 132). The reader's horror at the violent escalation in the text may be tempered by a horrified aesthetic pleasure resulting from the game of recognition and repetition the reading-process necessarily becomes.

[45] Tournier, *Les Météores*, 523: *Gemini*, 435 ('as the soft, slithering jaws closed slowly over his crucified body he felt the hard edges grinding into it like teeth of steel').

[46] Plato, *The Symposium*, trans. W. Hamilton (Harmondsworth, 1967), 60.

discussion is how Tournier attempts to recuperate and legitimize both the representation and the experience of violence against the body.

The final chapter of *Les Météores*, 'L'Ame déployée', differs radically from the rest of the novel. As Colin Davis comments: 'By far the largest part of *Les Météores* portrays loss, separation, and quest; in less than twenty pages the final chapter attempts to reverse these terms and show reconciliation, presence, and discovery.'[47] Yet, ironically, this expression of plenitude emerges specifically from an acceptance of loss and fragmentation. Paul has experienced vivisection; he lies in bed, a mutilated victim, drugged with novocaine. 'L'Ame déployée' is formed from a series of sensations, illusions, and fantasies, where Paul learns to create a sense of identity through the agency of his agony. As he says: 'tout doit être recréé à partir de ces élancements, torsions, crispations, crampes, ardillonnements, brûlures et martèlements qui habitent mon pauvre corps'.[48] His lacerated body becomes a crucial locus of sensation; indeed Paul claims figuratively: 'Mes plaies sont l'étroit théâtre dans les limites duquel il m'incombe de reconstruire l'univers'.[49]

Where Paul has literally lost his left arm and leg, he gradually discovers that he retains their sensations. He claims, early in the chapter, 'de ma jambe gauche, de mon bras gauche, je vis, je sens, je m'étends'.[50] Tournier's text extends into escalating fantasy as he balances magic realism with mental delusion. Paul details his experiences, at first with caution as he senses movement in his bandages and hazards the remark: 'tout se passe comme si de mes deux plaies émergeaient parfois ici une minuscule main, là un petit pied, doués de mouvement et de sensibilité'.[51] Tournier adds substance to Paul's illusion and the missing limbs come to appear in corporeal form. As Paul relates,

---

[47] Colin Davis, *Michel Tournier: Philosophy and Fiction* (Oxford, 1988), 106.

[48] Tournier, *Les Météores*, 527: *Gemini*, 440 ('all these will be re-created out of the stabbings, wrenchings, tensions, cramps, barbs, burnings and hammerings that occupy my poor body').

[49] *Les Météores*, 527: *Gemini*, 440 ('My injuries are the narrow scene within whose confines I must rebuild the universe').

[50] *Les Météores*, 525: *Gemini*, 438 ('in my left leg and my left arm I am alive, I can feel and stretch').

[51] *Les Météores*, 530: *Gemini*, 442 ('It was just as though a tiny foot here and a little hand there were now and then emerging from my two stumps and endowed with the power of movement and feeling').

with bizarre lucidity: 'depuis deux heures, ma jambe gauche—l'amputée, l'invisible—débordant du pansement, du drap, du lit, pendait sur le plancher de la chambre'.[52] The amputated limbs are assimilated with an imaginary 'corps gauche' which becomes the key to diversity of sensation and ubiquity. This 'corps gauche' is, further, associated specifically and finally with the lost twin as Paul comes to the realization that this 'corps gauche', 'c'est Jean, incorporé désormais à son frère-pareil'.[53] Tournier appears to show that beyond the bodily inscription of absence and loss, imaginary plenitude may be found in the incorporation of the Other and in the flowering of illusion.

• Le Corps morcelé

As he approaches his theory of the mirror stage, Lacan questions the function of role models adopted (like the mirror image) in the assumption of identity, and he wonders: 'Cette formule est-elle confirmée par l'étude des jumeaux?'[54] This is a question Tournier may be seen to take up in his novel Les Météores. This text enacts a protracted performance of identity formation. Tournier engages in a productive and antagonistic dialogue with psychoanalytic discourse, and with that of Lacan in particular.[55] In this novel of reflections, doubling, and twinship, it is highly apt that Tournier takes Lacan's essay 'Le Stade du miroir comme formateur de la fonction du Je' as formative intertext. His reference to the paper is signalled, as often in Tournier's

---

[52] Les Météores, 534: Gemini, 445 ('for the past two hours my left leg—the unseen, amputated one—had been oozing out of the bandages, the sheets and the bed and dangling onto the floor of the room').

[53] Les Météores, 535–6: Gemini, 447 ('It is Jean, now become a part of his identical brother').

[54] Jacques Lacan, Les Complexes familiaux dans la formation de l'individu (Paris, 1984). 48 ('Is this formula confirmed by the study of twins?').

[55] Tournier claims, however, to be resistant to psychoanalysis, since he is troubled by the question of whether a 'cure' may or should be achieved. He states: 'il y a dans l'ethnologie, la sociologie et la psychanalyse un biologisme de principe qui voudrait que tous les ressorts de l'homme favorisent son intégration au corps social. C'est de là que découle directement l'aspect réducteur de la cure psychanalytique' ('Tristan et Iseut', Le Vol du vampire: Notes de lecture (Paris, 1983), 28–37: 34) ('ethnology, sociology and psychoanalysis work from a basic biological principle that all man's motivating forces favour his integration into the social body. The reductive aspect of the psychoanalytic cure derives directly from this').

games of textual appropriation, by his echoing of the language of another writer (here Lacan). Paul ends his lament for the non-geminate singleton by saying: 'les miroirs ne lui renvoient qu'une image figée et inversée'.[56] Here the text would seem to reflect Lacan's description of 'la forme totale du corps', which appears to the individual 'dans un relief de stature qui la *fige* et sous une symétrie qui l'*inverse*'.[57] *Les Météores* may indeed be read as a lucid critique of Lacan's theory of the mirror stage, and the novel identifies a specific locus of discussion in Lacanian criticism.

The disparity between the texts of Tournier and Lacan lies precisely in the relation between the mirror image and the *corps morcelé* and the affective associations of each. In 'Le Stade du miroir comme formateur de la fonction du Je', Lacan defines 'une image morcelée du corps'[58] which exists as the inverse of the unified reflected image which the infant assumes and assimilates in the drama of the mirror stage. There are, it seems, uncanny resemblances between Lacan's images of the *corps morcelé* and Tournier's visions of fragilized flesh in *Les Météores*. This intertextual link may be felt particularly keenly in the instance of the final chapter of *Les Météores* where Paul's fantasies might be compared with the imagery of the paper 'Some Reflections on the Ego' in which Lacan refers to 'disjointed limbs . . . rearranged as strange trophies', and continues to question both 'the phenomenon called "phantom limb"' and indeed 'the strange fact of the persistence of pain with the removal of the subjective element of distress'.[59]

There is an element of the baroque and the macabre in Lacan's evocations of the *corps morcelé* and this itself serves to bring his texts closer to the violent mythologies of Tournier's own. Lacan encourages his reader to visualize the fragmented body 'sous la forme de membres disjoints et de ces organes

---

[56] Tournier, *Les Météores*, 247: *Gemini*, 204 ('mirrors give him back only a fixed, reversed image').

[57] Jacques Lacan, 'Le Stade du miroir comme formateur de la fonction du Je', in *Écrits* (Paris, 1966), 95: 'The Mirror Stage as Formative of the Function of the I', in *Écrits: A Selection*, 2 (my emphasis) ('the total form of the body . . . in a contrasting size that *fixes* it and in a symmetry that *inverts* it').

[58] Lacan, 'Le Stade du miroir comme formateur de la fonction du Je', 97: 'The Mirror Stage as Formative', 4 ('a fragmented body-image').

[59] Jacques Lacan, 'Some Reflections on the Ego', *International Journal of Psychoanalysis*, 34/1 (1953), 11–17: 13. This paper was read to the British Psycho-Analytical Society on 2 May 1951 and was published in English.

figurés en exoscopie, qui s'ailent et s'arment pour les per-
sécutions intestines, qu'à jamais a fixées par la peinture le
visionnaire Jérôme Bosch'.[60] This poetic evocation of the body in
pieces, winged and armed, reveals the very excess and elabora-
tion inherent in Lacan's development of the concept.

In *Les Complexes familiaux dans la formation de l'individu*
Lacan describes 'toute une série de fantasmes de morcellement
du corps qui vont en régression de la dislocation et du démembrement, par l'éviration, l'éventrement, jusqu'à la dévoration et
à l'ensevelissement'.[61] In 'L'Agressivité en psychanalyse' this
escalating series is enlarged to include 'les images de castration,
d'éviration, de mutilation, de démembrement, de dislocation,
d'éventrement, de dévoration, d'éclatement du corps'.[62]
Lacan shows a predilection for multiple variations: he undermines any stability in the concept of the *corps morcelé*, and
allows the image itself (appropriately) to metamorphose and
mutate.[63]

The experience of the *corps morcelé* has been seen specifically
to pre-date the discovery of mirroring plenitude and the
identification with a cohesive mirror image. It has been identified literally with the infant's experience of disparate sensory
perceptions and his lack of motor control. Elizabeth Grosz
comments that the infant's 'body is an uncoordinated *aggregate*,
a series of parts, zones, organs, sensations, needs and im-
pulses rather than an integrated totality'.[64] Grosz stresses that
the child experiences his body in parts, as do John P. Muller and
William J. Richardson, who describe 'the newly born human

[60] Lacan, 'Le Stade du miroir comme formateur de la fonction du Je', 97: 'The
Mirror Stage as Formative', 4 ('in the form of disjointed limbs, or of those organs
represented in exoscopy, growing wings and taking up arms for intestinal
persecutions—the very same that the visionary Hieronymus Bosch has fixed, for all
time, in painting').

[61] Lacan, *Les Complexes familiaux dans la formation de l'individu*, 60 ('a whole
series of fantasies of the fragmenting of the body which descend from dislocation
and dismemberment, through castration and disembowelling, to devouring and
burying').

[62] Jacques Lacan, 'L'Agressivité en psychanalyse', in *Écrits*, 101–24: 104:
'Aggressivity in Psychoanalysis', in *Écrits: A Selection*, 8–29: 11 ('the images of
castration, mutilation, dismemberment, dislocation, evisceration, devouring, burst-
ing open of the body').

[63] Indeed, as Malcolm Bowie comments revealingly: 'one of Lacan's recurrent
purposes as a writer is to amplify theories to the point where they become deranged'
(*Lacan* (London, 1991), 35).

[64] Elizabeth Grosz, *Jacques Lacan: A Feminist Introduction* (London, 1990), 33.

infant, initially sunk in motor incapacity, turbulent movement, and fragmentation'.[65] The *corps morcelé* is seen to pre-date the mirror stage and to be evidence of what Lacan describes as 'une prématuration natale physiologique'.[66] However, Jane Gallop suggests that 'actually, *that* violently unorganized image *only comes after* the mirror stage so as to *represent what came before*'.[67] Malcolm Bowie's reading of Lacan's paper argues that the anxious, vertiginous experience of the *corps morcelé* both pre-dates *and* inhabits the mirror stage. As he writes persuasively: 'the unity invented at these moments, and the ego that is the product of successive inventions, are both spurious; they are attempts to find ways round certain inescapable factors of lack, absence and incompleteness in human living'.[68]

Now, I have suggested that *Les Météores* may be seen to diverge from Lacan's account of the formation of the ego. While retaining the central drama enacted in Lacan's theory, Tournier makes an implicit critique of the notion of any security of identity resting on the identification with an *imago*. *Les Météores*, in its critique of Lacan, would seem to take Bowie's argument about 'inescapable factors of lack and absence' one stage further. Paul criticizes specifically the fixity and singular plenitude of the mirror image. As Grosz notes, similarly, 'the mirror stage is a necessarily alienating structure because of the unmediated tension between the fragmented or "fragilized" body of experience, and the "solidity" and permanence of the body as seen in the mirror'.[69] For Paul, this tension between experience and perception is conceived as destructive; the *corps morcelé* is constructed as the product of the mirror stage. The singleton experiencing a multiplicity of sensations and perceptions is traumatized by the very unity of his reflection. The twin, with his living image, is repeatedly fulfilled in his relation to an ever different and diverting image.

[65] John P. Muller and William J. Richardson, *Lacan and Language* (New York, 1982), 29.

[66] Lacan, 'L'Agressivité en psychanalyse', 113: 'Aggressivity in Psychoanalysis', 19 ('physiological natal prematuration').

[67] Jane Gallop, *Reading Lacan* (Ithaca, NY, 1985), 80.

[68] Malcolm Bowie, *Freud, Proust and Lacan: Theory as Fiction* (Cambridge, 1987), 106.

[69] Grosz, *Jacques Lacan*, 42.

Critique of the fixity of the mirror image is further substanti-
ated by Tournier in a seeming celebration of the potential
ecstasy of the *corps morcelé*. This would appear to be Tournier's
aim in the last chapter of the novel where Paul states (echoing
Eluard): 'la douleur est un capital qui ne doit pas être dilapidé.
C'est la matière brute qu'il faut travailler, élaborer, déloyer.'[70]
If Paul's mutilation is read as a literal experience of the
corps morcelé it may be seen as the product of the failure of
mirroring relations. *Les Météores* is fired by a desire to render
similar within the knowledge of impossible difference. Paul's
'salvation' comes in his peculiar recognition of pleasure in pain
and his discovery of the imaginary potential of his phantom
limbs.

Any sense of identity comes through carnal mutilation rather
than mirroring plenitude. Indeed mirrors in *Les Météores* are
seen as delusory, distressing, and disturbing. Jean, Paul's twin,
enters an irresistibly Lacanian scenario in a department store
changing-room. He confronts the reflection in a three-panelled
mirror, recognizing the triply reproduced image in an instant
not as himself but as his brother.[71] Jean is alienated from his
image, which he sees as his twin, and he describes the experience
as one of mutilation, saying: 'je m'avançai sans méfiance dans le
piège, et aussitôt ses mâchoires miroitantes se refermèrent
sur moi et me broyèrent si cruellement que j'en porte les traces
à tout jamais'.[72] This psychological fragmentation is figured as
an experience of the *corps morcelé*; indeed the very language of
the text looks forward to the savaging of Paul in the escape
tunnel.

The three-sided mirror corrodes Jean's sense of self; a
Venetian mirror placed later in the novel similarly dissipates and
disseminates reality. A guide describes to Paul the mirror's
frame, composed of smaller glasses offering alternate reflections,
and reveals: 'C'est un miroir *dérapant*, distrayant, un miroir
centrifuge qui chasse vers sa périphérie tout ce qui approche son

---

[70] Tournier, *Les Météores*, 527: *Gemini*, 440 ('Pain is a capital which must not be
dissipated. It is the raw material which must be worked, transformed and used to
best advantage').

[71] *Les Météores*, 246: *Gemini*, 203.

[72] *Les Météores*, 246: *Gemini*, 203 ('I walked forward unsuspectingly into the trap
and instantly its reflecting jaws closed on me and mangled me so cruelly that I shall
carry the marks with me always').

foyer.'[73] Tournier's mirrors distress and disturb integrity and identity, always foregrounding the experience of dislocation and the *corps morcelé*. It remains to question how this relates to the questions of identity and sexuality posed by *Les Météores*.

• 'Les Sables mouvants'

Les Météores is a novel whose representation of desiring relations cuts across the common axes of homosexual and heterosexual. At the centre of the novel is an incestuous and frustrated gay relationship upon whose failure the text depends. Writing about twinship in *Le Vent Paraclet*, Tournier tends to emphasize the positive aspects of such relations. He notes: 'Je n'ai pas inventé le bonheur gémellaire. Je l'ai rencontré dans les entretiens que j'ai eus avec des jumeaux, dans de nombreuses études consacrées à la gémellité.'[74] He goes on to suggest that if fewer twins marry or rise to the top of their professions, it is because they have a perfect partner from birth, and know greater satisfaction in themselves. It is then a further irony of *Les Météores* that Tournier should take in his terms the most perfect relationship in order to wreck it in his most poignant and wrenching tale of loss, passion, and solipsistic desire.

For Paul, his twin, the guarantor of identity, content, and completion, becomes the agent of dissociation. In the sixteenth chapter of the novel, Paul finally laments: 'O Jean, mon frère-pareil, quand cesseras-tu de glisser sous mes pas des sables mouvants, de dresser des mirages devant mes yeux?'[75] Paul, who has followed his brother on to the beach at night, pursuing 'sa mince silhouette courant sur le sable glacé',[76] finds his progress through the novel increasingly unsteady, hazardous, and illusory as Jean's very absence corrodes his identity and leaves

---

[73] *Les Météores*, 373: *Gemini*, 310 ('This is a distracting, a *diverting* mirror, a centrifugal mirror that throws everything that approaches its centre outward to the edge').

[74] Tournier, *Le Vent Paraclet*, 244: *The Wind Spirit*, 208 ('I did not invent gemel happiness but discovered it in my conversations with twins and in numerous studies of twinship').

[75] Tournier, *Les Météores*, 413: *Gemini*, 343 ('O Jean, my twin, when will you stop placing quicksands beneath my feet and building mirages before my eyes?').

[76] *Les Météores*, 152: *Gemini*, 128–9 ('his slim figure running over the ice-cold sands').

him, as we have seen, finally prey to exultant illusion. What we might question further is the effect this may have on the desiring reader. We begin a polyphonic and panoramic novel which stretches from the beaches of Brittany across the prairies of Canada, to Greenland and beyond. We end with a single insistent interior voice, anchored in space in a fragilized body and seeming delirium. The reader is stripped of any confirming specular relation with Paul, who is, nevertheless, an impeccable and imperious decoder. In his desire for Jean he has embarked on an impossible quest for possession and interpretation as hopeless as that of Proust's narrator. The attempts of Tournier's protagonist to retain his object of desire prove as vain as his wish to make a geminate reading of reality.

In *Les Météores* the reader may be led to equate the role of the deluded decoder with that of the despairing lover. The novel offers, however, a scenario of identity formation which refuses the illusion of secure identification and emphasizes the necessary instability mirroring relations with the Other may be seen to entail. Tournier shows identity to be fictive and fractured: his means of revelation are typically corporeal and gory as a psychic compulsion is written in the flesh.

Yet Paul is not the only decoder whose drama of desire is represented in *Les Météores*. He comes near to being upstaged, indeed, by his uncle, Alexandre. Why, we may wonder, does Tournier choose this dual focus for his novel? Why deplace the drama of twinship at its centre? Why allow, what he himself describes as 'le déséquilibre en faveur d'Alexandre'?[77]

• *'The Gay Deconstructor'*

It is, significantly, also in the figure of Alexandre Surin, insatiable cruiser, aesthete and gay uncle, that the reader finds his/her double in the text. It is, I will argue, Alexandre's failed passion which mimics and dictates the reader's desire.

Tournier places Alexandre as, in the words of Colin Davis, 'the gay deconstructor of *Les Météores*'.[78] This appellation is

---

[77] Tournier, *Le Vent Paraclet*, 250: *The Wind Spirit*, 213 ('the imbalance in favour of Alexandre').

[78] Davis, *Michel Tournier*, 78.

somewhat ambiguous, affording the questions: is Alexandre the deconstructor of *Les Météores* (who happens to be gay), does Alexandre deconstruct from the basis of a specifically gay ideology (due to his own sexual identity or not as the case may be), or is there in fact some more intrinsic, intuitive, or perhaps artificial relation between Alexandre's sexuality and his textual practice?

What is Alexandre's relation to the text he inhabits? How far is his role crucial to the reader's understanding of the dynamics of textual production in *Les Météores*? What implications may it have for our own reading practice that Alexandre should so flamboyantly be privileged as viewer and dealer in Tournier's strategies of seductive textual production?

Alexandre is an ardent theorist who constructs his own post-modernist aesthetics. He privileges the copy over the model, stating: 'L'idée est plus que la chose, et l'idée de l'idée plus que l'idée. En vertu de quoi l'imitation est plus que la chose imitée, car elle est cette chose plus l'effort d'imitation.'[79] In this sense, the text appears to construct a value system which is comparable in implication to that reconstructed by Butler in *Gender Trouble*. In Alexandre's terms at least, the copy, the imitation, the parody, is seen to acquire a higher value, to be more seductive than the model. Both Tournier and Butler appear to stress that the parodic replica supersedes the original in value. It is noticeable that, in *Les Météores*, this aesthetic and theoretical stance is associated implicitly with Alexandre's sexual identity and explicitly with his specific desiring practice. What we may question further is how far the text may be seen to pose a threat to the heterosexual matrix, through the agency of the protagonist Alexandre. Does the deconstruction Alexandre effects hold subversive power? Further, how formative may we assume the external reader's possible identification with Alexandre to be?

Alexandre's desire is revealed to be determined by an abstract concept he attempts to actualize in flesh and blood, and which directs and distorts his analysis of his desires. In the text, Alexandre's complex desire for Eustache and Daniel (rendered

---

[79] Tournier, *Les Météores*, 86: *Gemini*, 74 ('The idea is more than the thing and the idea of the idea more than the idea. Wherefore the imitation is more than the thing imitated, because it is the thing plus the effort of imitation').

doubly unobtainable by their desire for each other) is provoked
by the discovery that between them they actualize the concept of
'la copie de la copie'. The theoretical construct is recognized in
flesh and comes to exist with illusory power outside Alexandre's
imagination; as he says: 'Je n'imaginais pas que mes terrains
de chasse dans leur sublime et surprenante abondance me
livreraient l'équivalent érotique de l'idée de l'idée, de la copie de
la copie: la proie de la proie.'[80]

The intellectual and imagined concept fleshed out in corporeal
figures allows a charged exchange between the senses and the
imagination. While a compulsion is incarnated in erotic forms,
desire for these forms is idealized and sublimated; as Alexandre
claims: 'Eustache et Daniel—ces fleurs de gadoue—devaient
ensuite me faire accéder à un amour ricochant vers l'abstraction
par cet étrange objet, la proie de la proie.'[81] Alexandre's move
towards sublimation is always haunted by erotic images.
Michael Worton suggests that Tournier's 'sustained challenge to
contemporary attitudes to sexuality'[82] comes to advocate 'fulfilment and stable identity through sublimation'.[83] Analysing patterns of desire in the texts, Worton concludes: 'Tournier's
characters rarely remain satisfied with solutions and their lives
reveal themselves to be continuing, if vain, quests for the
Other—and especially for a new, *sublimated* relationship.'[84]

Whilst Worton's diagnosis of desire in Tournier's texts appears entirely apt, I might choose to disagree with his contention
that fulfilment and stable identity are found through sublimation. It might be argued that this is the implication of Tournier's
earliest text, *Vendredi; ou, Les Limbes du Pacifique*, which
closes on an exultant, cerulean scene dependent on the repres-
sion of desire for a seductive child.[85] For Robinson fulfilment is

[80] *Les Météores*, 93: *Gemini*, 79 ('I had no idea that my hunting grounds in their
astonishing and sublime abundance were going to furnish me with the erotic
equivalent of the idea of the idea, the copy of the copy: the quarry of the quarry').

[81] *Les Météores*, 100: *Gemini*, 85 ('Eustache and Daniel, those flowers of the
muck, introduced me to a love veering back to abstraction through that curious
thing, the quarry of the quarry').

[82] Michael Worton, 'Michel Tournier and the Nature of Love', *European Gay
Review*, 3 (1988), 36–46: 41.

[83] Ibid. 42.

[84] Ibid. 44.

[85] See my reading of this ending in Brian Stimpson and Lieve Spaas (eds.),
Robinson Crusoe (London, 1996).

certainly found, although any stable identity is dependent on death to the temporal world and illusory mirroring identification with a juvenile double and Other.[86] In Tournier's subsequent fictions, however, any possibility of stable identity is rendered despairingly hazardous and fragile. Tournier may reveal the search for stable identity through sublimation and through the rejection of the infidelity, shattering intimacy, and unknowability of engaged relations with the Other. Yet he appears to reveal emphatically that this stability remains necessarily an illusion.

This illusory rejection of alterity in quest of stable identity is of course found in *Les Météores* where Alexandre is seen to attempt to persuade himself that he finds in material reality the compulsions of his imagination. But surely Tournier stresses ultimately (and unwillingly) to his reader that Alexandre is a misguided fantasist, who eventually falls prey to his own delusions? Alexandre constructs his life as a quest which moves between sentient reality and the imagination. For Alexandre texts are seen to be so formative that they entirely condition his conception of his existence and his perception of the world around him.

Alexandre conceives of reality in terms of a text to be read with the senses. As he says of 'la gadoue', the staple substance of the refuse company he comes to command, 'c'est un grimoire infiniment complexe que ma narine n'en finit pas de déchiffrer'.[87] Reading is, for Alexandre, a perpetual, addictive activity resting on the belief that all can be deciphered. He affirms, for example: 'chaque homme est une certaine formule'.[88] Yet Alexandre's reading practice is such that it undermines any (de)finite ascription of meaning to a specific

---

[86] *Vendredi* might be compared with 'Barbedor', in *Gaspard, Melchior et Balthazar*, 107–17, which images succession without recourse to reproduction. Tournier himself teasingly expresses the desire to have a clone, saying: 'Je pourrais ainsi non seulement m'élever moi-même, mais éventuellement me suicider, soit en tuant mon clone, soit en me faisant tuer par lui' ('Plus encore qu'un jumeau j'aimerais avoir un clone', interview with Olivier Frébourg, *Contre Ciel*, 8 (Dec. 1984), 81–3: 82) ('Thus I could not only bring myself up, but eventually kill myself, either killing my clone or getting myself killed by him').

[87] Tournier, *Les Météores*, 84: *Gemini*, 72 ('It is an infinitely complex cipher which my nose is never done with decoding').

[88] *Les Météores*, 90: *Gemini*, 77 ('every man is made up according to a particular formula').

formula. His reading practice is necessarily more contingent and more tentative. Alexandre constructs his encounters with the world of privileged signs he perceives around him as continually disorientating, shattering, and transformative. Where Barthes evokes a textual encounter in the terminology of the casual pick-up, Alexandre in *Les Météores* is seen to construct the accounts of his cruising as hermeneutic adventure dependent, for its allure, on the changing of signs. As Alexandre writes of his sexual prey: 'Je l'avais vu et j'avais vu qu'il m'avait vu le voir, délicieux et vertigineux miroitement qui fait du chasseur une proie et du gibier un prédateur.'[89]

The passages of the text given over to Alexandre's outlandish theorizing and minute analysis serve, as we have seen, to embed within the text an emphatic and passionate deconstruction of any hierarchical relation between copies and models. In his privileging of mirroring and inversion, Alexandre produces a theory which effectively authorizes his sexual fantasies. But does his stance as 'gay deconstructor' offer further implications for the questioning of identity categories? Does *Les Météores* pose its own threat to the regulatory matrix of heterosexuality?

• *'Le Père-jumeau'*

'Alexandre', Tournier claims, 'c'est l'hybride, c'est le bâtard, beaucoup plus intéressant et romanesque comme tel que les êtres d'ordre et de légalité.'[90] Alexandre is constructed as a character whose identity category is unintelligible within the regulatory matrix of heterosexuality. It is important to argue, I think, that this unintelligibility arises not only from his homosexual identification but also from the threat Alexandre poses to patriarchal society in, as we shall see, emphatically countering 'le non du père'. In *Les Météores* Tournier contests the taboo surrounding incest as much as that surrounding homosexuality. In these terms it is important that *Les Météores* should be read as family

---

[89] *Les Météores*, 93: *Gemini*, 79 ('I had seen him and I had seen that he had seen me see him, a deliciously dizzying reflection which makes me a quarry of the hunter and a predator of the game').

[90] Tournier, *Le Vent Paraclet*, 251: *The Wind Spirit*, 214 ('Alexander . . . is a hybrid, a bastard, and as such a much more interesting character for fiction than the lawful and orderly').

drama which draws into question the central issue of the construction of identity through identification and desire.

Freud, in constructing theories of 'inversion', concentrates, largely on desire between mother and male child.[91] What remains effectively occluded is the possibility of a desiring relation between father and son. As Butler remarks: 'With the postulation of a bisexual set of libidinal dispositions, there is no reason to deny an original sexual love of the son for the father, and yet Freud implicitly does.'[92] Paternal–filial desire is, however, central to representations of homosexuality and can even be found inscribed in certain versions of the Oedipus legend.[93]

In *Les Météores*, Tournier calls on his reader to draw into question the construction of sexual identity by dramatizing a scenario of paternal–filial incest. Following Gide, perhaps, he makes his seductive elder not a father but an uncle. The uncle is a paternal figure (allowing the *hantise* of incest to exist), but he is himself childless, ensuring that the seduction of the son is always in the order of fantasy, however real the sexual relations may be. Tournier writes succinctly: 'Le père c'est l'ordre, l'honorabilité, la sagesse. L'oncle appartient à la même génération, mais dénué d'autorité et de responsabilité. Quelle n'est pas sa séduction!'[94] If we make use of the deciphering grid with which Alexandre himself decodes his textual reality, we will assume then that Alexandre, the uncle, is the father's copy and his mirror inverse. Does he then hold the power to subvert the system which the father's authority necessarily secures?

Alexandre stands by analogy as what Tournier describes as a 'père-jumeau'.[95] He is the youngest of three brothers and comes

[91] Sigmund Freud, *Three Essays on the Theory of Sexuality*, in *The Standard Edition of the Complete Psychological Works of Sigmund Freud*, 24 vols. (London, 1981), vii. 145. Here Freud writes: 'the future inverts, in the earliest years of their childhood pass through a phase of very intense, but short-lived fixation to a woman (usually their mother) and . . . after leaving this behind, they identify themselves with a woman and take *themselves* as their sexual object'.

[92] Judith Butler, *Gender Trouble: Feminism and the Subversion of Identity* (New York, 1990), 59.

[93] See Lowell Edmunds, *Oedipus: The Ancient Legend and its Later Analogues* (Baltimore, 1985). Edmunds draws principally on Apollodorus and Athenaeus to substantiate his contention that Laius was a pederast, see 7–9.

[94] Tournier, *Le Vent Paraclet*, 254: *The Wind Spirit*, 217 ('The father stands for order, honour, and wisdom. The uncle belongs to the same generation yet is stripped of authority and responsibility. How attractive that makes him!').

[95] Tournier, *Les Météores*, 335: *Gemini*, 277 ('the father-twin').

to mirror both his siblings. When Gustave, the eldest brother, dies, Alexandre will assume his position as chief of refuse collection. Through the death of one brother he will become the 'dandy des gadoues'.[96] While death determines one relation of imaginary twinship, seduction determines the other.[97] Alexandre describes his brother Édouard in alluring terms, saying: 'Jeune, il était beau, il était mieux que beau. Il émanait de lui une force, un goût de la vie, un dynamisme calme qui vous atteignaient en vagues chaleureuses.'[98] Alexandre feels fraternal attraction, but the seduction is not enacted. Alexandre becomes not Édouard's lover but his double, with relation to his nephews the twins Jean and Paul.

Édouard, the father of the twins, is described in specifically non-paternal terms. Jean says of him: 'il n'était pas trop doué pour le rôle paternel. Ami, amant, frère à la rigueur—encore qu'il ait bien peu fait, que je sache, pour se rapprocher de l'oncle Alexandre—mais père . . .'.[99] For the twins, Édouard is an imaginary, not actual (or gay), lover. They fantasize about his seduction, about his fraternity. Paul says: 'Edouard m'aurait compris, suivi, obéi. C'est le père-jumeau qu'il m'aurait fallu. Au lieu que Jean . . .'.[100] The desired seductive father is, ironically, incarnated in the text in the figure of Alexandre, who experiences the pederastic longings the twins seek in vain in

[96] *Les Météores*, 86: *Gemini*, 74 ('the dandy garbage man').

[97] Tournier draws attention to the ambivalence of geminate relations in *Vendredi ou les limbes du Pacifique* (Paris, 1967) where Robinson writes in the last entry in his log-book: 'Des êtres semblables, des jumeaux sont en gestation dans la lune, des gémeaux naissent de la lune. Noués l'un à l'autre, ils remuent doucement, comme s'éveillant d'un séculaire sommeil. Leurs mouvements qui paraissent d'abord de molles et rêveuses caresses prennent un sens tout opposé: ils travaillent maintenant à s'arracher l'un à l'autre' (p. 186: *Friday*, trans. Norman Denny (New York, 1985), 213: 'Two similar beings, twins, are in process of gestation; Gemini are being born on the moon. Linked together they gently move, as though awakening after a centuries-long sleep. Their movements which at first are like soft and drowsy caresses, suddenly change and now they are struggling to detach themselves from one another').

[98] Tournier, *Les Météores*, 32: *Gemini*, 30 ('As a young man he was handsome, he was more than handsome. He radiated a strength, a zest for living, a calm dynamism that came at you in warm waves').

[99] *Les Météores*, 401–2: *Gemini*, 334 ('he was not really cut out for a father's role. Friend, lover, even brother in a pinch—although he did little enough, as far as I know, to keep on close terms with Uncle Alexandre—but father . . .').

[100] *Les Météores*, 335: *Gemini*, 277 ('Edouard would have understood me, followed and obeyed me. He was the father-twin I should have had. Whereas Jean . . .').

their father. Alexandre becomes a mirror image of Édouard. Yet once more the seduction is deferred and the veiled incest of relations between uncle and nephew is forbidden.

Alexandre falls in love with a blond child he names his *ubiquiste*. Since he sees the child repeatedly he begins to be haunted by the idea that the child may have a twin: 'et si mon ubiquiste était deux? S'il s'agissait de deux frères jumeaux, parfaitement indiscernables, mais assez indépendants pourtant pour choisir des occupations, des promenades différentes?'.[101] His suspicion is confirmed when he finds the two boys asleep, in the sand: 'Ils sont là tous les deux, parfaitement indiscernables, enlacés dans un trou de sable.'[102] The union of the twins excludes Alexandre, who must stand apart from 'la proie et la proie de la proie'.[103] Each twin desires the other in the cellular unit and either (or both) is/are desired by Alexandre. The twins' status is underlined when Alexandre realizes that the boys are his nephews. If Édouard is, for his brother, 'la proie', and the twins are the implicit objects of paternal desire, then they are further confirmed as 'la proie' (for Édouard) and 'la proie de la proie' (for Alexandre). It is ironic that Alexandre, who writes, 'Le sexe, c'est la force centrifuge qui vous chasse dehors . . . C'est le sens de la prohibition de l'inceste,'[104] should in fact succumb to 'incestuous' desire for his nephews and should be conditioned always by the desire of fraternal incest.

Alexandre's death ends the scene of imagined and doubly displaced paternal seduction. The stabbing of Alexandre comes as the supremely apt culmination of a life devoted to 'cet acte d'amour et de mort qui mêle une épée et deux hommes'.[105] The text does not allow Alexandre to become the paternal twin of Jean and Paul: his life is curtailed before this fantasy can be put into subversive and substantial practice. The illicit incestuous

---

[101] *Les Météores*, 330: *Gemini*, 273 ('What if my ubiquitous boy were two? Suppose they were two identical twins, quite indistinguishable but yet sufficiently independent from one another to prefer to do different things and go to different places?').

[102] *Les Météores*, 333: *Gemini*, 276 ('There they are, the two of them, utterly indistinguishable, entwined together in a hollow in the sand').

[103] *Les Météores*, 333: *Gemini*, 276 ('the quarry and the quarry's quarry').

[104] *Les Météores*, 73: *Gemini*, 63–4 ('Sex is the centrifugal force that drives you out of doors . . . That is what the ban on incest is all about').

[105] *Les Météores*, 44: *Gemini*, 40 ('that act of love and death which involves two men and a sword').

séduction remains an alluring illusion. The seduction of the 'son' would allow Alexandre to discover and become the twin he desires ardently throughout his life. It is essential to the representation of sexual identity enacted throughout *Les Météores* that this role should never in fact be played, and that Alexandre's desire should never be requited. It is thus, indeed, that Tournier reflects on the formative potential of fiction, and warns against its insidious power, as I shall reveal below.

Alexandre's existence is largely directed by the search for a doubling Other. Tournier writes of him: 'il cherche en gémissant un frère jumeau qui n'existe pas'.[106] Alexandre tries to deny his natural position as 'sans-pareil'. Tournier states: 'il est singulier, étant né sans frère jumeau. Mais il refuse sa condition et revendique des privilèges gémellaires.'[107] Jean and Paul actualize in flesh the state Alexandre desires and attempts to replicate in amorous relations.

This can be seen particularly clearly in his relationship with Daniel, which is structured according to the obsessive paradigm of paternal seduction. In the first place it is Daniel's childlike appearance, '[l]a fragilité enfantine de son cou',[108] 'sa médaille virginale',[109] which attract Alexandre. Later he will outline what he sees as the dangers of pederasty when he says: 'Homosexuel oui, mais pas pédéraste. Déjà avec Dani, j'ai été cruellement puni, il me semble, pour m'en être pris à un âge beaucoup trop tendre.'[110] Yet the text makes explicit that the motivating force behind Alexandre's desire for Daniel is the seductive illusion of fraternity. Alexandre does not find a son in Daniel but rather, and more ambiguously, a 'fils-jumeau'.[111] Desire is seen to enact the crossing of boundaries between father and brother in the equalizing and uterine bed of consummation. Alexandre expresses himself thus: 'Fraternel. Le grand mot est tombé de ma

---

[106] Tournier, *Le Vent Paraclet*, 251–2: *The Wind Spirit*, 214 ('he longs for a twin brother who does not exist').

[107] *Le Vent Paraclet*, 251: *The Wind Spirit*, 214 ('He was born a single individual, without a twin brother, but he refuses to accept his condition and claims the privileges of a twin').

[108] *Les Météores*, 210: *Gemini*, 174 ('The childish fragility of his neck').

[109] *Les Météores*, 210: *Gemini*, 174 ('his medal of the Virgin').

[110] *Les Météores*, 326: *Gemini*, 271 ('I'm a homosexual, yes, but not a pederast. Already, with Dani, I feel that I have been cruelly punished for falling for someone much too young').

[111] *Les Météores*, 216: *Gemini*, 179 ('my twin son').

plume. Car si le lit est le ventre maternel, l'homme qui vient, dénaissant, m'y rejoindre ne peut être que mon frère. Frère jumeau, s'entend. Et tel est bien le sens profond de mon amour pour Daniel, épuré par les bras d'Eustache, apitoyé par mon petitchagrin.'[112]

The elision of the difference of generation rejuvenates Alexandre and revivifies for him the emotive image of himself as child. Alexandre is stirred by memories of his own child-hood vulnerability. These coalesce with the ambiguous and arousing *pitié* provoked by Daniel. Offering a definition of the peculiar erotic charge of this emotion, Alexandre claims: 'la pitié est la forme vicieuse de l'amour'.[113] Alexandre is drawn to what touches him, painfully. The culmination of his desire for Daniel comes in a horrifying scenario of mutilation where Alexandre sees his young lover's body eaten away before his eyes.

As we have seen, Paul's final trauma is imaged in terms of a harrowing and crucifixion. His bodily disintegration is prefigured in the novel in the death of Daniel. Alexandre sees his body: 'une forme humaine, étendue sur le ventre, les bras en croix'.[114] Where I have claimed previously that Paul lives out and lives through a fleshed experience of the 'corps morcelé', Tournier's choice of vocabulary may lead us to suggest that Lacan's imagery of mutilation subtends the evocation of Daniel's macabre torment. Alexandre narrates, with a bizarre lucidity, 'Je m'absorbe dans la contemplation de ce pauvre mannequin désarticulé qui n'a plus d'humain que l'obscénité des cadavres.'[115] But it is not the image of the mannequin alone which recalls Lacan's drama (and trauma) of the formation of the ego. In a following chapter, Alexandre is seen significantly to question: 'Suis-je encore vivant? Ce que j'ai identifié à Miramas comme le corps déchiqueté de Dani, n'était-ce pas en vérité mon

[112] *Les Météores*, 215: *Gemini*, 178 ('Fraternal. The big word slipped from my pen. For if the bed is the mother's womb, the man who comes, becoming unborn, to join me there can only be my brother. My twin brother, of course. And that is really what my love for Daniel is all about, purged by Eustache's arms, moved to pity by my little sorrow').

[113] *Les Météores*, 191: *Gemini*, 160 ('pity is the vicious form of love').

[114] *Les Météores*, 261: *Gemini*, 217 ('a human form, stretched on its face with outflung arms').

[115] *Les Météores*, 263: *Gemini*, 218 ('I stand lost in contemplation of the poor disjointed puppet which has no more humanity now than the obscenity of dead bodies').

propre cadavre rendu méconnaissable par les dents de la lune et les becs du soleil?'[116]

Alexandre identifies himself with the disarticulated image of his lover's body. His identity is seen to be dependent on the mirroring relation which is his perpetual erotic obsession. The text itself enacts its own internal mirroring as Paul's experience of dissociation through loss is prefigured in Alexandre's own inability or unwillingness to dissociate self and Other. With relation to Alexandre, Tournier's text appears unequivocal in its denial of the possibility of secure mirroring relations, and of the securing of identity in the replication of an image. *Les Météores* may be seen to explore the creation and dissociation of identity through identification. Alexandre may be seen to identify in his nephews' twinship an ultimate of desiring reciprocity to which he painfully desires to accede. The text is particularly shattering firstly in its undermining of any possibility of finding the mirroring Other and replicating geminate security, and secondly in its insistent rupture of the very security it takes as obsessive paradigm and alluring ideal. And it is in this way, I will argue, that Tournier creates a peculiarly cautionary tale for his reader.

• *Reflecting Reading*

We may be led to question here whether Alexandre's desiring encounters may be seen to reflect upon the position of the external reader. What are the implications, indeed, of the text's use of Alexandre as failed lover, reading hero, and decoder of sexual identities?

Here it may be useful to pursue a comparison between *Les Météores* and *Un Amour de Swann*. Proust's text appears to be used by Tournier as a conscious intertext. Alexandre shares, indeed, Swann's desire to deny distinctions between psychical reality and material reality, between representations and animate objects of desire. Like Swann in love with Odette, for example, Alexandre desires an Arab boy precisely because he

[116] *Les Météores*, 283–4: *Gemini*, 236 ('Am I still alive? Was the thing that I identified at Miramas as Dani's torn body not in truth my own corpse made unrecognizable by the moon's teeth and the sun's beaks?').

gives the illusion of existing as a Murillo painting in corporeal form. Alexandre is revealed to be prey to the delusion that he has conjured up the child and he is shown to be concerned to test the child's physical reality.[117] The force of the scene derives from Alexandre's belief that an image has been fleshed out in three dimensions. Claiming agency and power he says: 'J'ai fait descendre un jeune garçon d'un tableau de la Pinacothèque de Munich, et il est là, chaud et loqueteux à côté de moi.'[118]

As I have been demonstrating, unlike Paul, for whom his drama and trauma are written in the flesh, Alexandre finds his compulsions fleshed in corporeal forms. In a sense his reading and engagement with fictions forms the world he perceives around him. This, of course, has particular implications for the external reader of the text, who may in some senses be encouraged to identify with Alexandre. Does Tournier's text require from its readers the belief in illusion betrayed in the figure of Alexandre?

Alexandre's ultimate object of desire, as we have seen, is the twin he imagines will become his double, his 'fils-jumeau'. The twin is shown significantly to be a reader: 'Il lisait. Extraordinaire acuité de ses traits, finement tirés et comme sculptés au rasoir. Lire—et peut-être mieux encore, déchiffrer, décrypter—telle paraît être la fonction naturelle de ce visage dont l'expression habituelle est une attention calme, studieuse.'[119] A complex play of mirroring is thus initiated. In intertextual terms Tournier underlines how far his text may be seen to mirror Proust's tale of displaced aesthetic desires. Making reference to the child's illusory ubiquity, Alexandre questions all too explicitly: 'Ce garçon qui paraît échapper à l'espace, vit-il également hors du temps?'[120] The concern with time and space evidently draws the reader's attention to the Proustian echoes of the passage. The text also signals the incongruity of Alexandre's

[117] *Les Météores*, 324: *Gemini*, 269.

[118] *Les Météores*, 324: *Gemini*, 269 ('I had conjured a boy out of a picture in the Munich Pinakotek and he was there, warm and ragged, beside me').

[119] *Les Météores*, 327: *Gemini*, 271–2 ('He was reading. His features were extraordinarily sharp and fine-drawn, as though carved with a razor. Reading—and even more perhaps deciphering, decoding—would seem to come naturally to that face with its habitual expression of calm, studious concentration').

[120] *Les Météores*, 327: *Gemini*, 272 ('Can this boy, who seems not to be bound by space, exist equally outside time?').

quasi-incestuous desire as he laments his attraction to 'ce garçon qui n'est pas mon type'.[121] Alexandre finds himself placed in this instance in the text, and in this specific and culminating erotic scenario, as double of Swann. It might be argued that Proust's text stands momentarily as father and double of *Les Météores*. The paradigm of the 'père-jumeau' is realized then in textual, not sexual, terms. Tournier's texts might be seen to look towards a rereading of intra-poetic relationships in terms of doubling and seduction, rather than difference and contest, as outlined in Harold Bloom's *The Anxiety of Influence*. While this may go some way towards increasing our understanding of, what has seemed to some, Tournier's rather over-indulgent use of intertextuality, what bearing may this compulsion with reflection and replication in desire have upon the role of the reader?

To return to the scenario where Alexandre finds his last, elusive object of desire: what further patterns of doubling and reflection may be perceived? I have argued that Alexandre may seek in the child reading his double and juvenile Other. But what of the reader? If the reader is seen as double of Alexandre, then does the text not beg the question: who is the model, who the copy, and who the 'copie de la copie'? Further, what, we might wonder, are the implications for the reader of the emphatic suggestion that mirroring relations fail, that they undo rather than uphold any security of identity since they are fated by the rupture afforded necessarily by difference and alterity? Alexandre, after all, dies in a quasi-suicidal act very soon after he has discovered the love-object from whom he must necessarily be divided and whom he has always implicitly desired. The failure in desiring relations between Jean and Paul themselves is reflected indeed at one remove in the failure of their uncle's desire for them.

Tournier's texts leave his protagonists divided, it seems, between death and delusion. This is of course the very literal fate of Paul Surin. It would appear that Tournier takes as his central and compelling subject in many of his fictions the drama of identity formation, yet what seems to interest him precisely is the possibility of malfunction, distortion, and even, we might

---

[121] *Les Météores*, 332: *Gemini*, 275 ('this boy who was not my type').

argue, distress. What we need to question is whether the mal-functioning in the formation of identity revealed in these texts is unequivocally pathological, or whether it becomes the means by which, as Tournier himself claims, he comes to question and challenge the normative function of such regulatory systems as the psychoanalytic academy and the Catholic Church. The subversive intent behind Tournier's fictions is perhaps unques-tionable. In this sense his fictions may be seen admirably, in Butler's terms, to challenge the power of the regulatory matrices by which our society may be seen to be constructed and policed. But can Tournier's texts be seen to have further political import and impact? Does Tournier, whose texts so emphatically offer a subversive parody of the system-building we might argue is central to the policing of social and sexual identities, conceive of a possible move, as outlined by Butler, from parody to politics?

It seems necessary to argue, I think, that these texts work paradoxically. In the first place Tournier may be seen to reflect and reveal the formative power of fiction. His characters com-pulsively map out their lives with reference to a series of textual precedents. Their trajectories may diverge from their pre-in-scribed paths, but this is seen disturbingly in each case not to shake their faith in the wisdom of following textual precedents and putting fictions into practice, but rather to work instead to undo their very identity and identify a necessary fracture in the construction of the self. Whilst Tournier would appear to dem-onstrate the dangers of identification with a fiction in the con-struction of the self, he may be seen to present a cautionary tale to his reader. Yet the reader is by no means free to disengage from the text itself, and this is perhaps what may be seen to be most disturbing about Tournier's fiction. By means of the construction of characters who are themselves engaged in a drama of decoding, by the careful placing of signs which them-selves can be read in a manner seductively congruent with the deciphering grids constructed by the characters within the texts, Tournier, like Proust, allows his readers no privileges over the protagonists with whom they are led to identify. The reader is, I suggest, necessarily involved in a formative mirroring rela-tion, to the very dangers of which the text itself may be seen to testify.

Such, then, is the paradox of Tournier's fiction. But how further may this ambivalent postulation of formative power be related to the question of the regulatory matrix of heterosexuality within and against which I have been working in this study? Here I would argue, following Tournier himself it seems, that the placing, for example, of a flamboyantly queer character within *Les Météores* is in itself a far from subversive or challenging act. Even placing Alexandre as desiring subject in certain erotic scenarios does little other than offer the straight reader the possibility of crossing sexual identifications for a couple of chapters and enjoying thus Alexandre's engagement with his prey and 'la proie de la proie'. Where Tournier's text may be seen to offer some more disruptive charge, however, is in its focus on the formation of identity. In the thematics of his texts Tournier challenges the possibility of securing identity through an essentially deceptive relation of mirroring. If at all, identity is to be located, it seems, in the very experience of harrowing, dislocation, and bodily fragmentation. This thematic obsession is played further, as I have been arguing, on a metatextual level and determines the nature of the engagement between text and reader.

In Tournier's texts social and sexual identities are shown to be fictive, constructed, and precarious. It is in this sense that his texts may be seen, in keeping with Butler's propositions, to show up the constructed status of what has been seen to be the heterosexual original and norm. These texts lay emphasis on the fragility and fallibility of the process of the construction of identity, undermining thus the illusory power if not the possible seduction of the perfect performance of a heterosexual identity. Tournier's fictions engage the reader in a disturbing performance of the imperfections and impossibilities of identity formation. It is thus that they themselves may be seen to pose their challenge to the heterosexual matrix by prescribing a reading encounter which, regardless of the sexual identification of the reader him/herself, will necessarily be shattering, dislocating, and delusory. Tournier may be said to seek to create in his novels his own queer readers, yet his conclusions as to their fate would appear to undermine the celebration of subversive power to be found in Butler's texts.

Perhaps this ultimate pessimism, this refusal to choose between death and delusion, serves to explain Tournier's apparent fear of the readers he has sought to construct. His words before Cerisy testify to the tenuous nature of the writer's identity as his authority and integrity are not secured but undermined in failed mirroring relations with his reader. Fear, betrayal, and despair haunt relations between self and Other in Tournier's texts. He seeks both signification and significance through pain, making his reader his victim, and bearing witness, it seems, to the sinister motto: 'les signes ont besoin de la chair pour se manifester.'[122]

[122] Tournier, *Le Roi des Aulnes*, 109: *The Erl-King*, 89 ('signs need flesh to make themselves manifest').

6

'Mon histoire de Lol V. Stein': Duras, Reading, and Amnesia

> I let her go, I let her go
> Diminished and flat, as after radical surgery
> How your bad dreams possess and endow me
>
> (Sylvia Plath, 'Elm')

> There is, in each survivor, an imperative need to *tell* and thus to come to *know* one's story, unimpeded by ghosts from the past
>
> (Shoshana Felman and Dori Laub, *Testimony: Crises of Witnessing in Literature, Psychoanalysis and History*)

• *'Au ras de la maladie'*

In her essay 'La Maladie de la douleur: Duras', Julia Kristeva writes: 'il ne faut pas donner les livres de Duras aux lecteurs et lectrices fragiles'.[1] How, we might wonder, may the fragile reader become a victim of Duras's texts? Is it possible, indeed, that Duras's texts work to undermine the reader's certainty and sanity, forming, rather than reflecting, the trauma of non-cathartic identification Kristeva has sought to analyse? And might this be understood in positive rather than negative terms?

Kristeva's argument works to suggest that Duras's texts confront her readers with madness and horror, in unspeakable intimacy. She writes: 'les textes apprivoisent la maladie de la mort, ils font un avec elle, ils y sont de plein-pied, sans distance

---

[1] Julia Kristeva, 'La Maladie de la douleur: Duras', in *Soleil noir: Dépression et mélancolie* (Paris, 1987), 227–65: 235: 'The Malady of Grief: Duras', in *Black Sun: Depression and Melancholia*, trans. Leon S. Roudiez (New York, 1990), 219–59: 227 ('Duras's books should not be put into the hands of oversensitive readers').

et sans échappée. Aucune purification ne nous attend à la sortie de ces romans au ras de la maladie.'[2] In analysing the strategies by which Duras's texts may seem to achieve their task of confronting the reader, Kristeva favours a vocabulary of seduction and enchantment. She appears to claim for Duras's texts a malign force and intent; as she suggests: 'Sans catharsis, cette littérature rencontre, reconnaît, mais aussi propage le mal qui la mobilise'.[3] Duras's fiction is endowed, it seems, with the power to contaminate its readers. Kristeva suggests, indeed, that '[cette littérature] est l'envers du discours clinique—tout près de lui, mais jouissant des bénéfices secondaires de la maladie, elle la cultive et l'apprivoise sans jamais l'épuiser'.[4] Kristeva might be seen to claim for Duras's texts a troublingly formative power, which she then moves to disclaim as disintegrative, disruptive, and plainly dangerous.

Kristeva works, essentially, within a normative framework. Her analysis of Duras reveals how very integrally and intimately Duras's texts may be seen to trouble the drama of identity formation. This leads Kristeva to a revelatory diagnosis of the 'maladie' reflected in Duras's texts and infecting their readers. What her study might be seen to deny, or repress, however, is any substantial threat this 'maladie' might pose to our understanding of the veracity and stability of theories of the assumption of identity through identification. It is in these terms, I will argue, that Duras's texts are most radical, and pose their most cogent threat to the normative and curative power of clinical discourse.

In order to make this reading of Duras, I will concentrate primarily on her novel *Le Ravissement de Lol V. Stein*, published in 1964, and paradoxically located as a focal point in Duras's examination of passion and analysis, desire, insanity, and obsessive re-creation.[5] Duras herself said of the novel, here

---

[2] 'La Maladie de la douleur', 235: 'The Malady of Grief', 227–8 ('the texts domesticate the malady of death, they fuse with it, are on the same level with it, without either distance or perspective. There is no purification in store for us at the conclusion of these novels written on the brink of illness').

[3] 'La Maladie de la douleur', 237 'The Malady of Grief', 229 ('Lacking catharsis, such a literature encounters, recognizes, but also spreads the pain that summons it').

[4] 'La Maladie de la douleur', 237 'The Malady of Grief', 229 ('[this literature] is the reverse of clinical discourse—very close to it, but as it enjoys the illness' secondary benefits cultivates and tames it without ever exhausting it').

[5] Marguerite Duras, *Le Ravissement de Lol V. Stein* (Paris, 1964): *The Ravishing of Lol Stein*, trans. Richard Seaver (New York, 1986).

designated only by the name of its protagonist: 'Lol V. Stein, c'est ce que vous en faites, ça n'existe pas autrement, je crois que je viens de dire quelque chose là sur elle.'[6] Duras herself may be seen to collaborate in the framing of her novel as a case history, whose subject and heroine becomes synonymous with the complex the text itself may seek to analyse. Yet Duras works to undermine, too, any possibility of finite analysis or knowledge within the text. Her own remarks are suitably tenuous, dissolving any fixed interpretation the reader may have salvaged.

Duras denies any grasp on her character or her text, claiming instead: 'D'habitude, quand je fais un livre, je sais à peu près ce que j'ai fait, j'en suis quand même un peu le lecteur ... Là non. Quand j'ai eu fait Lol V. Stein, ça m'a totalement échappé.'[7] The reader becomes aware of how far Duras's words only ever reflect and displace the drama of her text, never attempting to offer further insight. Tatiana, the novel's central female figure engaged in the analysis of Lol, reveals early in the course of the narrative: 'au collège on se la disputait bien qu'elle vous fuît dans les mains comme l'eau'.[8] Duras herself claims to have no privileged knowledge of Lol. She constructs herself as author engaged in this teasing, tenuous game of love of Lol. She says in interview with Xavière Gauthier, with a characteristic tone of helplessness: 'Il y a une chose troublante, c'est que je l'aime infiniment, cette Lol V. Stein, et je peux pas m'en débarrasser. Elle a pour moi une ... une sorte de grâce inépuisable.'[9] This desire is seen to surpass the text itself and to be generative of further fictions; as Duras comments: 'Mes films et mes livres sont des histoires d'amour avec elle depuis des années.'[10]

---

[6] Marguerite Duras and Michelle Porte, *Les Lieux de Marguerite Duras* (Paris, 1977), 101 ('Lol V. Stein is what you make of it, it doesn't exist in any other way, I think I've just said something about her there').

[7] Ibid. 99–100 ('Usually when I write a book, I know just about what I've done, even so I am in some ways its reader ... But it wasn't like that with this one. When I had created Lol V. Stein, it entirely escaped me').

[8] Duras, *Le Ravissement de Lol V. Stein*, 13: *The Ravishing of Lol Stein*, 3 ('they vied for her affection at school—although she slipped through their hands like water').

[9] Marguerite Duras and Xavière Gauthier, *Les Parleuses* (Paris, 1974), 160 ('There's something troubling: I love her inifinitely much this Lol V. Stein, and I can't rid myself of her. For me she has a ... a sort of undying charm').

[10] Duras and Porte, *Les Lieux de Marguerite Duras*, 69 ('My films and my books have been love stories with her for many years').

My interest, evidently, is in how the reader of the text may find him/herself implicated and insinuated in the performance of these 'histoires d'amour'. How far does the reading of the text necessitate the creation of the reader's own 'histoire de Lol V. Stein'? How far does this become a fragile, unending, and despairing task? In order to pursue these questions, and their interrelation with the questions of binary gender positions and of the regulatory matrix of heterosexuality as examined through the course of this study, I will pursue a reading of *Le Ravissement de Lol V. Stein* as text which undoes certainty and reason. I will look first at the questions of gender, desire, and narrative position the text inevitably raises, before going on to look at relations between doubling and identity, and finally at the necessary attack on interpretation the text poses in its suicidal refusal of closure. It will be my intention to analyse thus the reader's troubled encounter with a text which obsessively inscribes and prefigures 'la fin sans fin, le commencement sans fin de Lol V. Stein'.[11]

• *The Female Reader*

Duras places at the start of Lol's story a distressing scene of closure and abandonment to which the text incessantly returns. The interpretation of this scene appears to determine the text as a whole, or at least this appears to be the wish of its intradiegetic narrator. *Le Ravissement de Lol V. Stein* is, importantly, a first-person narrative: Lol's story is told by a 'je' whom we discover, approximately one-third of the way into the novel, to be one of the characters, Jacques Hold. The text makes it clear that Jacques is telling his own tale of Lol, which he carefully orchestrates. He even admits to not knowing Lol at the time of her abandonment at T. Beach. He tells us that his narration will be mingled with 'ce que j'invente sur la nuit du Casino de T. Beach'[12] and he shows that it will be his own 'histoire de Lol V. Stein' written to convince the reader, as he

---

[11] Duras, *Le Ravissement de Lol V. Stein*, 184: *The Ravishing of Lol Stein*, 175 ('the endless end, the endless beginning of Lol Stein').

[12] *Le Ravissement de Lol V. Stein*, 14: *The Ravishing of Lol Stein*, 4 ('what I have been able to imagine about that night at the Town Beach Casino').

says, of 'l'écrasante actualité de cette femme dans ma vie'.[13] From its very opening, then, Duras draws both desire and doubt into the narrative, showing that Jacques's desire for Lol is the pre-condition for his assumption of subject position within the text, yet also the very factor which will undermine the stability of this position and the security of the reader's faith in the veracity of his narrative. Jacques Hold is placed not to be an unbiased witness to Lol's life. His text does not acquire the status of testimony but exists, rather, between fantasy and confession, becoming the means to a wish-fulfilling construction of a tenuous identity. His claiming of the narrative allows Jacques Hold, so it seems, to perform a role which defines him as determining agent in Lol's life. Yet his bid to be the author of her destiny fails, undermined as we will see, by the conflictual function of the female decoder.

Jacques Hold is seen to read the night at the Casino in T. Beach as the first moment when Lol enters his destiny. He claims: 'Je vais donc la chercher, je la prends, là où je crois devoir le faire, au moment où elle me paraît commencer à bouger pour venir à ma rencontre.'[14] Duras underlines how far the self, in this case Jacques, is constructed in illusory relation to the Other. Lol becomes, in effect, the guarantor of Jacques's identity as author. The scene of closure and ending at T. Beach is re-viewed conversely as an opening, and as a formative scenario in the formation of the identity of Jacques Hold. This identity is revealed, however, to be in its origins fragile since Jacques lacks knowledge of the first moments when Lol enters his destiny. His narrative is undermined by his failure to witness the events he describes. Jacques Hold is seen to question, for example, the very first moment when Anne-Marie Stretter and Michael Richardson notice each other, the first sign of Lol's rejection: 'Avait-elle regardé Michael Richardson en passant? L'avait-elle balayé de ce non-regard qu'elle promenait sur le bal? C'était impossible de le savoir, c'est impossible de

---

[13] Le Ravissement de Lol V. Stein, 14: The Ravishing of Lol Stein, 4 ('the overwhelming actuality of this woman in my life').

[14] Le Ravissement de Lol V. Stein, 14: The Ravishing of Lol Stein, 4–5 ('I am therefore going to look for her, I shall pick her up at that moment in time which seems most appropriate, at that moment when it seems to me she first began to stir, to come toward me').

savoir quand, par conséquent, commence mon histoire de Lol V. Stein.'[15]

It might be argued that Duras tantalizes her reader with a refusal to focus. She allows both unknowability and, as we shall see below, amnesia, to become dispersive agents of the narrative, which necessarily guarantee its perpetual, desired unintelligibility. Duras works thus to attack stable interpretation. What is particularly interesting is how far this fallibility of interpretative prowess on the part of both the protagonists and the external reader is seen to have a disruptive bearing on the integrity of identity.

As we have seen, the stability of Jacques Hold's story is undermined by his avowed partiality and his tentative search for plausibility. We may well wish as readers to endorse the words of Lacan, who suggests in his celebrated reading of the text that Jacques is not so much 'la voix du récit': 'bien plutôt est-il son angoisse'.[16] It is possible to argue that Duras seeks thus to dismantle the authority of the masculine subject position and undermine the autocratic male 'I' who might seek to construct and regulate the (re)presentation of an elusive female object of desire. Martha Noel Evans argues convincingly, for example, 'Duras uses this male narrator as a kind of front: first to present and explore the characteristics of traditional male narrative and then to dramatize the undoing of that very narrative.'[17] While I would agree that such a strategy appears to be at work in *Le Ravissement de Lol V. Stein*, I think it could be argued that many critics are too ready to privilege the role of Jacques Hold as interpreter and inventor of Lol's tale. This leads to a reading of the text which reveals Jacques's failure to remain holder of the signifier (as Sharon Willis puts it). Yet it shows him defeated primarily by the absences and incoherencies in his narrative, and

[15] *Le Ravissement de Lol V. Stein*, 16. *The Ravishing of Lol Stein*, 6 ('Had she looked at Michael Richardson as she passed by? Had this non-look of hers swept over him as it took in the ballroom? It was impossible to tell, it is therefore impossible to know when my story of Lol Stein begins').

[16] Jacques Lacan, 'Hommage fait à Marguerite Duras du ravissement de Lol V. Stein', in *Marguerite Duras* (Paris, 1975), 93–9: 94 ('he is much more its anxiety'). For an important and instructive reading of Lacan's essay on Duras, seè Leslie Hill, *Marguerite Duras: Apocalyptic Desires* (London, 1993), 64–73.

[17] Martha Noel Evans, 'Marguerite Duras: The Whore', in *Masks of Tradition: Women and the Politics of Writing in Twentieth-Century France* (Ithaca, NY, 1987), 123–56: 125.

by Lol's perpetual ability to elude definition. Duras may well attack traditional male narrative thus, but this is not the only threat to stable gender positions posed by her text.

While Jacques Hold's role is undeniably important to the text, an interpretation of the novel as dependent on the couple formed by Jacques Hold and Lol V. Stein, on 'his need to dominate and possess Lol',[18] works to deny the necessarily triangular nature of relations between the characters and effectively to minimize the role of Tatiana Karl in the imagining and constructing of an 'histoire de Lol V. Stein'. Crucially, it seems, her witnessing of Lol pre-dates and surpasses that of Jacques Hold. Tatiana is revealed at the outset to be a physical presence in Lol's story and the protagonist best placed to mediate between lived experience and its placing in narrative.

Most importantly, Tatiana is with Lol on the formative evening at the casino in T. Beach. She is Lol's comforter in her moment of abandonment. She is shown to shadow Lol at the ball, to wait with her behind green plants and stroke her hand in a gesture of tenderness. This physical intimacy between Lol and Tatiana, the privileging of language over touch in their relations, is interwoven as a thread throughout the novel. *Le Ravissement de Lol V. Stein* opens with an image of Lol and Tatiana dancing together.[19] As they dance to tunes from a radio in a neighbouring building, the text initiates the motif of the dance with its exchange of partners, which creates a replicated pattern of displacement.

In interview with Xavière Gauthier, Duras speaks of her film *Nathalie Granger*, a film about two women. Gauthier questions her about what she perceives as 'cette complicité, entente entre les deux femmes'[20] as represented in the film. Duras comments: 'C'est deux mouvements, quelquefois ça se touche. Les deux mouvements se touchent et puis se séparent, c'est comme une seule et même personne, voyez.'[21] Duras's comments may offer some insight into the focus on relations between Lol and Tatiana in the text. Their intimacy may introduce images of female

---

[18] Ibid. 139.

[19] Duras, *Le Ravissement de Lol V. Stein*, 11: *The Ravishing of Lol Stein*, 2.

[20] Duras and Gauthier, *Les Parleuses*, 73 ('this complicity, harmony between the two women').

[21] Ibid. 74 ('They are two movements, sometimes they come together. The two movements come together and then separate, it's like one single person, you see').

homoeroticism into the text, possibly indicative of the wish-fulfilling fantasy of the male narrator. Yet it may also allow the text to analyse further a seemingly seductive merging of identities. Lol is seen to stroke Tatiana's hair, to approach her, and, as the text reveals, 'elle l'enlace légèrement',[22] as Jacques Hold and the reader hear 'leurs voix entrelacées, tendres'.[23] Tatiana is shown to know a physical closeness with Lol, an intuitive intimacy, ever denied Jacques Hold despite Lol's seduction of him and his ever iterated attempts to become her author.

Tatiana's reading of Lol is lent authority, then, by her privileged access to both her friend's trauma and her friend's body. The reader gradually becomes aware that Jacques's fragile position as narrator is dependent, up to a certain point, on what Tatiana has told him. Yet she works not to authenticate but to destabilize his narrative. Where Jacques Hold takes control of the text from its opening, he requires Tatiana as informed interlocutor. The 'histoire de Lol V. Stein' created is framed in part as a lovers' dialogue. Tatiana tells Jacques of her childhood with Lol: 'Elles, on les laissait faire, dit Tatiana, elles étaient charmantes.'[24] Not only does Tatiana produce the images projected in Jacques's fantasies, she is also shown to undo his story. Jacques Hold asserts, troublingly: 'Tatiana ne croit pas au rôle prépondérant de ce fameux bal de T. Beach dans la maladie de Lol V. Stein.'[25] Where one purpose of the text appears to be to posit the ballroom scene as originary, Tatiana privileges indeterminacy over the specific teleology Jacques favours. Tatiana's own statements about Lol are, appropriately, tentative: 'Au collège, dit-elle, et elle n'était pas la seule à le penser, il manquait déjà quelque chose à Lol pour être—elle dit: là.'[26]

[22] Duras, *Le Ravissement de Lol V. Stein*, 92: *The Ravishing of Lol Stein*, 83 ('[she] puts her arm around her lightly').

[23] *Le Ravissement de Lol V. Stein*, 92: *The Ravishing of Lol Stein*, 83 ('their voices, interwoven, tender').

[24] *Le Ravissement de Lol V. Stein*, 11: *The Ravishing of Lol Stein*, 2 ('And they knew how to get their way too, Tatiana said, they were a beguiling pair').

[25] *Le Ravissement de Lol V. Stein*, 12: *The Ravishing of Lol Stein*, 2 ('Tatiana does not believe that this fabled Town Beach Ball was so overwhelmingly responsible for Lol Stein's illness').

[26] *Le Ravissement de Lol V. Stein*, 12: *The Ravishing of Lol Stein*, 3 ('She says that in school—and she wasn't the only person to think so—there was already something lacking in Lol, something which kept her from being, in Tatiana's words, "there"').

It is important to recognize here how far the text troubles the origins of Lol's 'maladie', her madness, her absence. While Jacques privileges an 'histoire de Lol V. Stein' which locates her trauma, and in so doing allows at least for the tentative plausibility of a cure through retelling and re-enactment, *Le Ravissement de Lol V. Stein* as text exceeding the control of its narrator allows for a traumatic reckoning with the possibility that Jacques is deluded and that Lol's 'maladie' radically predates his temporal construction. Tatiana's function in the text appears to be to unsettle conviction in a logical relation between trauma and cure, between narrative and knowledge. The text exists thus as a dispute over an ever elusive Lol. Tatiana's reading of Lol as ever decentred and absent is rejected by Jacques, but it necessitates the rejection of his certainty as well. He states simply: 'Je ne crois plus rien de ce que dit Tatiana, je ne suis convaincu de rien.'[27]

What, then, is the place of the external reader in this drama of desire and decoding? I would argue that the reader engaged in a quest for knowledge of the text is, as we have seen Duras suggest, engaged necessarily in a search for knowledge of Lol V. Stein. We are presented with two undecidable positions. Duras offers the possibility of identification with a male desiring subject: her text would appear to offer a specular security of identity to a privileged male reader. Yet a reader who engages in identification with Jacques Hold rapidly becomes aware that his subject position affords none of the privileges of stability, certainty, and knowledge conventionally awarded the male viewer within the protective structures of the regulatory matrix of heterosexuality. Jacques's desire for Lol is hazardous, his identity as a result precarious, and his narrative crosscut with assertions of knowledge which are then troublingly undermined.

Does the text then offer the alternative option of identification with the female 'reader' Tatiana Karl, who enjoys at least access to knowledge of Lol? This position again becomes tenuous and disturbing as a result, I shall argue, of the very merging of identities which has been seen to place Tatiana as a privileged witness.

[27] *Le Ravissement de Lol V. Stein*, 14: *The Ravishing of Lol Stein*, 4 ('I no longer believe a word Tatiana says. I'm convinced of absolutely nothing').

• *Loving Tatiana*

The text shows Lol as one of those 'femmes au cœur déchiré',[28] loved for her absence and indifference by the man she later marries, for 'cette virtualité constante et silencieuse qu'il nommait sa douceur, la douceur de sa femme'.[29] Lol creates a world of perfect order, of 'ordre glacé'.[30] She lives within 'l'échafaudage de son ordre',[31] her life becomes 'la célébration de cet ordre si rigoureux qu'elle seule avait la force et le savoir de faire régner'.[32] Her behaviour is obsessive; the text stresses that she is playing a role: 'Lol imitait, mais qui?'[33] It is important that the act of imitation precedes the (re)discovery of a model to copy. Lol is shown to live within the confines of a compulsive pattern of replication; her identity is constantly reperformed, but she derives from this no integrity, only the comfort of ritual repetition.

In the midst of the structures and immobility of her adult life Lol is seen to re(-)cover the stage of her childhood. In this pattern of repetition, 'elle prit l'habitude de se promener dans la ville de son enfance'.[34] Lol is shown by Jacques Hold to embark on a journey of re-creation and commemoration. What the reader may question is whether this effectively allows her to reread her past unimpeded by the phantom presence of her former self, or whether indeed she is perpetually trapped in a spiralling drama of re-enactment.

Lol begins to fit material reality to the patterns of her psychical reality; she begins to gain some access to the language and names of the past: 'Alors, seulement, croit-elle, depuis des

[28] *Le Ravissement de Lol V. Stein*, 30: *The Ravishing of Lol Stein*, 20 ('women whose hearts had been broken').

[29] *Le Ravissement de Lol V. Stein*, 33: *The Ravishing of Lol Stein*, 24 ('this constant, silent promise of something different which he called her gentleness, the gentleness of his wife').

[30] *Le Ravissement de Lol V. Stein*, 35: *The Ravishing of Lol Stein*, 25 ('icy order').

[31] *Le Ravissement de Lol V. Stein*, 43: *The Ravishing of Lol Stein*, 33–4 ('her fixed routine').

[32] *Le Ravissement de Lol V. Stein*, 44: *The Ravishing of Lol Stein*, 35 ('the observance of that strict order that she alone had the strength and ability to impose').

[33] *Le Ravissement de Lol V. Stein*, 34: *The Ravishing of Lol Stein*, 24 ('Lol was imitating someone, but who?').

[34] *Le Ravissement de Lol V. Stein*, 36: *The Ravishing of Lol Stein*, 26 ('she got into the habit of taking walks through this town where she had grown up').

semaines qu'il flottait, ça et là, loin, le nom est là: Tatiana Karl.'[35] In her repeating trajectories Lol re-views Tatiana, watches her meet a lover, and follows them to a hotel. Lol's obsessional observation of the scene is doubly motivated: not only does she recognize Tatiana but, further, she recognizes the hotel. As the text informs the reader: 'Lol connaît cet hôtel pour y être allée dans sa jeunesse avec Michael Richardson';[36] and it was there indeed that Michael Richardson declared his love for her.[37] By following Tatiana's lead Lol has walked back into the scenario of her own failed passion. Tatiana once again marks the transition between experience and its fictionalization as she and her lover come to reincarnate and dramatize Lol's memories of her encounter with Michael Richardson.

Lol becomes obsessed now with refinding Tatiana Karl: it is indeed the search for Tatiana that attracts Lol. She seeks again to circle round her past history.[38] Tatiana becomes a focus for her imaginings and for the fragile mental structures she creates. Before Lol lets herself encounter Tatiana once more, 'Tatiana Karl lui est devenue en peu de jours si chère que si sa tentative allait échouer, si elle allait ne pas la revoir, la ville deviendrait irrespirable, mortelle.'[39] Locating Tatiana is motivated, it seems, by the avoidance of suicide, of the collapse of identity. Tatiana is placed to ensure survival and mirroring identity. Yet her ability or desire to fulfil this role is largely drawn into question within the text.

When the desired encounter between Lol and Tatiana takes place, Tatiana quite literally questions rather than restores Lol's identity. She says: 'Non, mais c'est Lol? Je ne me trompe pas?'[40]

---

[35] *Le Ravissement de Lol V. Stein*, 58: *The Ravishing of Lol Stein*, 50 ('Then, and only then, she believes, the name that had been hovering on the edge of her consciousness for weeks was there: Tatiana Karl').

[36] *Le Ravissement de Lol V. Stein*, 61: *The Ravishing of Lol Stein*, 52 ('Lol remembers this hotel from the times she went there as a young girl with Michael Richardson').

[37] *Le Ravissement de Lol V. Stein*, 61: *The Ravishing of Lol Stein*, 52.

[38] *Le Ravissement de Lol V. Stein*, 68: *The Ravishing of Lol Stein*, 60.

[39] *Le Ravissement de Lol V. Stein*, 71: *The Ravishing of Lol Stein*, 62 ('In the course of the past few days, Tatiana Karl has become so dear to her that, if her attempt were to fail, if she were not able to see her again, the town would become unlivable, stifling and deadly').

[40] *Le Ravissement de Lol V. Stein*, 73: *The Ravishing of Lol Stein*, 64 ('But, is it Lol! I'm not mistaken?').

Lol then announces herself in the third person. The text maintains a constant and troubling play of doubt in relations between Lol and Tatiana. The reader is forever caught in
contradictions. Lol, remembering or fantasizing her friendship
with Tatiana, speaks of a photograph she has found in her attic.
In this photograph they stand hand in hand, in their school
uniform.[41] Where, in *L'Amant*, Duras alludes to photographs
which are absent since they have never been taken, in *Le
Ravissement de Lol V. Stein*, whether the photograph exists or
not remains uncertain. The text states categorically that Tatiana
did not remember the photograph.[42] She casts doubt on Lol's
image and, by association, on their intimacy. Tatiana is seen to
ask:

—Est-ce que nous étions tellement amies, à ce collège? Sur cette
photo comment sommes-nous?
    Lol prend un air désolé:
—Je l'ai de nouveau égarée, dit-elle.'[43]

Either Lol lies and the photo does not exist at all, or she refuses
to confront her image with the reality of Tatiana, apparently the
clear-sighted decoder within the text. Tatiana listens to Lol; she
is an attentive reader and makes the most acute analysis of her
friend, saying: 'Tu parles de ta vie comme un livre.'[44] Tatiana is
placed to play the role of analyst talking through Lol's story
with her and revealing it to her. Tatiana is shown to be capable
of giving Lol access to a memory (or narration?) of the night at
the Casino in T. Beach, allowing her to see herself from outside,
as she might be viewed by a witness. Tatiana says to Lol: 'Tu es
toujours restée là où tu étais près de moi, derrière les plantes
vertes.'[45] Lol replies, distractedly: 'Ainsi cette femme qui me
caressait la main, c'était toi, Tatiana.'[46] Note here that the

---

[41] *Le Ravissement de Lol V. Stein*, 75: *The Ravishing of Lol Stein*, 67.
[42] *Le Ravissement de Lol V. Stein*, 75: *The Ravishing of Lol Stein*, 67.
[43] *Le Ravissement de Lol V. Stein*, 96: *The Ravishing of Lol Stein*, 87 (' "Were we
actually such close friends in school? How do we look in that photograph?" Lol
seems distressed. "I'm afraid I've mislaid it again", she says.').
[44] *Le Ravissement de Lol V. Stein*, 76: *The Ravishing of Lol Stein*, 67 ('You speak
of your life as though you were reciting from a book').
[45] *Le Ravissement de Lol V. Stein*, 104: *The Ravishing of Lol Stein*, 95 ('You were
there with me the whole time, behind the green plants at the end of the room.').
[46] *Le Ravissement de Lol V. Stein*, 104: *The Ravishing of Lol Stein*, 95 ('You
mean the woman who was caressing my hand was you, Tatiana').

realization of Tatiana's physical presence within the scenario is made only after she has been implicated in Lol's drama of repetition. Lol herself is shown to have been entirely unaware of this convergence between past action and restorative narrative. While it is Tatiana who will seek to tell Lol how she suffered her abandonment, while Tatiana says to Lol, 'Je suis ton seul témoin,'[47] Lol herself will, it seems, reject the access to memory Tatiana offers, and adopt instead (consciously or not) a more dangerous strategy of erasure through re-enactment.

Instead of accepting the reality of memory as narrated by another, Lol appears to withdraw within the limbo of her amnesia. She will attempt instead to relive the past in the present, deny Tatiana's status as witness, and make her the centre of a new, repeating fantasy. The reader's identification with Tatiana is thus unsettled by her implication within the narrative and the rejection of her stance as analyst.

Tatiana as lover, not analyst, becomes the key to both reincarnation and carnality within the text. This can be demonstrated in a rare scene where the three major protagonists are found centre-stage together. Jacques Hold and Lol go to tea with Tatiana: 'Tatiana sert le thé. Lol la suit des yeux. Nous la regardons, Lol V. Stein et moi.'[48] The text dwells on Tatiana's sensuality, her graceful movements. Lol is given brief access to a memory or fantasy of Tatiana as a girl: 'Ah! tes cheveux défaits, le soir, tout le dortoir venait voir, on t'aidait.'[49] And as Tatiana adjusts her hair again Jacques Hold writes: 'je me souviens d'hier—Lol la regarde—je me souviens de ma tête à ses seins mêlés, hier.'[50] Lol's gaze literally breaks into the sentence: the present tense elides difference between the dormitory memory or fantasy, the watching of Tatiana naked in the bedroom at the Hôtel des Bois, and the scene in the sitting-room as Lol watches now. What is crucial to the text is that Jacques Hold is

---

[47] *Le Ravissement de Lol V. Stein*, 99: *The Ravishing of Lol Stein*, 90 ('I'm your only witness').

[48] *Le Ravissement de Lol V. Stein*, 79: *The Ravishing of Lol Stein*, 70 ('Tatiana serves tea. Lol's eyes follow her. We are both watching her, Lol and I').

[49] *Le Ravissement de Lol V. Stein*, 79: *The Ravishing of Lol Stein*, 70 ('Ah, when you unpinned your hair and let it down in the evening, the whole dormitory would come and watch. We used to give you a hand').

[50] *Le Ravissement de Lol V. Stein*, 79: *The Ravishing of Lol Stein*, 71 ('I am thinking back to yesterday—Lol is watching her—I remember my head buried in her breast, yesterday').

captivated by the fantasy of Lol watching his passion with Tatiana. Not only is the scene of female voyeurism erotic for him, also Lol's gaze serves to embed his affair with Tatiana into the story of *Le Ravissement de Lol V. Stein*. Jacques and Tatiana become images of Michael Richardson and Lol V. Stein. Lol herself in her own rehearsal and re-enactment of her story will return as Anne-Marie Stretter and seduce Jacques Hold.

It is integral to this reading, then, that Lol fails to accept Tatiana's lucid role as witness, and seeks in her instead a seductive mirror image, a lost self incarnate. Yet Lol seeks not to rescue this past self but to dispossess herself of her, to stand outside herself and displace her history in a re-enacted fiction. Thus Tatiana would appear to serve the perpetuation of delusion; she becomes in effect an accessory to Lol's amnesia. The reader has been offered the illusion that the text will enact the discovery of curative analysis. But this is in no sense achieved.

It is important to stress that my reading differs from Kristeva's at this point. Kristeva describes Tatiana as 'le substitut de la première rivale, Anne-Marie Stretter, et, en dernier ressort, de la mère'.[51] This reading leads her to suggest that in relations between Lol and Tatiana, and more generally in the female homoeroticism of her texts, Duras 'raconte le sous-sol psychique antérieur à nos conquêtes de l'autre sexe, qui reste sous-jacent aux éventuelles et périlleuses rencontres des hommes et des femmes'.[52] Kristeva's reading suggests that *Le Ravissement de Lol V, Stein* works to restage a primal trauma of separation and loss. In this sense the text is seen as retrospective and even nostalgic, yet it is seen to offer no balm for the wound of separation it perpetually reopens. Kristeva challenges thus the trauma of the reader confronted with the very *douleur* of Duras's fictions.

To argue, as I have done, that Tatiana represents not the first rival and lost mother, but an image of the self, has altogether differing implications which I shall discuss below. But first to

---

[51] Kristeva, 'La Maladie de la douleur', 257: 'The Malady of Grief' ('the subsitute for the first rival, Anne-Marie Stretter, and, in the last instance, for the mother').

[52] 'La Maladie de la douleur', 263: 'The Malady of Grief', 256–7 ('She relates the psychic substratum previous to our conquests of the other sex, and which still underlies the eventual, perilous encounters between men and women').

substantiate my claim. If Lol locates Tatiana as an image of her past self, then her passionate interest in Tatiana's affair with Jacques makes more sense. Lol's seduction of Jacques Hold, indeed, despite its sexual intensity, becomes another excuse to tell a story. When they are alone together Lol narrates to Jacques: 'Votre chambre s'est éclairée et j'ai vu Tatiana qui passait dans la lumière. Elle était nue sous ses cheveux noirs.'[53] The immediacy and charge of Lol's voyeuristic vision is such as to call up a hallucinatory Tatiana Karl before the lovers: 'La voici, Tatiana Karl nue sous ses cheveux, soudain, entre Lol V. Stein et moi.'[54] And when Jacques next meets Tatiana at the Hôtel des Bois he relates: 'c'était la fin du jour, et . . . j'ai cru voir à mi-distance entre le pied de la colline et l'hôtel une forme grise, une femme, dont la blondeur cendrée à travers les tiges du seigle ne pouvait pas me tromper.'[55] Lol is watching, perceived, or fantasized, by Jacques. When Jacques and Lol make love again, what Lol desires most are the details of Jacques's love-making with Tatiana. Lol is caught in a double bind; as Jacques Hold says: 'Elle aime, aime celui qui doit aimer Tatiana.'[56] Lol tries to enter the relationship from which she is always already excluded: in literal terms because it takes place between Jacques and her real rival (and self-identified friend) Tatiana, in metaphoric terms because their couple represents, as I have been arguing, that formed by Michael Richardson and Lol V. Stein which is precisely what is destroyed and unobtainable for her. Lol is entrapped in her desire; she says to Jacques: 'Ce qui s'est passé dans cette chambre entre Tatiana et vous je n'ai pas les moyens de le connaître. Jamais je ne saurai. Lorsque vous me racontez il s'agit d'autre chose.'[57] She cannot relive her own love

[53] Duras, Le Ravissement de Lol V. Stein, 115: The Ravishing of Lol Stein, 104 ('The light went on in your room, and I saw Tatiana walk in front of the light. She was naked beneath her black hair').

[54] Le Ravissement de Lol V. Stein, 116: The Ravishing of Lol Stein, 106 ('Here she is, Tatiana Karl, suddenly naked beneath her hair, between Lol Stein and me').

[55] Le Ravissement de Lol V. Stein, 120: The Ravishing of Lol Stein, 109 ('dusk was just descending, and . . . I thought I could discern, between the hotel and the foot of the hill, a gray form, a woman about whose grayish blondness there could be no doubt whatsoever').

[56] Le Ravissement de Lol V. Stein, 133: The Ravishing of Lol Stein, 122 ('She loves, loves the man who must love Tatiana').

[57] Le Ravissement de Lol V. Stein, 136: The Ravishing of Lol Stein, 125 ('I have no way of knowing what went on in that room between Tatiana and you. I'll never know. When you tell me it's something else').

for Michael Richardson: it can only exist as a narrative, and a retelling which is essentially and necessarily elusive. She cannot synthesize past and present, memory and re-enactment, and this may be seen as a result of her inability to become or usurp Tatiana.

Tatiana is placed visually as Lol's double: in the absent photograph, apparently, they appear at the same age in the same uniforms; in the school playground they have danced together; later they walk with their arms wound round each other. Jacques Hold observes this illusion of doubling and similarity the last time all three are together in the text: 'Elles portent toutes deux ce soir des robes sombres qui les allongent, les font plus minces, moins différentes l'une de l'autre.'[58] Kristeva, depending on this insistent doubling, reads passion between Lol and Tatiana; she writes: 'la passion entre deux femmes est une des figures les plus intenses du dédoublement.'[59] She continues to suggest that Lol is in love with the couple formed between Jacques and Tatiana, and with Tatiana above all.

Kristeva's text depends on an elision of difference between doubling identification and homosexual desire. This serves, of course, to relegate lesbian desire to the imaginary, to diagnose such desire as at best illusory, at worst psychotic. Teresa de Lauretis challenges Kristeva sharply, writing with reference to *Histoires d'amour*: 'Lesbian sexuality, in other words, is a nonrelationship, or a *nonsexual* relationship: unless it is an adjunct, a sideline, an added attraction to the cutting edge of male sexuality . . . sex between women is a bland pre-oedipal soup.'[60] Now, it might be said, of course, that relations between Lol and Tatiana are indeed a sideline to male sexuality which is, I would argue, the privileged subject of *Le Ravissement de Lol V. Stein*. Yet this is precisely because *Le Ravissement de Lol V. Stein* does not, I think, represent female homosexuality. It dramatizes instead a merging of identities, a troubled play of identification, lubricated by lush female homoeroticism.

In these terms I would argue, following Leslie Hill, that *Le*

---

[58] *Le Ravissement de Lol V. Stein*, 147: *The Ravishing of Lol Stein*, 136 ('This evening they are both wearing dark dresses which make them seem taller and more slender and . . . less obviously different one from the other').

[59] Kristeva, 'Le Maladie de la douleur' 257: 'The Malady of Grief', 250 ('passion between two women represents one of the most intense images of doubling').

[60] Teresa de Lauretis, 'Film and the Visible', in Bad Object-Choices (ed.), *How do I Look? Queer Film and Video* (Seattle, 1991), 254.

Ravissement de Lol V. Stein prefigures the compulsive scenario within *L'Amant* where the young girl fantasizes about the body of her adored friend Hélène Lagonelle. Hill suggests persuasively that this scene in *L'Amant* offers the most forceful commentary on the desire that inhabits *Le Ravissement de Lol V. Stein*. His reading reveals how far Duras's texts may be seen to cut across the axes of binary gender, and of homosexuality and heterosexuality, where he looks at how the text of *L'Amant* describes '[an] indeterminate process of simultaneous fusion and division, identification and detachment, a mingling of bodies and sexes by which male and female are no longer discrete positions, but become joined in a round of desire in which neither the subject nor the object of desire can reliably be placed'.[61]

In this round of desire, I would suggest that Hélène is in herself not simply an object of erotic obsession for the young girl. It is instead the possibility that the self-identified friend may be drawn into desiring relations between the protagonist and her lover which proves such a powerful source of erotic tension. The text dissects vicarious pleasures and the desire to displace reality lived with reality viewed, fiction consumed. The young girl says: 'Je voudrais donner Hélène Lagonelle à cet homme qui fait ça sur moi pour qu'il le fasse à son tour sur elle.'[62] And she continues to draw out her wish: 'Ceci en ma présence, qu'elle le fasse selon mon désir, qu'elle se donne là où moi je me donne.'[63] The wish to see the lover making love with a cherished friend appears to achieve a specific desire in Duras's texts. In *L'Amant*, the young girl states: 'Ce serait par le détour du corps de Hélène Lagonelle, par la traversée de son corps que la jouissance m'arriverait de lui, alors définitive.'[64] There is a voyeuristic desire to observe the self which can only be satisfied at one remove. This desire generates the narrative of *L'Amant*, indeed, which is constructed from the older narrator's desiring observation of her younger self. This device is further set *en*

[61] Hill, *Marguerite Duras*, 79.

[62] Marguerite Duras, *L'Amant* (Paris, 1984), 92: *The Lover*, trans. Barbara Bray (London, 1985), 79 ('I'd like to give Hélène Lagonelle to that man who does that to me, so he may do it in turn to her').

[63] *L'Amant*, 92: *The Lover*, 79 ('I want it to happen in my presence, I want her to do it as I wish, I want her to give herself where I give myself').

[64] *L'Amant*, 92: *The Lover*, 79 ('It's via Hélène Lagonelle's body, through it, that the ultimate pleasure would pass from him to me').

abîme as the young girl wishes again to take her pleasure from the observation of her lover and her friend. This is the model which is copied, insistently, in *Le Ravissement de Lol V. Stein*.

I wish to argue that Lol's fascination with Tatiana does not represent a return to 'la symbiose mortifère avec les mères',[65] as Kristeva would seem to imply. This depends on both an interpretation of the text as enactment of female homosexuality, and on a disturbingly normative psychoanalytic interpretation of female homosexuality itself. In fact, I would argue further, and more simply, that Lol's fascination with Tatiana is in fact in no sense a return. Not only does Duras preclude catharsis and disrupt the curative function of psychoanalytic discourse, I would argue that more radically in her texts, she emphatically refuses access to past trauma, never curing the amnesia of her characters. Her texts depend on emphatic repetition and, seemingly, on the return to the scenes and scenarios of past trauma. Yet where they are in fact most traumatic for their reader is in their refusal to allow the integration or coexistence of past and present. Identity in Duras's texts appears to be contingent and to depend on a performance which (in Butler's terms) is repeated, but which offers no illusion of coherence or cohesion. It is only in creating re-enactments, effectively in fictionalizing the self, that her protagonists are allowed any vision of the performances which have prefigured and conditioned their present trauma. Duras replaces testimony with fantasy, creating her characters as no more than blind witnesses to the events by which they are harrowed.

In loving Tatiana, in identifying her as mirror image, Lol achieves no control over her sanity. She creates herself instead as fascinated viewer of a fiction of her past projected perpetually in 'le cinéma de Lol V. Stein'.[66]

• *'La Fin sans fin'*

'C'est ça, Lol V. Stein, c'est quelqu'un qui chaque jour se souvient de tout pour la première fois, et ce tout se répète

---

[65] Kristeva, 'Le Maladie de la douleur', 257: 'The Malady of Grief', 250 ('death-bearing symbiosis with the mothers').

[66] Duras, *Le Ravissement de Lol V. Stein*, 49: *The Ravishing of Lol Stein*, 39 ('the cinema of Lol Stein').

chaque jour, elle s'en souvient chaque jour pour la première fois comme s'il y avait entre les jours de Lol V. Stein des gouffres insondables d'oubli. Elle ne s'habitue pas à la mémoire. Ni à l'oubli, d'ailleurs.'[67] So speaks Duras about Lol V. Stein. Elsewhere she likens Lol to someone drowning: 'C'est comme ça que je la vois, Lol V. Stein, elle apparaît à la surface des eaux et elle replonge.'[68] If the reading encounter entails the fantasizing of an 'histoire de Lol V. Stein', what then is the impact on the reader of such a despairing, discontinuous text?

I would argue that the reader necessarily follows Lol's suicidal acts of remembering. The text may be made up of a series of metaphoric dives beneath the surface without ever reaching dry land, closure, finite meaning. Duras's narration reiterates and imitates Lol's inability to remember and her refusal to forget as the reader fails to assimilate the text, and doubt destabilizes interpretation. Lacan claims that as we read we are following in Lol's footsteps and he questions: 'Mais si, à presser nos pas sur les pas de Lol, dont son roman résonne, nous les entendons derrière nous sans avoir rencontré personne, est-ce donc que sa créature se déplace dans un espace dédoublé?'[69] The reader finds him/herself following a circular and sense-less trajectory.

Duras's text ends with a suspension of sense, denying any resolution in closure. In its parting image night is falling, Jacques Hold arrives at the Hôtel des Bois. He writes: 'Lol nous avait précédés. Elle dormait dans le champ de seigle, fatiguée, fatiguée par notre voyage.'[70] The image of Lol sleeping in a field of rye is one of the most captivating in Duras's fictions, and has drawn much interpretation. Martha Noel Evans writes, for

[67] Duras and Porte, *Les Lieux de Marguerite Duras*, 99 ('That's what she is, Lol V. Stein, she's someone who remembers everything for the first time every day, and everything is repeated every day, she remembers it every day for the first time, as if there are unfathomable gulfs of forgetting between the days of Lol V. Stein. She doesn't get used to memory. Nor indeed to forgetting').

[68] Ibid. ('This is how I see Lol V. Stein, she appears on the surface of the water and is immersed again').

[69] Lacan, 'Hommage fait à Marguerite Duras du ravissement de Lol V. Stein', 93 ('But if, in following Lol's footsteps, which echo through her novel, we hear them behind us when we have met no one, is it then true that her creature moves in a double space?').

[70] Duras, *Le Ravissement de Lol V. Stein*, 191: *The Ravishing of Lol Stein*, 181 ('Lol had arrived there ahead of us. She was asleep in the field of rye, worn out, worn out by our trip').

example: 'Lol returns to S. Tahla, posts herself in the rye field outside the hotel of public love, and, waiting for Jacques and Tatiana to appear, falls asleep. With that obliviousness, that indifference, the book ends.'[71] Béatrice Didier, in her analysis of the ending, explores the significance of the field of rye in terms of the play between opening and closure, seeing it as an 'espace circonscrit, circulaire, mais d'où la vue s'étend au loin, jusqu'à percer l'intimité de la chambre'.[72] She states neatly: 'Paradoxe suprême, il possède une fenêtre, sans être clos de murs.'[73] This is the type of paradox, of play between presence and absence, with which Duras's work abounds. It might also be seen as a feature of the figure of the sleeping Lol.

Lol's reclining figure implicitly commemorates her collapse after the ball at T. Beach. While this echo of an unconscious Lol remains subliminal, others are more consciously rehearsed, and it is through a reading of these scenes that the reader may come to a closer understanding of the ending. The first scene where Lol lies in a field of rye comes when she has followed Tatiana to the Hôtel des Bois. Here, as in the final scene of the novel, she lies down and sleeps. The text is heavy with sensuality: 'Vivante, mourante, elle respire profondément, ce soir l'air est de miel, d'une épuisante suavité. Elle ne se demande pas d'où vient la faiblesse merveilleuse qui l'a couchée dans ce champ. Elle la laisse agir, la remplir jusqu'à la suffocation, la bercer rudement, impitoyablement jusqu'au sommeil de Lol V. Stein.'[74] Lol's sleep at the end of the text (with its aura of closure and finality, of exhaustion at the end of a voyage of remembering and textual existence) is already specifically inscribed. The ending is shown to be a repetition, not a resolution. And the first scene where Lol sleeps in the field of rye is deliberately shown to be non-originary, and as itself a repetition. Once Lol has succumbed to

[71] Evans, 'Marguerite Duras: The Whore', 152.

[72] Béatrice Didier, 'Le Ravissement de Lol V. Stein', in L'Écriture-femme (Paris, 1981), 275–86: 280 ('a space which is confined and circular, but which has an extensive view, right into the privacy of the hotel room').

[73] Ibid. ('A supreme paradox, it has a window, without being enclosed in walls').

[74] Duras, Le Ravissement de Lol V. Stein, 62–3: The Ravishing of Lol Stein, 54 ('Living, dying, she breathes deeply, tonight the air is like honey, cloyingly sweet. She does not even question the source of the wonderful weakness which has brought her to lie in this field. She lets it act upon her, fill her until she thinks she will suffocate, lets it lull her roughly, pitilessly, until Lol Stein is fast asleep').

sleep, Duras writes: 'le souvenir d'une certaine mémoire passe. Elle frôle Lol peu après qu'elle s'est allongée dans le champ, elle lui montre à cette heure tardive du soir, dans le champ de seigle, cette femme qui regarde une petite fenêtre rectangulaire, une scène étroite.'[75] The narrative moves almost imperceptibly into Lol's tantalizing memory of herself, into what seems to be a dream of the events taking place. Duras leads us to question whether the view of Jacques Hold and Tatiana making love is a dream within a dream. Lol's sleeping leads to a destabilizing of narrative security: it may also be seen to open the way to forgetting and absence. The next time Jacques and Tatiana meet in the hotel, Lol is again lying in the field, is again observed by Jacques. Yet, as he takes Tatiana, in their pleasure Lol is annihilated. He tells us: 'Cet instant d'oubli absolu de Lol, cet instant, cet éclair dilué, dans le temps uniforme de son guet, sans qu'elle ait le moindre espoir de le percevoir, Lol désirait qu'il fût vécu. Il le fut.'[76]

Lol's sleep in the field of rye becomes hauntingly suicidal: she is left poised by the text, alive and acting out her own death. This last scene, despite its grace and seeming tranquillity, should be reread as one of troubling irresolution. Jacques Hold admits earlier in the text: 'L'image du champ de seigle me revient, brutale, je me demande jusqu'à la torture, je me demande à quoi m'attendre encore de Lol.'[77] I feel this is the question Duras leaves the reader with in her closing scene; the text may be seen to inscribe thus 'la fin sans fin, le commencement sans fin de Lol V. Stein'.[78] The novel seeks perpetually to restage an ending and to undo closure.

---

[75] Le Ravissement de Lol V. Stein, 63: The Ravishing of Lol Stein, 54 ('the recollection of a certain memory flits past. It grazes Lol not long after she has lain down in the field, it portrays for her, at this late evening hour in the field of rye, this woman who is gazing up at a small rectangular window, a narrow stage').

[76] Le Ravissement de Lol V. Stein, 123: The Ravishing of Lol Stein, 112 ('That moment when Lol was completely forgotten, that extended flash, in the unvarying time of her watchful wait, Lol wanted that moment to be, without harboring the slightest hope of perceiving it. It was').

[77] Le Ravissement de Lol V. Stein, 152: The Ravishing of Lol Stein, 141 ('Suddenly, like a slap, the image of the field of rye comes back to me, I ask myself, and the question is sheer torture, I ask myself what I may expect next from Lol').

[78] Le Ravissement de Lol V. Stein, 184: The Ravishing of Lol Stein, 175 ('the endless end, the endless beginning of Lol Stein').

• *'Regarde, comme je t'oublie'*

Crucial to Duras's texts, I would argue, is a pained reckoning with the survivor's inability to gain access to her narrative. It is in this way that Duras so emphatically counters the claim of psychoanalysis to effect even a contingent or transitory cure. For Duras, narrative cure, reintegration, and memory are no longer viable options. She posits instead a fragile and hazardous possibility of displacement and diversion into fiction. Her texts are intimately bound up with the compulsion to renarrate, to review. Her protagonists are in some senses always already spectators of their own dramas. This has, in itself, peculiar repercussions for the reader and viewer of Duras's fictions, who is placed in a position that is necessarily complicit with these pained and desiring voyeurs. That these intradiegetic spectators should themselves be desiring viewers is of course significant for the external reader. The lovers' dialogue which constructs an 'histoire de Lol V. Stein' is interwoven throughout Duras's texts. Text is shown to be dependent on desiring exchange, on the interdependent performance of contingent identities. Conversely, desire itself is generated in the passionate engagement in the rereading and renarrating of an erotic history. For Duras, desire is interpretative, is dependent on an infrastructure of fiction.

Identity is revealed to be tenuous and performative, dependent on fictions which are as much created as copied. This may be illustrated particularly well with reference to *Hiroshima mon amour*, a text which, I suggest, allows specific insight into the interdependence between identity, amnesia, and desire I have been arguing is generative of *Le Ravissement de Lol V. Stein*.

In *Hiroshima mon amour*, the Frenchwoman is placed on the stage of Hiroshima. This notion of theatricality is emphasized by the fact that she is an actress who has come to Japan to act in a film about peace which depends on the re-viewing and reconstitution of Hiroshima. In the film itself, and in the film within the film, Hiroshima is a set which becomes the stage for the performance of the Frenchwoman's identity.

Hiroshima mon amour depends on anonymity. In the film the viewer never knows the characters' names nor how they meet; as Duras specifies in her synopsis: 'Les conditions de leur rencontre ne seront pas éclaircies dans le film. Car ce n'est pas là la question.'[79] Instead this is necessarily a fleeting 'amour de rencontre' which has no past and is already pre-inscribed by its own ending. It is indeed a pre-condition of the relationship that it should end. The film echoes constantly with the desire to re-view, to see again, as the Japanese lover repeats his wish to 'revoir' the woman, yet, as in *Le Ravissement de Lol V. Stein*, it is to the impossibility of re-viewing or retaining the self that Duras would appear to testify. Before the encounter is over, when the lovers are still together, the Frenchwoman cries out painfully: 'Je t'oublierai! Je t'oublie déjà! Regarde, comme je t'oublie! Regarde-moi!'[80] Amnesia becomes the very pre-condition of their relationship.

Hiroshima mon amour denies the fixity of memory, and in these terms too denies the fixity of identity. The Frenchwoman's identity is not self-identical, pre-given, or even pre-constructed. Instead her self at Hiroshima is the product of a perpetual, repeated performance which takes place through the agency and in the arms of the Japanese lover. As in *Le Ravissement de Lol V. Stein* identity is seen to be transactional and dependent on the gaze and desire of the Other.

Hiroshima mon amour opens in dialogue and is generated out of dialogue between the lovers. In the opening sequences of the film Resnais uses voice-off so that the direct relation between words and images is dissociated. It is also significant that the film opens in negation. The opening line, spoken by the Japanese lover is: 'Tu n'as *rien* vu à Hiroshima. Rien.'[81] In this first sequence the woman's voice calls forth the images she has recorded and recalled in her mind, only to be reminded constantly of the impossibility of viewing Hiroshima. She claims that she has invented nothing, but her lover replies: 'Tu as *tout* inventé.'[82] The dialogue works to cast doubt over the veracity of the woman's statements; Duras works to weave unease into her script, as later the Japanese lover admits to the Frenchwoman:

[79] Marguerite Duras, *Hiroshima mon amour* (Paris, 1960), 9: *Hiroshima mon amour*, trans. Richard Seaver (London, 1966), 9 ('How they met will not be revealed in the picture. For this is not what really matters').

[80] Ibid. 124: 79 ('I'll forget you! I'm forgetting you already! Look how I'm forgetting you! Look at me!').

[81] Ibid. 22: 19 ('You saw nothing in Hiroshima. Nothing').

[82] Ibid. 28: 21 ('You made it *all* up').

'Quand tu parles, je me demande si tu mens ou si tu dis la vérité.'[83] The text draws attention to how far the woman's performance of her identity at Hiroshima is in no way inspired by a commitment to truthfulness, but rather, it seems, by a desire to justify her own position as actress on the stage of Hiroshima. And this is demonstrated specifically to the viewer in the narrating of the trauma of Nevers, which takes place in the third and fourth parts of the script.

In an interview about the making of *Hiroshima mon amour* Alain Resnais comments about the Frenchwoman: 'On location, we used to spend evenings making up all kinds of stories about her. For instance, she is really a compulsive liar and the Nevers story she tells the Japanese lover is nothing but a fabrication. Or maybe she has just been released from an asylum and she has made up the complete story.'[84] Resnais adds: 'You can see to what degree her personality could evade us as well as the spectator.'[85] Resnais's comments are useful in drawing our attention to the very unknowability of the woman's identity. He would seem to suggest that the spectator is, like the reader of *Le Ravissement de Lol V. Stein*, involved in creating his/her own *histoire* to piece together the fragments of evidence we are given. Yet Resnais's sense that the woman may be entirely and arbitrarily fabricating this performance of her identity can and perhaps should be denied. I would argue indeed that where we might be left to doubt whether the events at Nevers took place, the specificity of this narrative nevertheless determines the relations between the Japanese lover and the Frenchwoman in Hiroshima. In a sense it provides them with a script to follow.

As the woman begins to recount the narrative of Nevers, she asks her lover why she should talk about this episode in her life rather than about others. He replies: 'A cause de Nevers, je peux seulement commencer à te connaître. Et, entre les milliers et les milliers de choses de ta vie, je choisis Nevers.'[86] We note that the

[83] Marguerite Duras, 54: 35 ('When you talk, I wonder whether you lie or tell the truth').

[84] Alain Resnais, '*Hiroshima mon amour*: A Composite Interview with Alain Resnais', in Robert Hughes (ed.), *Film*, ii: *Films of Peace and War* (New York, 1962), 49–66: 63.

[85] Ibid.

[86] Duras, *Hiroshima mon amour*, 80: 50–1 ('Because of Nevers. I can only begin to know you, and among the many thousands of things in your life, I'm choosing Nevers').

performance of the narrative of Nevers is his choice, not hers. As for Jacques Hold, a trauma is framed by the Japanese lover as the moment when the elusive 'elle' enters his destiny. He explains his choice of Nevers as fiction and origin, saying: 'C'est là, il me semble l'avoir compris que j'ai failli . . . te perdre . . . et que j'ai risqué ne jamais te connaître'[87] or further: 'C'est là, il me semble l'avoir compris, que tu as dû commencer à être comme aujourd'hui tu es encore.'[88]

The narrative of Nevers has been chosen, and orchestrated, by the Japanese lover. It serves to create the actress for him as fictional heroine, it serves to re-create trauma in fantasy but not to effect narrative cure. As I have suggested, Nevers provides the conditions for the living out of the relationship at Hiroshima. In both its script and its images *Hiroshima mon amour* depends on equivalences between the two love affairs it stages. In cinematic terms Resnais several times makes use of the form dissolve, where an image of the Japanese lover dissolves into one of the German soldier. This happens in narrative terms too. It would appear that the Frenchwoman slips from speaking of her lover in the third-person singular, to speaking of him and to him in the second-person singular, beginning directly to address the man now present with her. Yet on close analysis we note that it is in fact the Japanese lover who gives her the cue to confuse or associate their identities. He says to her: 'Quand tu es dans la cave, je suis mort?'[89] And she replies then, tentatively: 'Tu es mort . . . et . . .' and then continues: '. . . comment supporter une telle douleur?'[90]

The remainder of the recalling of Nevers depends on her address to the Japanese lover. We are reminded crucially that the relationship in Hiroshima is always necessarily a re-enactment of the trauma and loss of Nevers. Notably the re-enactment allows the Frenchwoman not to recall, but in fact to forget, her past passion. Duras reveals this most specifically when the Frenchwoman, now alone, speaks to her reflection, admitting to the German soldier: 'J'ai raconté notre histoire. Elle

[87] Ibid. 81: 52 ('It was there, I seem to have understood, that I almost . . . lost you . . . and that I risked never knowing you').

[88] Ibid. 81: 52 ('It was there, I seem to have understood, that you must have begun to be what you are today').

[89] Ibid. 87: 57 ('When you are in the cellar, am I dead?').

[90] Ibid. 87: 57 ('You are dead . . . and . . . how is it possible to bear such pain?').

était, vois-tu racontable.'[91] Her speech ends in voice-off as the viewer appears to have privileged access to her thoughts, as her inner voice says:

> Regarde comme je t'oublie . . .
> —Regarde comme je t'ai oublié.
> Regarde-moi.[92]

As we have seen, these words are almost, but imperfectly, repeated in the last few lines of the script. Duras's texts frequently depend on sonorous, incantatory repetitions creating a cumulative effect. Apparently single statements often depend on echoes which at once add emphasis, yet also may serve to displace the seemingly originary meaning. This stylistic device is also copied and re-enacted in the structure of Duras's narratives, and in the relations between her texts, where scenarios are compulsively restaged, displaced, and deformed through repetition.

In *Hiroshima mon amour* the relations between the scenario at Nevers and the love affair at Hiroshima are established above all by citation: images are copied, words reiterated, but with some minor degree of difference. And it is indeed this degree of difference that is crucial to this reading of Duras, and which relates specifically to the issue of performative identities, beyond that of identity as performance.

The text may be seen to suggest that the performance of identity enacted by the Frenchwoman in her love affair at Hiroshima is conditioned by a preceding and enabling narrative. Her performance at Hiroshima repeats her trauma at Nevers. Yet this repetition is traumatically imperfect. The distress at the loss of one lover has been displaced, the words reiterated: yet no access to a continuity of identity has been achieved. Duras reveals that a further dislocation and dissociation will take place, that the Japanese lover will also be lost and forgotten. Their literal separation will in time be re-enacted and repeated in the gradual loss of memory.

Duras's text may be seen to reveal that identity is dependent on a compulsory and repeated performance. Identity is shown

---

[91] Duras, 110: 72 ('I told our story. It was, you see, a story that could be told').
[92] Ibid. 110: 72 ('Look how I'm forgetting you . . . Look how I've forgotten you. Look at me').

further to be tenuously constructed in time. In her interest in repeating narrative patterns and the internalizing of further prior performances of the self, Duras shows identity to be always in process, always unstable and non-self-identical. Her textual practice radically displaces any notion of primary and stable identity. Yet her texts revolve around, rework, and re-enact performances of identity. The self is shown to be always already in performance; identity is shown to be performatively constituted through the citation and displaced repetition of pre-existent texts. Yet a reading of these performances of identity reveals, I think, how far any notion of a unified self is distressingly fictive, disparate, and insubstantial.

Such, then, are the texts with which Duras's desiring reader contends. It might be argued that her fictions pose no ostensible threat to the compulsory matrix of heterosexuality in their privileging of dialogic desiring relations *between* the sexes. This Duras herself would appear to underline in an enigmatic statement from a brief text about sexuality where she says: 'Là où l'imaginaire est le plus fort c'est entre l'homme et la femme.'[93] Thus she defines the imaginary spaces her texts inhabit, showing her fictions to depend on (sexual) difference, desire, and unknowability.

Duras works, nevertheless, to destabilize the structure she apparently upholds within her texts. In the first place, the power balance between male viewer and female object of desire is disrupted since, as in Proust, physical possession no longer guarantees knowledge, and thus doubt precludes domination. This will also necessarily be the experience of the desiring reader, who is offered no further purchase on Duras's elusive objects of desire. The reader who identifies, then, with the seemingly secure position of the male desiring subject is effectively dispossessed of the dominant role within the libidinal economy to which Duras's texts would give the appearance of subscribing.

What is important to note here is that stable identification is dramatically disrupted. In this way Duras may be seen to draw into question the possibilities of identity constructed with relation to a fiction. Mirroring relations in her texts are, as we have

[93] Marguerite Duras, *La Vie matérielle* (Paris, 1987), 39 ('The imaginary dimension is strongest between a man and a woman').

seen, fraught with difference, and dependent upon the ways in which identification may undo the fragile fictions of identity the self has salvaged. Repetition and replication work as much to corrode as to corroborate the individual's performances of identity. Yet where Duras shows no stable reflection between self and *imago*, between protagonists and past histories, between reader and text, she nevertheless does not eschew the necessity to negotiate these relations. Indeed Duras's texts may be seen to exist in moments of dislocation, of failed identification, which are emphatically dependent still on the belief that copying a fiction can restore identity.

Duras shows identity to be disturbingly dependent on identification, yet paradoxically she denies and undermines the normative function of fictions. She attacks the regulatory mechanisms of texts by testifying to the impossibility of replication and the inevitability of distortion. Her conclusions with relation to identity are fairly shattering: Duras emphatically refuses to construct a reassuring image of reintegration. In interrelation her protagonists discover how far the necessary Other serves to disperse and disrupt any security of identity or stability of knowledge. Duras's texts appear to approach Butler's rereading of Lacan where, as we have seen, she diagnoses the delirium which we are forced to live.

To return to Kristeva, then, I would argue that Duras's texts may be seen, more profoundly than Kristeva would allow, to attack our foundational illusions of identity. Where Kristeva suggests of our complicity with Duras's texts that 'Elle nous conduit à radiographer nos folies, les bords dangereux où s'écroule l'identité du sens, de la personne et de la vie,'[94] she herself appears still to have faith in some notion of the unity and integrity of meaning and identity, fostered and upheld by the normative and curative enterprise of psychoanalysis. Duras, in denying a specific teleology in her accounts of trauma, in refusing closure and cure, in dispersing identity, effectively seeks to disempower such discourse.

Duras's reader encounters texts which emphatically testify to the formative power of fictions, to the ways by which we are

---

[94] Kristeva, 'Le Maladie de la douleur', 236: 'The Malady of Grief', 228 ('It leads us to X-ray our madness, the dangerous rims where identities of meaning, personality, and life collapse').

compelled to live in relation to elusive *imagos*. Desire in Duras's texts is scripted, fictions are re-enacted. The reader engages in an activity which is distressingly mirrored in the text s/he consumes, but this mirroring offers only insecurity. Duras succeeds thus in disrupting any hierarchization of reading positions, or any claims to prominance and pre-eminence in the reading encounter.

Where her texts are particularly radical is in their denial of any stable relation between the protagonist and the fictions of her life the text performs. The reader is confronted with a perpetually divergent relation between the subject in front of the mirror and her reflected, and fictive, images. No integration is offered, and no authority is given to the reader's interpretations. In her texts Duras dramatizes lives in pieces, whose fragments are rearranged, replaced by a desiring viewer, whose efforts are revealed finally to be only ever hopeless and in vain.

Concluding Remarks

In a recent text, *Le Médianoche amoureux*, Michel Tournier creates a couple on the verge of separation. To announce their divorce they invite their friends to join them for 'un médianoche d'amour et de mer'.[1] Through the course of this evening their friends will tell a series of tales which will serve effectively to divide or unite the couple. In the text, Tournier frames these tales with a preview of their outcome as the male partner avows their renewed desire to stay together and reveals: 'Ce qui nous manquait en effet, c'était une maison de mots où habiter ensemble. Jadis la religion apportait aux époux un édifice à la fois réel—l'église—et imaginaire, peuplé de saints, enluminé de légendes, retentissant de cantiques, qui les protégeait d'eux-mêmes et des agressions extérieures. Cet édifice nous faisait défaut. Nos amis nous en ont fourni tous les matériaux. La littérature comme panacée pour les couples en perdition. . .'.[2] In fairly unequivocal terms the text would appear to propagate a belief in the formative, and possibly also normative, function of fiction. Can the reader take this seeming testimony on Tournier's part at face value? Can we possibly subscribe to the view that fiction can form an edifice in our lives?

Throughout this study I have worked to analyse texts which figure the reading encounter as experiential, which deny discrete divisions between existence and text, which dramatize the

---

[1] Michel Tournier, *Le Médianoche amoureux* (Paris, 1989), 38–9: *The Midnight Love Feast*, trans. Barbara Wright (London, 1992), 27 ('a midnight love feast and a celebration of the sea').

[2] *Le Médianoche amoureux*, 42: *The Midnight Love Feast*, 30 ('What we lacked, in fact, was a house of words to live in together. In former times, religion provided couples with an edifice that was at the same time real—the church—and imaginary, peopled with saints, illuminated with legends, resounding with hymns, which protected them from themselves and from outside aggression. We lacked this edifice. Our friends have provided us with all the materials for it. Literature as a panacea for couples in distress . . .').

contagious and possibly insidious effect of fiction upon reality. I have been concerned to question whether these texts thus testify to their own power, imaging prospectively the response they will inspire. To end with reference to Tournier's comments within *Le Médianoche amoureux* might seem in some ways contradictory. Tournier offers what appears at first an all too simple and optimistic schema for the relations between fiction and reality. This schema is in part congruent with the argument I have been developing here since it emphasizes the primacy of fiction to existence, and their primary interdependence. Yet, Tournier's statement becomes more problematic in this context when one considers the implications of his comparison between the instructive potential of religion and the constructive potential of fiction.

Tournier creates an image of the religious edifice as protective. We might question whether, in so doing, he overlooks its explicitly regulatory function. It remains unclear whether Tournier envisages literature offering an equivalent or a different edifice to that offered by religion. The distinction between these two possibilities may appear slight, but I would argue that it is of prime importance to our understanding of Tournier's texts. Tournier's fictions may provide 'les couples en perdition' with a seductive and voluminous imaginary world, peopled by fantasists, decoders, and monsters. Tournier may readily invite his reader to inhabit the edifice of his fiction. But the possibility that these very fictions should structure a regulatory system which seeks in any way to police the morality and habits of their readers is highly disturbing.

In this sense, I think it is important to maintain that Tournier privileges difference over equivalance and that he seeks in his texts to question and trouble the regulatory function of fictions. I would argue that Tournier undermines the structure of religion and conventional morality, constructing in their place a mirroring, but different, edifice and economy of identification. His texts may be seen to deny the possibility of recognizing in their confines tenets by which to live, and images with which to identify positively. Instead he shows systems which malfunction, identities which corrode. Tournier's fiction becomes a study in delusion. His protagonists live lives in pieces.

The fracturing of identity has proved an obsession throughout this study and it might be said that the lives revealed in the texts of Proust, Cixous, Duras, and Tournier are all lives in pieces, harrowed and transformed by trauma and desire. In this sense I would argue that these dissociative fictions of identity serve a peculiarly salutary function in their disruption of secure mirroring relations. Mirroring fails within the relations represented in these texts, as it will fail also in relations between reader and text. These authors refuse an illusion of integrity and by this token they refuse ultimate authority too. The function of these texts is, it seems, to expose rather than conceal the mechanisms of the fragile fictions of identity by which we are forced to live.

These texts may be seen thus to eschew their normative function, by offering no stable identities or fixed regulatory structure. This denial of authority is achieved also by problematizing relations between writer and reader, eradicating any fixed hierarchy which may have subtended this relation, and showing instead how both writer and reader come to enjoy a tenuous and illusory freedom to choreograph desiring textual relations. In this sense the loss of the author's authority effectively undermines the words of the law in his texts.

I have contended that for a text to serve a normative function it should, then, offer the reader fixed, coherent, and intelligible *imagos* with which to identify and to incorporate in the construction of his/her identity. This I have seen to be dependent on a hierarchical relation between writer and reader, where the writer, in Lacanian terms, consciously initiates the movements of the images within the text which are copied by the reader. I have sought to show how the texts of Proust, Cixous, Tournier, and Duras, in their amply different ways, refract mirroring relations and deconstruct this hierarchical power structure. It has been crucial to my argument to suggest, however, that to contest the normative function of fictions should not necessarily be to deny their formative power and potential, and secondly that to deny the author's authority is by no means to ensure (or desire) his/her absence from the stage of textual reception.

I have sought to argue that the reading of fiction may be formative. This argument has depended on a recognition of the proximity between the process of identity formation through identification, and the act of identifying with a fiction. I would suggest that despite the apparent agency and freedom of the reader no unequivocal and clear-cut divisions can be made definitively between the two processes of identification. Such arguments, and evidence of the deleterious effects of, say, films as recent as *Reservoir Dogs* or *Natural Born Killers*, have provoked the sometimes heeded call for censorship. As stated in my introduction, I am loath here to enter into discussion of violence on screen, but I would tentatively suggest that the question of sexuality in texts might be less muddied and bloodied. Where, in Tournier's terms, some may feel the necessity of a protective edifice regulating the realm of video violence and policing its miscreants, in the infinitely subjective domain of erotic fictions and sexual identities, regulation appears instantly less protective than censorious. But if it is recognized that fiction may be formative, may we not suggest that its effect might be positive and, as is the case with the texts analysed in this study, its force might be seen, in liberating terms, to disrupt the regulatory function of the compulsory matrix of heterosexuality?

I would argue, then, that the reader is not in complete control of the text s/he consumes, and that s/he cannot necessarily at will, and without trauma, adopt a series of dissident identifications. If it is accepted that reading is not merely performance, but a potentially performative act, then closer attention should be paid to the scripts which narrate and orchestrate our identities. The texts studied here have all been selected by virtue of their seeming self-consciousness and the guarded attention they draw to their own formative yet deregulatory function. I have chosen texts which attack the foundational illusions of identity, and the illusory polarities of male and female, masculine and feminine, straight and gay. These are texts of dissociation and destabilization which seek finally a formative power through the unsettling rather than the securing of the reader's identity.

Where I have expressed some qualms about Butler's seeming championing of instability, it would seem that in conclusion I should confess, if not to the pleasure of distress, at least to its power. In these terms I would argue that, in a study of formative fictions, it may ultimately be in conflict rather than in confirming replication that sheer force may be found. Thus I would suggest that taut, tense, and imperfect mirroring relations are the most suggestive, and those texts which strive to disrupt, frustrate, and mispresent their readers may have the greatest force in changing the world they appear to reflect.

And this leads me back to Tournier and to the scenario from *Le Médianoche amoureux* with which I have chosen to end. In the closing lines of 'Les Amants taciturnes' the male lover, as we have seen, testifies simply to the restorative and reparative power of fiction. In an apparently metatextual gesture Tournier seems in fact to delude his reader once more. *Le Médianoche amoureux* appears to set out a fairly logical relation between fiction and its effect on the reader, allowing the couple to be drawn apart by the 'nouvelles, âprement réalistes, pessimistes, dissolvantes'[3] and drawn together by 'les contes, savoureux, chaleureux, affables'.[4] Yet this entirely occludes the sado-masochistic economy in which Tournier's texts so readily deal. And this he gestures towards earlier in the text in a savage and ethereal scene as the lovers walk on the seashore. They see what they take to be 'deux corps humains enlacés recouverts de sable'.[5] It is only as they approach that they realize that these are (merely) 'deux statues sculptées dans le sable d'une étrange et poignante beauté'.[6] Tournier dramatizes the shift from reality to fiction, from flesh to representation, yet allows the first shocked response, the charge of emotion, to colour over aesthetic appreciation. The tide begins to come in and dissolve the couple before their eyes: 'Nous regardions avec horreur cette dissolution capricieuse et inexorable de ce couple que nous persistions à sentir humain, proche de nous, prémonitoire peut-être. Une vague plus forte s'abattit sur la tête de la femme, emportant la moitié de son visage, puis ce fut l'épaule droite de l'homme qui s'effondra, et nous les trouvions encore plus émouvants dans leur mutilation.'[7] Distress is seen to heighten and rarefy

---

[3] *Le Médianoche amoureux*, 40: *The Midnight Love Feast*, 29 ('the short stories—grimly realistic, pessimistic and demoralizing').

[4] *Le Médianoche amoureux*, 40–1: *The Midnight Love Feast*, 29 ('the tales—delectable, warm-hearted and tender').

[5] *Le Médianoche amoureux*, 24: *The Midnight Love Feast*, 16 ('two human bodies clasped in each other's arms and covered in sand').

[6] *Le Médianoche amoureux*, 25: *The Midnight Love Feast*, 17 ('two statues sculpted in sand, of strange and poignant beauty').

[7] *Le Médianoche amoureux*, 17–18: *The Midnight Love Feast*, 17–18 ('Horrified, we watched the capricious and inexorable dissolution of this couple which we persisted in feeling to be human, close to us, perhaps premonitory. A stronger wave broke over the woman's head, carrying away half her face, then it was the man's right shoulder that collapsed, and we thought them even more touching in their mutilation', 26).

appreciation. The edifice Tournier builds in his fictions finds its foundations in moving sand; it is at once perilous and fragile; his readers are formed, I would suggest, not by the comfort but the trauma of his texts.

The texts I have studied offer their readers the troubled pleasures of pained identification. In these reading encounters sexual identities are revealed to be fragile, contingent, and constructed. Decoding lovers remain deluded, divisions between fantasy and sensation are denied to the point of insanity. Yet the possibility of vicarious existences, which may challenge or change the reader, remains endlessly alluring. In the seductive encounter that reading is, the reader survives unceasingly as lover and victim.

Bibliography

ANZIEU, DIDIER, *Le Corps de l'œuvre: Essais psychanalytiques sur le travail créateur* (Paris: Gallimard, 1981).

Bad Object Choices (ed.), *How do I Look?: Queer Film and Video* (Seattle: Bay Press, 1991).

BALZAC, HONORÉ DE, *Le Père Goriot* (Paris: Garnier-Flammarion, 1966).

BARTHES, ROLAND, *Fragments d'un discours amoureux* (Paris: Seuil, 1977).

——*Incidents* (Paris: Seuil, 1987).

——*Le Plaisir du texte* (Points; Paris: Seuil, 1973).

——*S/Z* (Points; Paris: Seuil, 1970).

——'Une idée de recherche', in *Recherche de Proust* (Points; Paris: Seuil, 1980), 34–9.

BAUDRILLARD, JEAN, *De la séduction* (Folio; Paris: Denoël, 1979).

BERSANI, LEO, 'Death and Literary Authority: Marcel Proust and Melanie Klein', in *The Culture of Redemption* (Cambridge, Mass.: Harvard University Press, 1990), 7–28.

——*The Freudian Body: Psychoanalysis and Art* (New York: Columbia University Press, 1986).

——*Homos* (Cambridge, Mass.: Harvard University Press, 1995).

BETTELHEIM, BRUNO, *The Uses of Enchantment* (London: Thames & Hudson, 1976).

BEVAN, D. G., *Michel Tournier* (Amsterdam: Rodopi, 1986).

BLOOM, HAROLD, *Agon: Towards a Theory of Revisionism* (New York: Oxford University Press, 1982).

——*The Anxiety of Influence* (New York: Oxford University Press, 1973).

——*A Map of Misreading* (Oxford: Oxford University Press, 1975).

——Paul de Man, Jacques Derrida, Geoffrey H. Hartman, and J. Hillis Miller, *Deconstruction and Criticism* (London: Routledge, 1979).

BOOTH, WAYNE C., 'Ten Literal "Theses"', in Sacks (ed.), *On Metaphor*, 173–4.

BOULOUMIÉ, ARLETTE, *Michel Tournier: Le Roman mythologique* (Paris: José Corti, 1988).

——and MAURICE DE GANDILLAC (eds.), *Images et signes de Michel Tournier* (Paris: Gallimard, 1991).

BOWIE, MALCOLM, *Freud, Proust and Lacan: Theory as Fiction* (Cambridge: Cambridge University Press, 1987).
——*Lacan* (London: Fontana, 1991).
——*The Morality of Proust* (Oxford: Clarendon Press, 1994).
BROWN, ANDREW, *Roland Barthes: The Figures of Writing* (Oxford: Oxford University Press, 1992).
BUTLER, JUDITH, *Bodies that Matter: On the Discursive Limits of 'Sex'* (New York: Routledge, 1993).
——*Gender Trouble: Feminism and the Subversion of Identity* (New York: Routledge, 1990).
——'Imitation and Gender Insubordination', in Fuss (ed.), *Inside/Out*, 13–31.
CALLE, MIREILLE, 'L'Écrire-penser d'Hélène Cixous', in Calle (ed.), *Du féminin*, 97–111.
——(ed.) *Du féminin* (Grenoble: Presses Universitaires de Grenoble, 1992).
CALVINO, ITALO, *If on a Winter's Night a Traveller* (London: Picador, 1982).
CAWS, MARY ANN, and EUGÈNE NICOLE (eds.), *Reading Proust Now* (New York: Peter Lang, 1990).
CHAMBERS, ROSS, *Story and Situation: Narrative Seduction and the Power of Fiction* (Minneapolis: University of Minnesota Press, 1984).
CHAMPAGNE, ROLAND, *Literary History in the Wake of Roland Barthes* (Birmingham, Ala.: Summa Publications, 1984).
CIXOUS, HÉLÈNÈ, *La Bataille d'Arcachon* (Laval: Québec, Éditions Trois, 1986).
——*Dedans* (Paris: Éditions des Femmes, 1986; first pub. Paris: Grasset, 1969).
——'Difficult Joys', in Wilcox *et al.* (eds.), *The Body and the Text*, 5–30.
——'En Octobre 1991 . . .', in Calle (ed.), *Du féminin*, 115–37.
——*Entre l'écriture* (Paris: Éditions des Femmes, 1986).
——*L'Heure de Clarice Lispector* (Paris: Éditions des Femmes, 1989).
——*Jours de l'an* (Paris: Éditions des Femmes, 1990).
——*LA* (Paris: Gallimard, 1976).
——*Le Livre de Promethea* (Paris: Gallimard, 1983).
——*Reading with Clarice Lispector* (London: Harvester Wheatsheaf, 1990).
——'Le Rire de la méduse', *L'Arc*, 61 (1975), 39–54.
——*Three Steps on the Ladder of Writing* (New York: Columbia University Press, 1993).
——and MIREILLE CALLE-GRUBER, *Hélène Cixous, photos de racines* (Paris: Éditions des Femmes, 1994).

CLOONAN, WILLIAM, *Michel Tournier* (Boston: Twayne, 1985).

COHEN, SUSAN, *Women and Discourse in the Fiction of Marguerite Duras* (London: Macmillan, 1993).

COLLIER, PETER, *Proust and Venice* (Cambridge: Cambridge University Press, 1989).

——and HELGA GEYER-RYAN (eds.), *Literary Theory Today* (Cambridge: Polity, 1990).

CONLEY, VERENA ANDERMATT, 'Délivrance', in Françoise van Rossum-Guyon and Myriam Diaz-Diocaretz (eds.), *Hélène Cixous: Chemins d'une écriture* (Amsterdam: Rodopi, 1990), 35–44.

——'Féminin et écologie', in Calle (ed.), *Du féminin*, 53–64.

——*Hélène Cixous* (London: Harvester Wheatsheaf-Modern Cultural Theorists, 1992).

——*Hélène Cixous: Writing the Feminine*, expanded ed. (Lincoln: University of Nebraska Press, 1991).

CORNELL, SARAH, 'Hélène Cixous and *les Études Féminines*', in Wilcox et al. (eds.), *The Body and the Text*, 31–40.

Criminal Justice and Public Order Act 1994 (London: HMSO, 1994).

CULLER, JONATHAN, *Barthes* (Glasgow: Fontana, 1983).

——'The Problem of Metaphor', in Hope (ed.), *Language, Meaning and Style*, 5–20.

DAVIS, COLIN, 'Les Interprétations', in Bouloumié and Gandillac (eds.), *Images et signes de Michel Tournier*, 191–206.

——*Michel Tournier: Philosophy and Fiction* (Oxford: Oxford University Press, 1988).

——'Michel Tournier between Synthesis and Scarcity', *French Studies*, 42 (July, 1988), 320–31.

DELEUZE, GILLES, *Logique de sens* (Paris: Minuit, 1969).

——*Présentation de Sacher-Masoch* (Paris: Minuit, 1967).

——*Proust et les signes* (Paris: Presses Universitaires de France, 1964).

DE MAN, PAUL, *Allegories of Reading* (New Haven: Yale University Press, 1979).

——*Blindness and Insight: Essays in the Rhetoric of Contemporary Criticism* (London: Methuen, 1983).

DERRIDA, JACQUES, *De la Grammatologie* (Paris: Minuit, 1967).

DIDIER, BÉATRICE, 'Le Ravissement de Lol V. Stein', in *L'Écriture-femme* (Paris: Presses Universitaires de France, 1981), 275–86.

DOANE, MARY ANN, 'Film and the Masquerade: Theorising the Female Spectator', *Screen*, 23/3–4 (Sept.–Oct. 1982), 74–87.

DODD, PHILIP, 'Editorial: Dog Days', *Sight and Sound*, 8 (Aug. 1994), 3.

DOLLIMORE, JONATHAN, *Sexual Dissidence: Augustine to Wilde, Freud to Foucault* (Oxford: Oxford University Press, 1991).

DOUBROVSKY, SERGE, *La Place de la madeleine: Écriture et fantasme chez Proust* (Paris: Mercure de France, 1974).

DUBOIS, COLETTE, *'La Maman et la putain' de Jean Eustache* (Paris: Éditions Yellow Now, 1990).

DUNCAN, ANN, 'Que ma joie demeure: Proust's cantata', *French Studies*, 434 (Oct. 1989), 437–51.

DURAS, MARGUERITE, *L'Amant* (Paris: Minuit, 1984).

——*Hiroshima mon amour* (Folio; Paris: Gallimard, 1960).

——*Le Ravissement de Lol V. Stein* (Folio; Paris: Gallimard, 1964).

——*Un Barrage contre le Pacifique* (Folio; Paris: Gallimard, 1950).

——*La Vie matérielle* (Paris: POL, 1987).

——and XAVIÈRE GAUTHIER, *Les Parleuses* (Paris: Minuit, 1974).

——and MICHELLE PORTE, *Les Lieux de Marguerite Duras* (Paris: Minuit, 1977).

——*et al.*, *Marguerite Duras* (Paris: Éditions Albatros, Collection Ça/Cinéma, 1975).

EDMUNDS, LOWELL, *Oedipus: The Ancient Legend and its Later Analogues* (Baltimore: Johns Hopkins University Press, 1985).

——and ALAN DUNDES, *Oedipus: A Folklore Casebook* (New York: Garland, 1983).

ÉLUARD, PAUL, *Capitale de la douleur* (Paris: Poésie Gallimard, 1966).

EPSTEIN, JULIA, and KRISTINA STRAUB (eds.), *Body Guards: The Cultural Politics of Gender Ambiguity* (New York: Routledge, 1991).

EVANS, MARTHA NOEL, 'Marguerite Duras: The Whore', in *Masks of Tradition: Women and the Politics of Writing in Twentieth-Century France* (Ithaca, NY: Cornell University Press, 1987), 123–56.

FELMAN, SHOSHANA, *Jacques Lacan and the Adventure of Insight* (Cambridge, Mass.: Harvard University Press, 1987).

——*Le Scandale du corps parlant* (Paris: Seuil, 1980).

——*Testimony: Crises of Witnessing in Literature, Psychoanalysis, and History* (New York: Routledge, 1992).

——*What does a Woman Want? Reading and Sexual Difference* (Baltimore: Johns Hopkins University Press, 1993).

FISH, STANLEY, *Is there a Text in this Class? The Authority of Interpretive Communities* (Cambridge, Mass.: Harvard University Press, 1980).

FORRESTER, JOHN, 'Rape, Seduction and Psychoanalysis', in Tomaselli and Porter (eds.), *Rape*, 57–83.

FOUCAULT, MICHEL, 'De l'amitié comme mode de vie', *Le Best of Gai Pied* (1991), 34–6.

——*Herculine Barbin dite Alexina B.* (Paris: Gallimard, 1978).

——*Histoire de la sexualité*, i: *La Volonté de savoir* (Paris: Gallimard, 1976).

——Introduction to *Herculine Barbin: Being the Recently Discovered Memoirs of a Nineteenth-Century French Hermaphrodite* (Brighton: Harvester, 1980), pp. vii–xvii.

——'Qu'est-ce qu'un auteur?', *Bulletin de la Société française de philosophie*, 63/1 (1969), 73–104.

FRAYLING, CHRISTOPHER, 'The House that Jack Built: Some Stereotypes of the Rapist in the History of Popular Culture', in Tomaselli and Porter (eds.), *Rape*, 174–215.

FREUD, SIGMUND, *The Standard Edition of the Complete Psychological Works of Sigmund Freud*, 24 vols (London: Hogarth Press, 1981).

FREUND, ELIZABETH, *The Return of the Reader: Reader Response Criticism* (London: Methuen, 1987).

FUSS, DIANA, *Essentially Speaking: Feminism, Nature and Difference* (New York: Routledge, 1990).

——(ed.), *Inside/Out: Lesbian Theories, Gay Theories* (New York: Routledge, 1991).

GALLOP, JANE, *Feminism and Psychoanalysis: The Daughter's Seduction* (London: Macmillan. 1982).

——*Reading Lacan* (Ithaca, NY: Cornell University Press, 1985).

GENETTE, GÉRARD, *Figures III* (Paris: Seuil, 1972).

——*Palimpsestes: La Littérature au second degré* (Paris: Seuil, 1982).

GIDE, ANDRÉ, *Les Faux-Monnayeurs* (Paris: Gallimard, 1925).

——*Les Nourritures terrestres* (Folio; Paris: Gallimard, 1972).

GIRARD, RENÉ, *Mensonge romantique et vérité romanesque* (Paris: Grasset, 1961).

GLASSMAN, DEBORAH, *Marguerite Duras: Fascinating Vision and Narrative Cure* (London: Associated University Presses, 1991).

GREIMAS, ALGIRDAS-JULIEN, *De l'imperfection* (Périgueux: Pierre Fanlac, 1987).

GROSZ, ELIZABETH, *Jacques Lacan: A Feminist Introduction* (London: Routledge, 1990).

GUICHARD, NICOLE, *Michel Tournier: Autrui et la quête du double* (Paris: Didier Érudition, 1990).

HESIOD, *Theogony* and *Works and Days*, in *The Homeric Hymns and Homerica* (London: Heinemann, 1967).

HILL, LESLIE, *Marguerite Duras: Apocalyptic Desires* (London: Routledge, 1993).

HOFMAN, CAROL, *Forgetting and Marguerite Duras* (Colorado: University of Colorado Press, 1991).

HOPE, T. E. (ed.), *Language, Meaning and Style* (Leeds: Leeds University Press, 1981).

IRIGARAY, LUCE, *Ce Sexe qui n'en est pas un* (Paris: Minuit, 1977).

——*Éthique de la différence sexuelle* (Paris: Minuit, 1984).

ISER, WOLFGANG, *The Implied Reader* (Baltimore: Johns Hopkins University Press, 1974).

——'Interaction between Text and Reader', in Suleiman and Crosman (eds.), *The Reader in the Text*, 106–19.

JARDINE, ALICE, 'Woman in Limbo: Deleuze and his Br(others)', *SubStance*, 44–5 (1984), 46–60.

JAUSS, HANS ROBERT, *Pour une esthétique de la réception* (Paris: Gallimard, 1978).

JEAN, RAYMOND, *Lectures du désir* (Paris: Seuil, 1977).

JOHNSON, BARBARA, *The Critical Difference* (Baltimore: Johns Hopkins University Press, 1980).

JOUVE, NICOLE WARD, '*Ananas*/Pineapple', in *White Woman Speaks with Forked Tongue: Criticism as Autobiography*, 37–45.

——'Oranges et sources: Colette et Hélène Cixous', in Rossum-Guyon and Diaz-Diocaretz (eds.), *Hélène Cixous: Chemins d'une écriture*, 55–73.

——'To Fly/to Steal: No More? Translating French Feminisms into English', in *White Woman Speaks with Forked Tongue: Criticism as Autobiography*, 46–58.

——*White Woman Speaks with Forked Tongue: Criticism as Autobiography* (London: Routledge, 1991).

KAFKA, FRANZ, *Letters to Friends, Family, and Editors* (New York: Schocken, 1978).

——*The Transformation and Other Stories* (London: Penguin, 1992).

KOFMAN, SARAH, *Lectures de Derrida* (Paris: Éditions Galilée, 1984).

KOSTER, SERGE, *Tournier* (Paris: Veyrier, 1986).

KRISTEVA, JULIA, *Histoires d'amour* (Folio; Paris: Gallimard, 1983).

——*Soleil noir: Dépression et mélancolie* (Folio; Paris: Gallimard, 1987).

——*Le Temps sensible: Proust et l'expérience littéraire* (Paris: Gallimard, 1994).

KUHN, ANNETTE, 'Introduction to Hélène Cixous's "Castration or Decapitation?"', *Signs*, 7/1 (1981), 36–40.

LACAN, JACQUES, 'L'Agressivité en psychanalyse', in *Écrits*, i. 101–24.

——*Les Complexes familiaux dans la formation de l'individu* (Paris: Navarin, 1984).

——*Écrits* (Paris: Seuil, 1966).

——'Hommage fait à Marguerite Duras du ravissement de Lol V. Stein', in Marguerite Duras et al., *Marguerite Duras* (Paris: Éditions Albatros, Collection Ça/Cinéma, 1975), 93–9.

——'Some Reflections on the Ego', *International Journal of Psychoanalysis*, 341 (1953), 11–17.

——'Le Stade du miroir comme formateur de la fonction du Je', in *Écrits* (Paris, 1966), i. 93–100.

LAGOS, PATRICIO, *Arena, bain de vie*, preface by Michel Tournier (Brussels: Édition de Lassa, 1990).

LAPLANCHE, JEAN, and J.-B. PONTALIS, *Vocabulaire de la psychanalyse* (Paris: Presses Universitaires de France, 1973).

LAURETIS, TERESA DE, 'Film and the Visible', in Bad Object-Choices (ed.), *How do I Look?: Queer Film and Video* (Seattle, 1991), 223–64.

LAVERS, ANNETTE, *Roland Barthes: Structuralism and After* (London: Methuen, 1982).

MAGNY, JOËL, 'Le Cri de l'écran', in *Marguerite Duras* (Paris: Cinémathèque française, 1992), 15–34.

MAKWARD, CHRISTINE, 'Structures du silence/du délire: Marguerite Duras/Hélène Cixous', *Poétique*, 35 (Sept. 1978), 314–24.

MALLARMÉ, STÉPHANE, *Oeuvres complètes* (Paris: Gallimard, 1945).

MERLLIÉ, FRANÇOISE, *Michel Tournier* (Paris: Belfond, 1988).

MODLESKI, TANIA, 'Some Functions of Feminist Criticism; or, The Scandal of the Mute Body', *October*, 49 (Summer 1989), 3–24.

MOI, TORIL, *Sexual/Textual Politics* (London: Harvester, 1985).

MORIARTY, MICHAEL, *Roland Barthes* (Cambridge: Polity, 1991).

MULLER, JOHN P., and WILLIAM J. RICHARDSON, *Lacan and Language* (New York: International Universities Press, 1982).

MULVEY, LAURA, *Visual and Other Pleasures* (London: Macmillan, 1989).

PENROD, LYNN KETTLER, 'Hélène Cixous: Lectures initiatiques, lectures centrifuges', in Calle (ed.), *Du féminin*, 83–95.

PLATH, SYLVIA, *Collected Poems* (London: Faber, 1981).

PLATO, *The Symposium*, trans. W. Hamilton (Harmondsworth: Penguin, 1967).

POLLOCK, GRISELDA, *Vision and Difference: Femininity, Feminism and the Histories of Art* (London: Routledge, 1988).

POSNER, GERALD L., and JOHN WARE, *Mengele: The Complete Story* (London: MacDonald, 1986).

POULET, GEORGES, *La Conscience critique* (Paris: José Corti, 1971).

PROUST, MARCEL, *A la recherche du temps perdu* (Paris: Gallimard, 1989).

——*Contre Sainte-Beuve* (Folio; Paris: Gallimard, 1954).

——*Pastiches et mélanges*, in *Contre Sainte-Beuve* (Paris: Gallimard, 1971), 5–207.

RESNAIS, ALAIN, '*Hiroshima mon amour*: A Composite Interview with

Alain Resnais', in Robert Hughes (ed.), *Film*, ii: *Films of Peace and War* (New York: Grove Press 1962), 49–66.

RICŒUR, PAUL, 'The Metaphorical Process as Cognition, Imagination and Feeling', in Sacks (ed.), *On Metaphor*, 141–57.

RIVERS, J. E., *Proust and the Art of Love: The Aesthetics of Sexuality in the Life, Times, and Art of Marcel Proust* (New York: Columbia University Press, 1980).

ROBERT, PIERRE-EDMOND, '*La Prisonnière*: Notice', in Proust, *A la recherche du temps perdu*, iii. 1628–93.

RODOWICK, D. N., *The Difficulty of Difference: Psychoanalysis, Sexual Difference and Film Theory* (New York: Routledge, 1991).

ROSE, JACQUELINE, *Sexuality in the Field of Vision* (London: Verso, 1986).

ROSELLO, MIREILLE, *L'In-différence chez Michel Tournier* (Paris: José Corti, 1990).

ROSSUM-GUYON, FRANÇOISE VAN, and MYRIAM DIAZ-DIOCARETZ (eds.), *Hélène Cixous: Chemins d'une écriture* (Amsterdam: Rodopi, 1990).

SACKS, SHELDON (ed.), *On Metaphor* (Chicago: University of Chicago Press, 1978).

SARTRE, JEAN-PAUL, *Qu'est-ce que la littérature?* (Paris: Gallimard, 1972).

SCHOR, NAOMI, 'Fiction as Interpretation/Interpretation as Fiction', in Suleiman and Crosman (eds.), *The Reader in the Text*, 165–82.

SEDGWICK, EVE KOSOFSKY, *Between Men: English Literature and Male Homosocial Desire* (New York: Columbia University Press, 1985).

——*Epistemology of the Closet* (Hemel Hempstead: Harvester Wheatsheaf, 1991).

SELLERS, SUSAN, 'Learning to Read the Feminine', in Wilcox *et al.* (eds.), *The Body and the Text*, 190–5.

SHERINGHAM, MICHAEL, *French Autobiography: Devices and Desires* (Oxford: Oxford University Press, 1993).

SHIACH, MORAG, *Hélène Cixous: A Politics of Writing* (London: Routledge, 1991).

SILVERMAN, KAJA, *Male Subjectivity at the Margins* (New York: Routledge, 1992).

SMITH, PAUL JULIAN, *Laws of Desire: Questions of Homosexuality in Spanish Writing and Film 1960–1990* (Oxford: Oxford University Press, 1992).

SOLLERS, PHILIPPE, 'Proust et Gomorrhe', *Théorie des exceptions* (Paris: Gallimard-Folio, 1986), 75–9.

SONTAG, SUSAN, *A Susan Sontag Reader* (Harmondsworth: Penguin, 1983), 95–101.

SPIVAK, GAYATRI, 'Cixous sans frontières', in Calle (ed.), *Du féminin*, 65–81.

STAMBOLIAN, GEORGE, and ELAINE MARKS (eds.), *Homosexualities and French Literature: Cultural Contexts/Critical Texts* (Ithaca, NY: Cornell University Press, 1979).

STILL, JUDITH, 'A Feminine Economy: Some Preliminary Thoughts', in Wilcox *et al.* (eds.), *The Body and the Text*, 49–60.

STIMPSON, BRIAN, and LIEVE SPAAS (eds.), *Robinson Crusoe* (London: Macmillan, 1996).

STONE, SANDY, 'The *Empire* Strikes Back: A Posttranssexual Manifesto', in Epstein and Straub (eds.), *Body Guards*, 280–304.

SULEIMAN, SUSAN, and INGE CROSMAN (eds.), *The Reader in the Text* (Princeton: Princeton University Press, 1980).

TILBY, MICHAEL, *Beyond the Nouveau Roman: Essays on the Contemporary French Novel* (Providence, RI: Berg, 1990).

TOMASELLI, SYLVANA, and ROY PORTER (eds.), *Rape* (Oxford: Basil Blackwell, 1986).

TOURNIER, MICHEL, *Le Coq de bruyère* (Paris: Gallimard, 1978).

——*Des Clefs et des serrures* (Paris: Chêne-Hachette, 1979).

——*Gaspard, Melchior et Balthazar* (Paris: Gallimard, 1980).

——*Gilles et Jeanne* (Paris: Gallimard, 1983).

——*La Goutte d'or* (Paris: Gallimard, 1985).

——*Le Médianoche amoureux* (Paris: Gallimard, 1989).

——*Les Météores* (Paris: Gallimard, 1975).

——*Petites proses* (Folio; Paris: Gallimard, 1986).

——'Plus encore qu'un jumeau j'aimerais avoir un clone', interview with Olivier Frébourg, *Contre Ciel*, 8 (Dec. 1984), 81–3.

——'Qu'est-ce que la littérature?', interview with Jean-Jacques Brochier, *Magazine littéraire*, 179 (Dec. 1981), 80–6.

——*Le Roi des Aulnes* (Paris: Gallimard, 1970).

——*Vendredi ou les limbes du Pacifique* (Paris: Gallimard, 1967).

——*Le Vent Paraclet* (Paris: Gallimard, 1977).

——*Le Vol du vampire: Notes de lecture* (Paris: Gallimard-Collection Idées, 1983).

ULMER, GREGORY L., 'Fetishism in Roland Barthes's Nietzschean Phase', *Papers on Language and Literature*, 14/3 (Summer 1978), 334–55.

UNGAR, STEPHEN, *Roland Barthes: The Professor of Desire* (London: University of Nebraska Press, 1983).

WILCOX, HELEN, KEITH MCWATTERS, ANN THOMPSON, and LINDA R. WILLIAMS (eds.), *The Body and the Text: Hélène Cixous, Reading and Teaching* (London: Harvester Wheatsheaf, 1990).

WILLIS, SHARON, *Marguerite Duras: Writing on the Body* (Urbana: University of Illinois Press, 1987).

WILSON, EMMA, 'Duras and the Female Reader: *Le Ravissement de Lol V. Stein*', *Dalhousie French Studies*, 26 (Spring/Summer 1994), 97–107.

——'Hélène Cixous: An Erotics of the Feminine', in Hughes and Ince (eds.), *Desiring Reading: French Women's Erotic Writing* (forthcoming).

——'Tournier, the Body and the Reader', *French Studies*, 47 (January 1993), 43–56.

——'*Vendredi ou les limbes du Pacifique*: Tournier, Seduction and Paternity', in Stimpson and Spaas (eds.), *Robinson Crusoe* (forthcoming).

WINTON, ALISON, *Proust's Additions* (Cambridge: Cambridge University Press, 1977).

WITTIG, MONIQUE, *The Straight Mind and Other Essays* (Hemel Hempstead: Harvester Wheatsheaf, 1992).

WORTON, MICHAEL, 'Michel Tournier and the Nature of Love', *European Gay Review*, 3 (1988), 36–46.

——'Use and Abuse of Metaphor in Tournier's "Le Vol du vampire"', *Paragraph*, 10 (Oct. 1987), 13–28.

——and JUDITH STILL (eds.), *Textuality and Sexuality* (Manchester: Manchester University Press, 1993).

WRIGHT, ELIZABETH, *Psychoanalytic Criticism: Theory in Practice* (London: Methuen, 1984).

ZAGDANSKI, STÉPHANE, *Le Sexe de Proust* (Paris: Gallimard, 1994).

Index